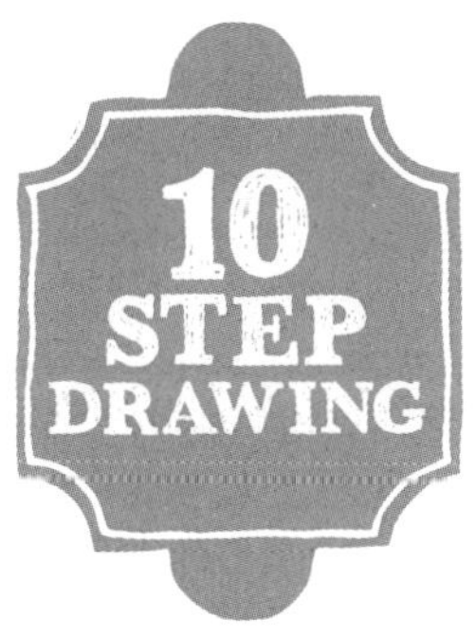

Flowers

DRAW 75 FLOWERS IN 10 EASY STEPS

Published in 2018 by Search Press Ltd.
Wellwood, North Farm Road
Tunbridge Wells
Kent, TN2 3DR

Reprinted 2020, 2021, 2023, 2024, 2025

This book is produced by
The Bright Press, an imprint of the Quarto Group,
1 Triptych Place, London
SE1 9SH, United Kingdom
T (0)20 7700 6700
www.quarto.com

Our EU representation is covered by information on our website
GPSR information can be found at www.searchpress.com

ISBN: 978-1-78221-661-2

Publisher: Mark Searle
Associate Publisher: Emma Bastow
Managing Editor: Isheeta Mustafi
Editors: Abi Waters and Abbie Sharman
Commissioning Editor: Emily Angus
Design: Les Hunt
Cover design: Tania Gomes and Katherine Radcliffe

10 9 8 7 6

Printed in Huizhou, Guangdong, China
TT/10/25

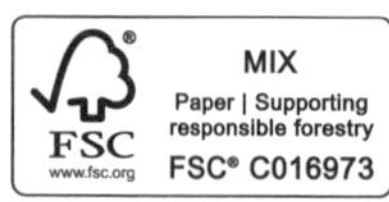

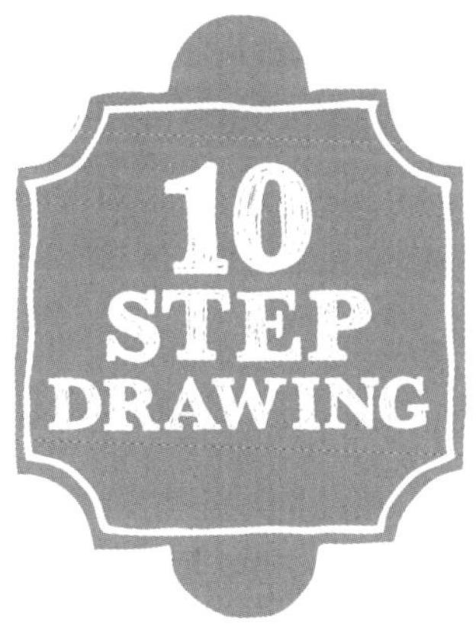

Flowers

DRAW 75 FLOWERS IN 10 EASY STEPS

MARY WOODIN

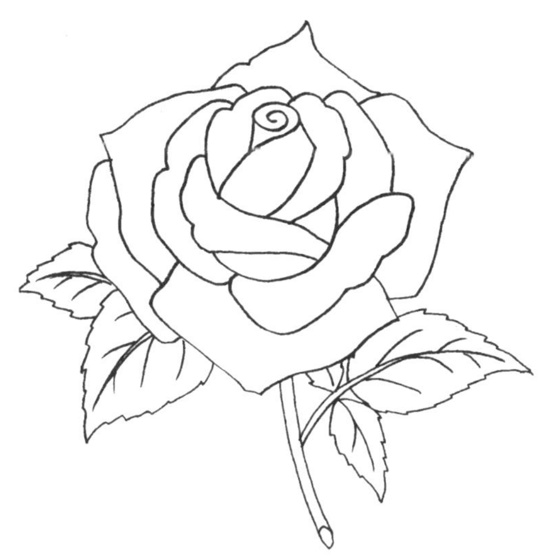

Search Press

Contents

Blooms

Blossoms

Botanicals

Displays

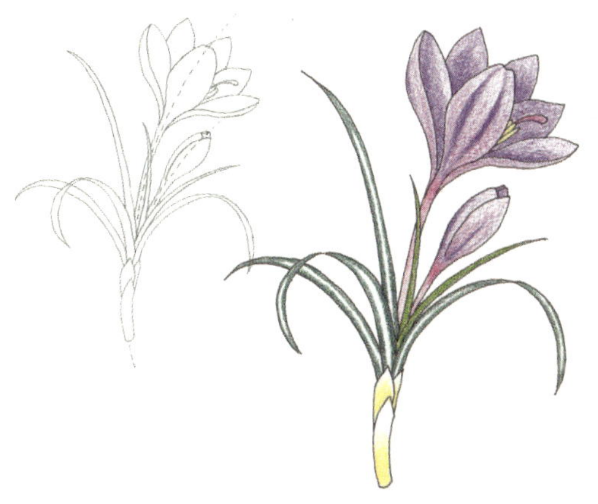

Introduction

In this book you will find 75 beautiful flower illustrations that have been created in just 10 simple steps. Whether it's a beautiful rose, a tall sunflower or a potted succulent, it's time to choose your favourite flower and get drawing.

Drawing flowers is easier than you think because many of them share the same basic shapes. Breaking the drawing down into smaller elements will help you place them in the correct position.

TACKLING DIFFERENT SHAPES

Flowers and plants come in many different shapes and sizes. Each drawing in this book begins with a simple shape or guide outline to begin with. The step-by-step instructions often also advise you to use further circle or other shape outlines as guides for placing flower heads, leaves or individual petals. This will enable you to get the proportions right.

All of the flower and plant drawings in this book also show the different shapes of petals and leaves – from the open, blousy shapes of a peony to the tiny, closed petals on a hyacinth. Following the instructions and guides on what shape the petals and leaves should be will help you achieve the overall appearance of different flowers.

We have also provided a colour palette at the end of each finished drawing. Use this as a guide, but feel free to experiment and use your favourite shades for different flowers and plants.

I hope you will enjoy creating the flowers in this book as much as I did. Drawing has never been easier!

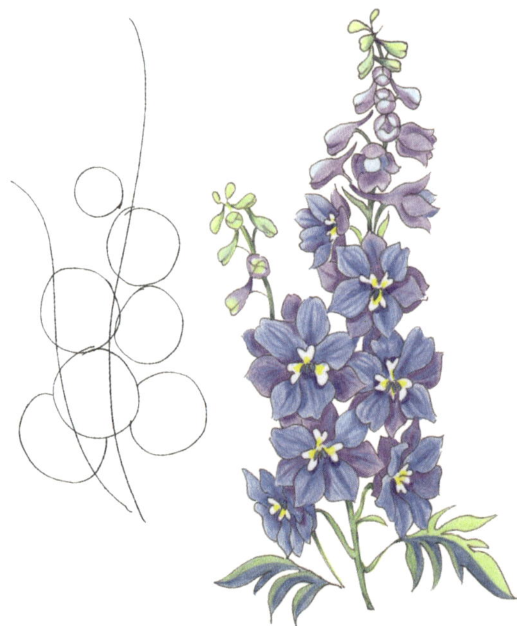

How to use this book

BASIC EQUIPMENT

Paper: any paper will do, but using sketch paper will give you the best results.

Pencil, rubber and pencil sharpener: try different pencil grades and invest in a good-quality rubber.

Pen: for inking the final image. A medium or fine ink pen is best (ink is better than ballpoint because it dries quickly and is less likely to smudge).

Small ruler: this is optional, but you may find it useful for drawing guide lines.

FOLLOWING THE STEPS

Use pencil and follow each step. When you are happy with the flower, draw over it in ink and leave it to dry. Then erase the underlying pencil. Finally, apply colour as you like.

COLOURING

Stay inside the lines and keep your pencils sharp so you have control in the smaller areas.

To achieve a lighter or darker shade, try layering the colour or pressing harder with your pencil.

Many flowers come in different colours and have different patterns, so once you're confident with where the shading should be on each flower, why not try varying the colours you use?

You have several options when it comes to colouring your drawings – why not explore them all?

Pencils: this is the simplest option, and the one I have chosen for finishing the pictures in this book. A good set of coloured pencils, with about 24 shades, is really all you need.

Paint and brush: watercolour is probably easiest to work with for beginners, although using acrylic or oil means that you can paint over any mistakes. You'll need two or three brushes of different sizes, with at least one very fine brush.

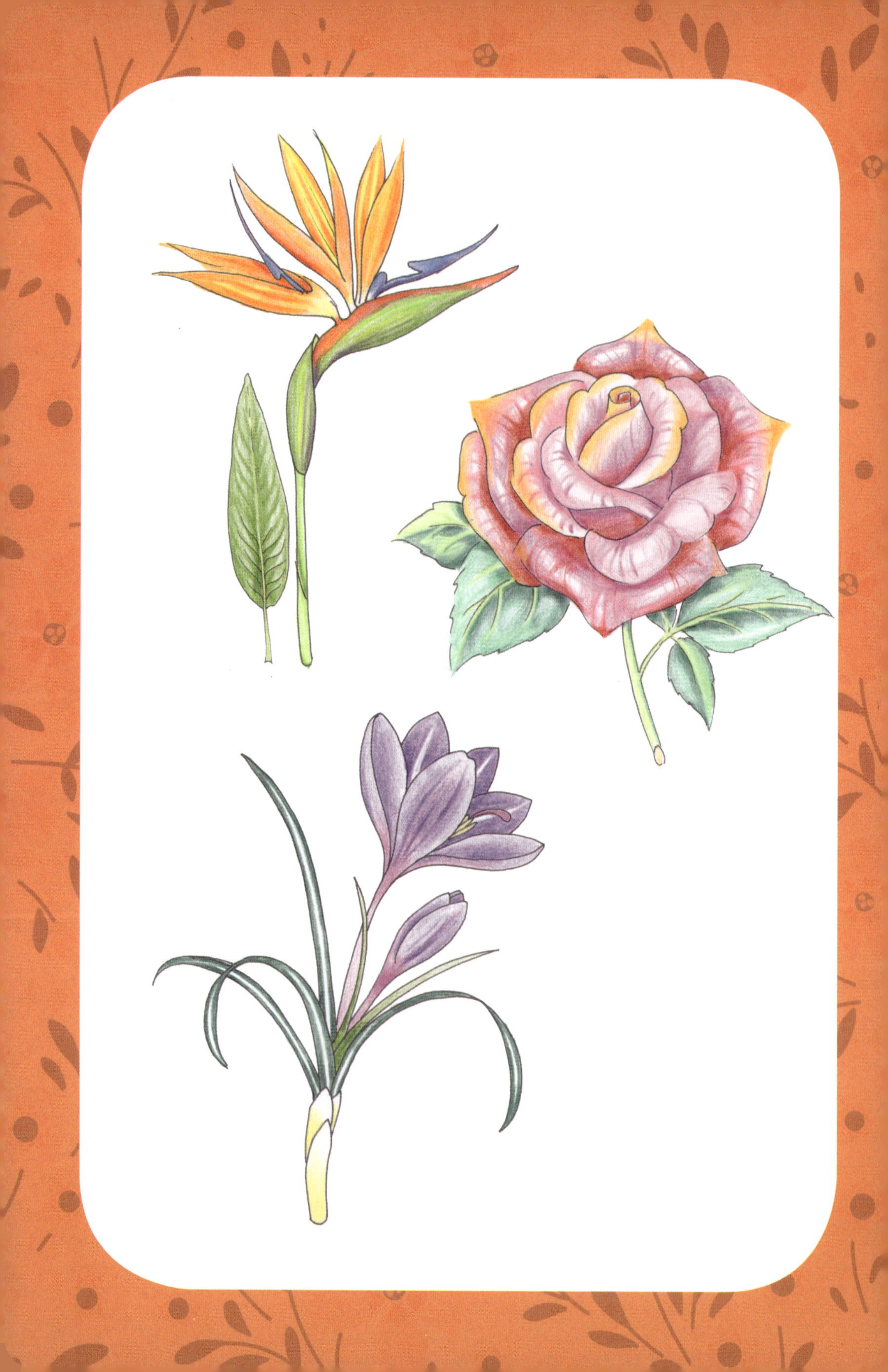

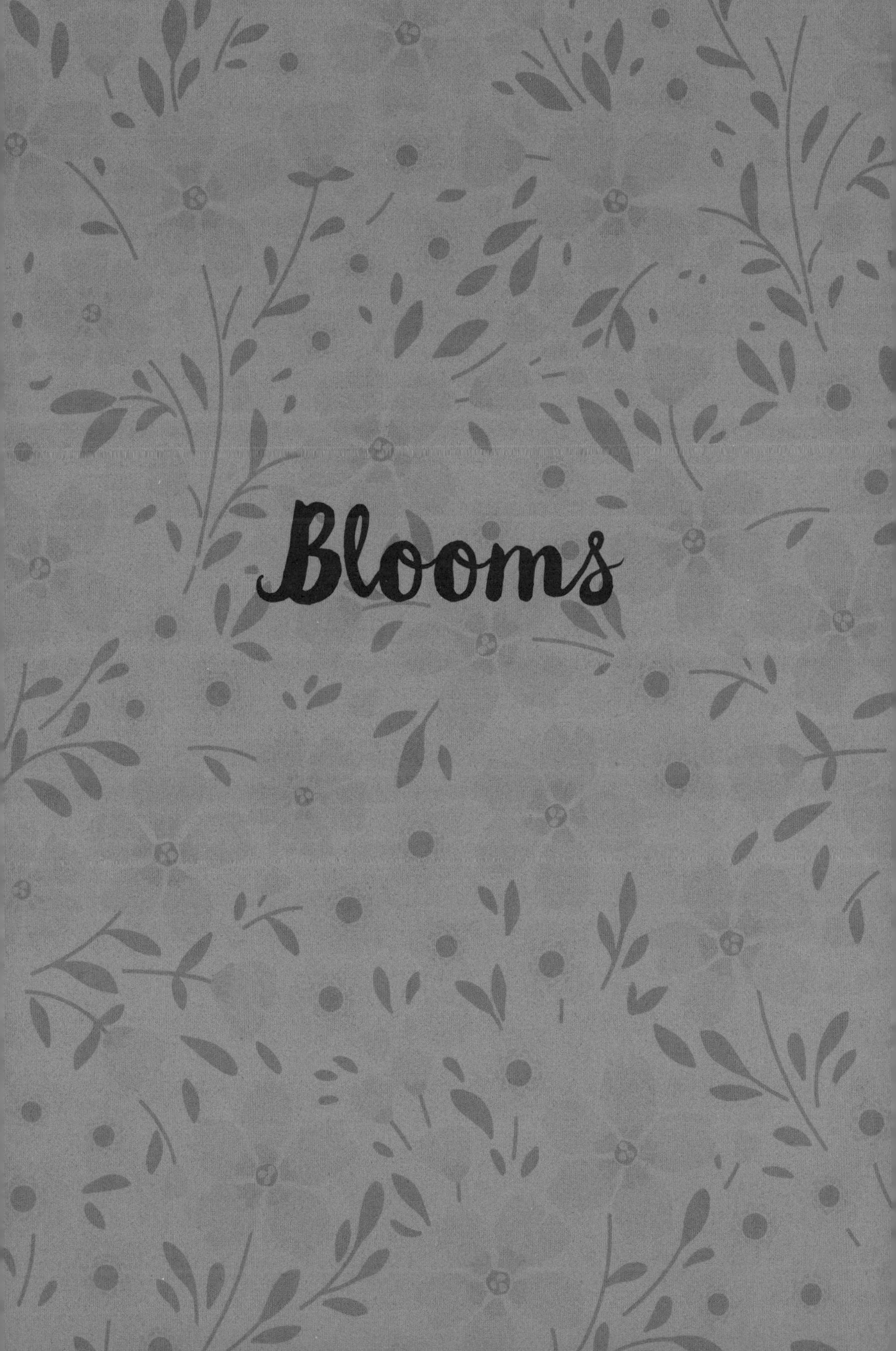

Blooms

Rose

Roses come in many variations and a multitude of colours. Learn the basic shape of this beautiful flower and you will be able to add variety to all of your flower drawings.

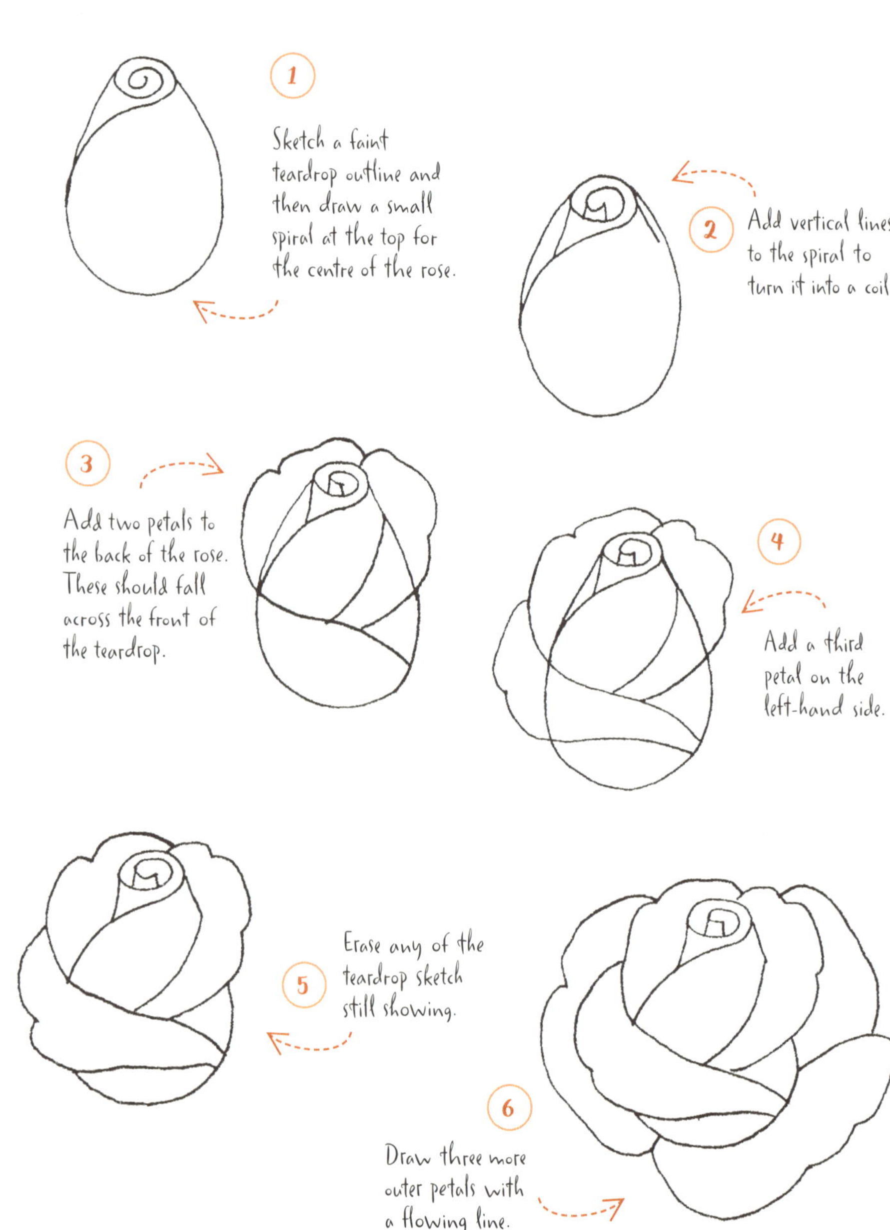

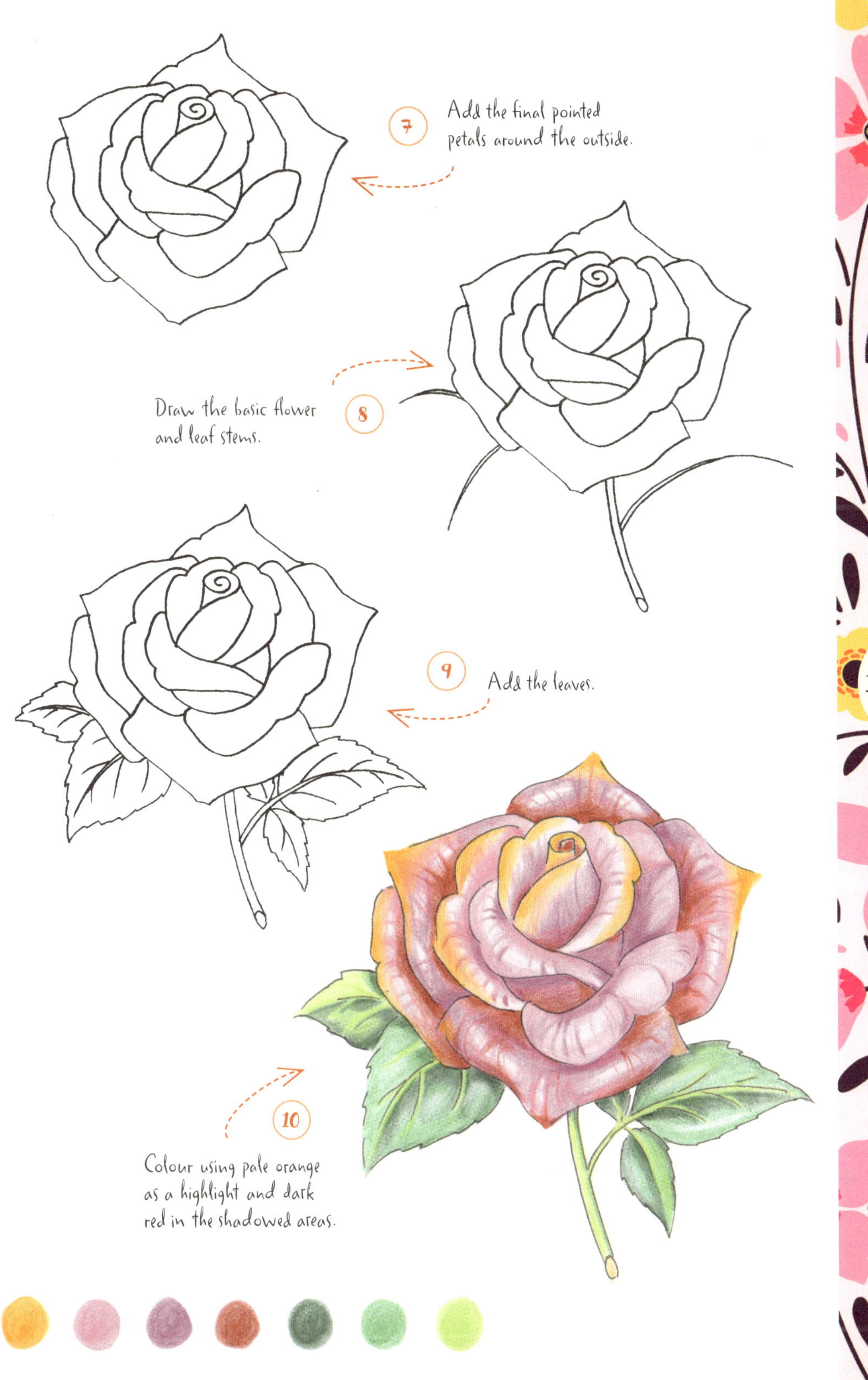
7
Add the final pointed petals around the outside.
Draw the basic flower and leaf stems.
8
9
Add the leaves.
10
Colour using pale orange as a highlight and dark red in the shadowed areas.

Iris

This tall flowering plant appears in beautiful shades of blue and purple and is a great way to practise blending of colours.

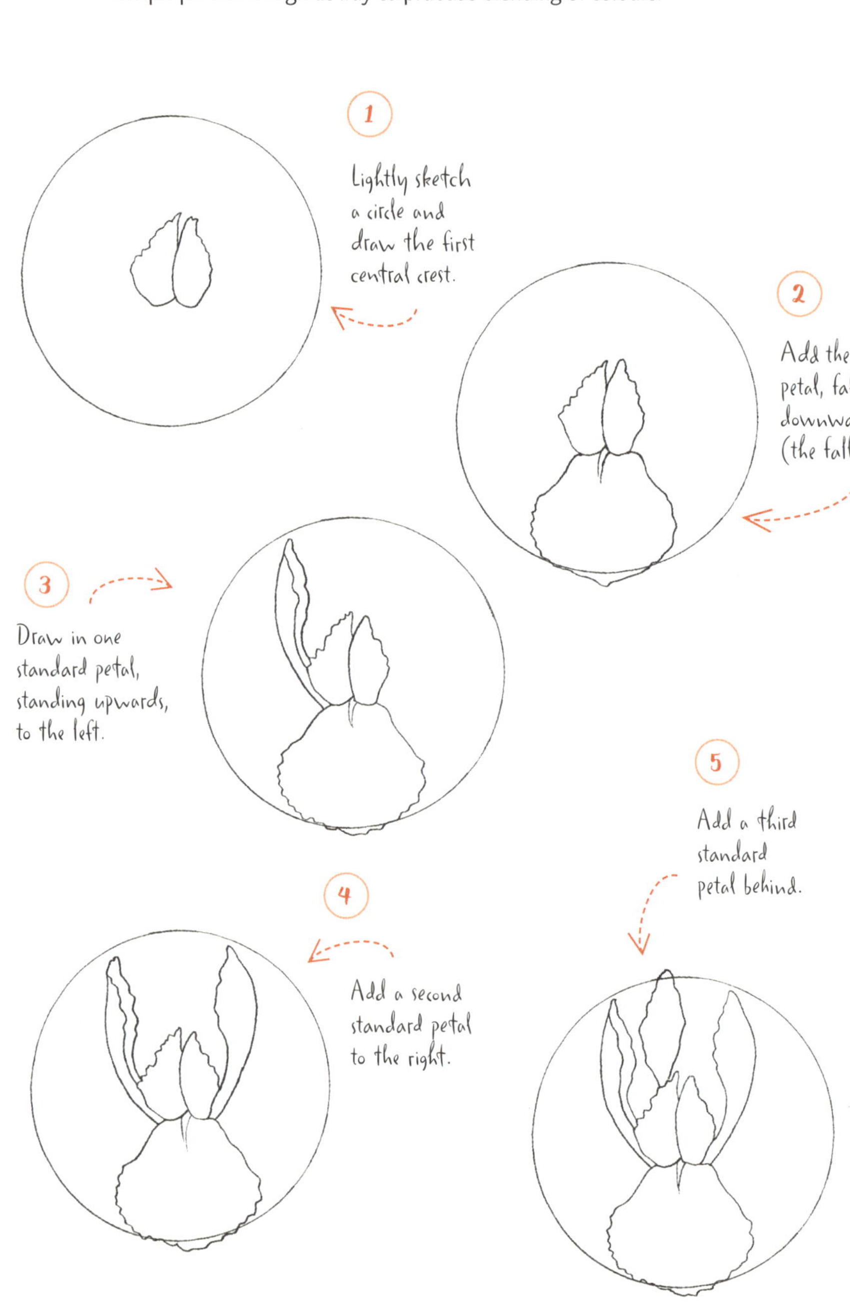

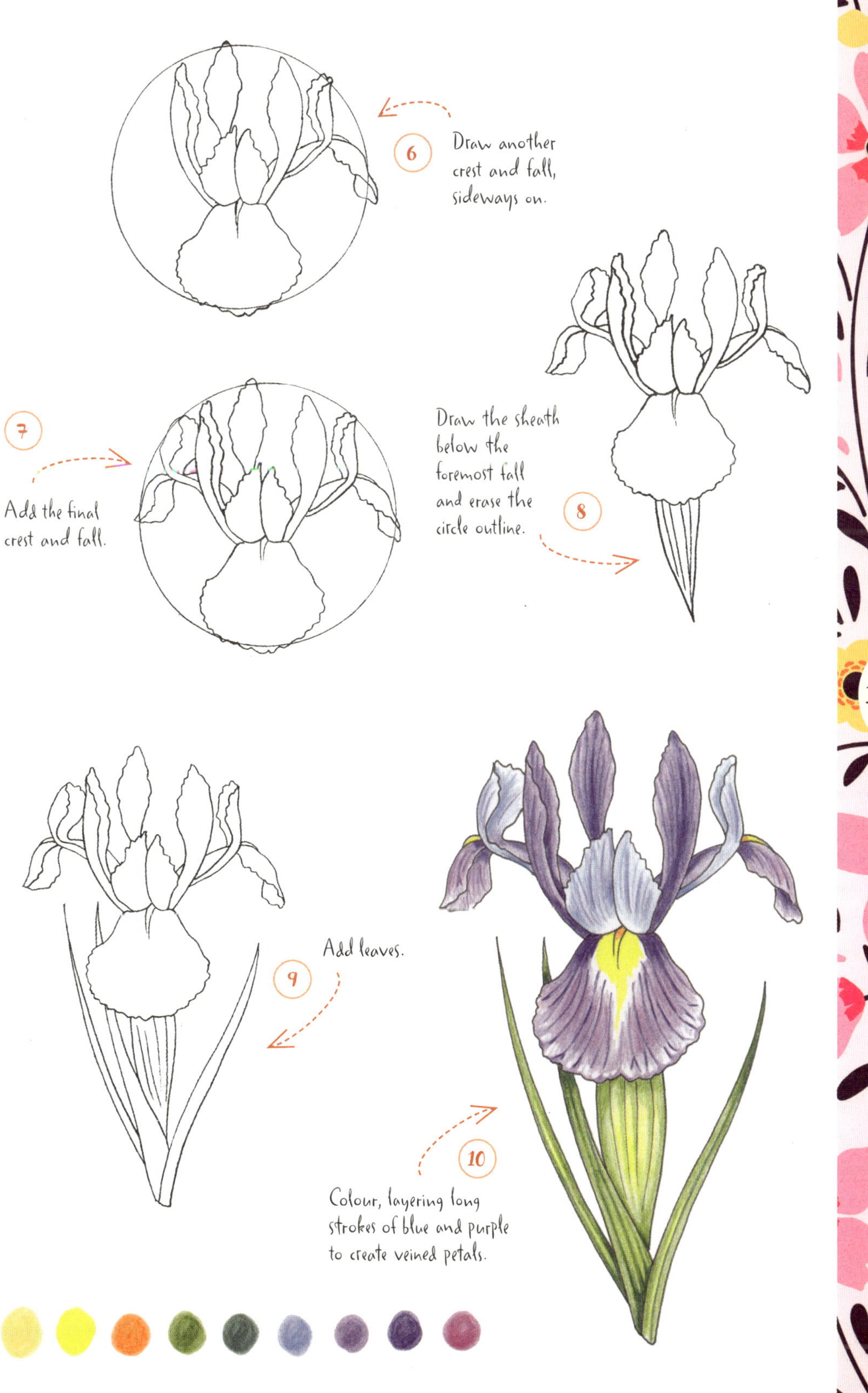
6
Draw another crest and fall, sideways on.
7
Add the final crest and fall.
Draw the sheath below the foremost fall and erase the circle outline.
8
Add leaves.
9
10
Colour, layering long strokes of blue and purple to create veined petals.

Jasmine

Learn to draw this pretty spray of small white flowers from the olive family to brighten and freshen up any sketch.

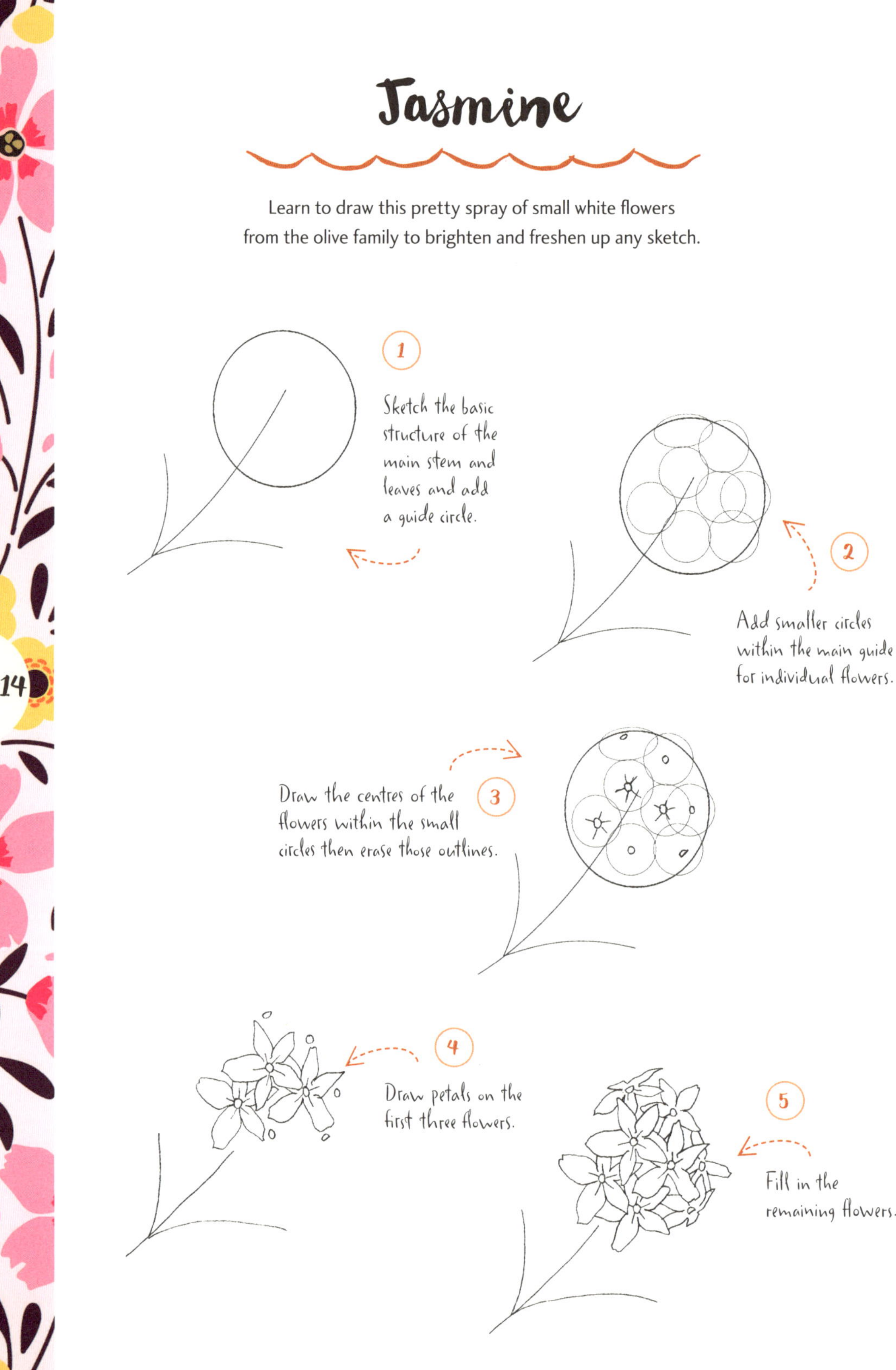

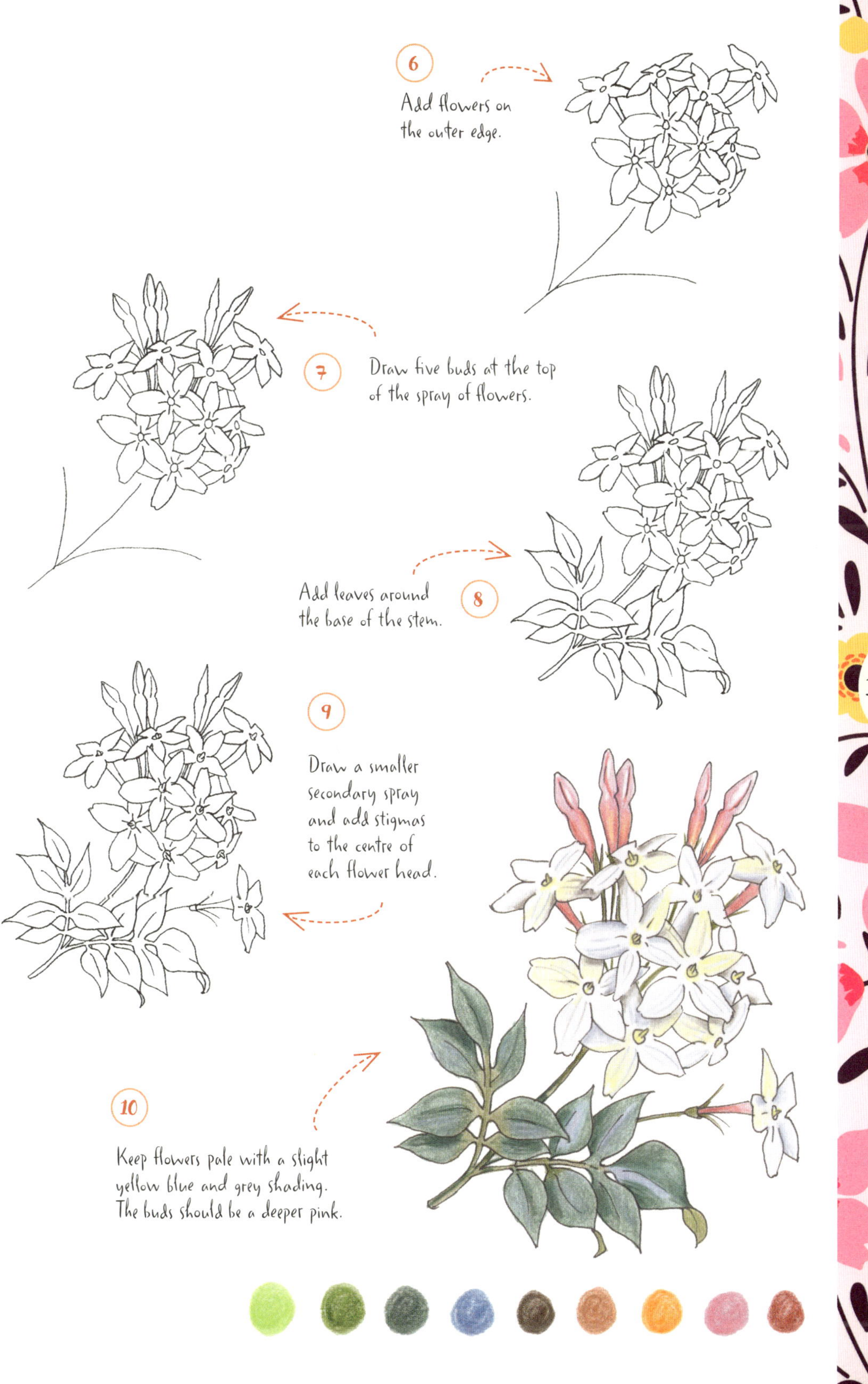
6
Add flowers on the outer edge.
7
Draw five buds at the top of the spray of flowers.
8
Add leaves around the base of the stem.
9
Draw a smaller secondary spray and add stigmas to the centre of each flower head.
10
Keep flowers pale with a slight yellow blue and grey shading. The buds should be a deeper pink.

Delphinium

The long stem of this plant is full of beautiful blue and purple flowers and is great for adding height to a drawing of a bouquet of flowers.

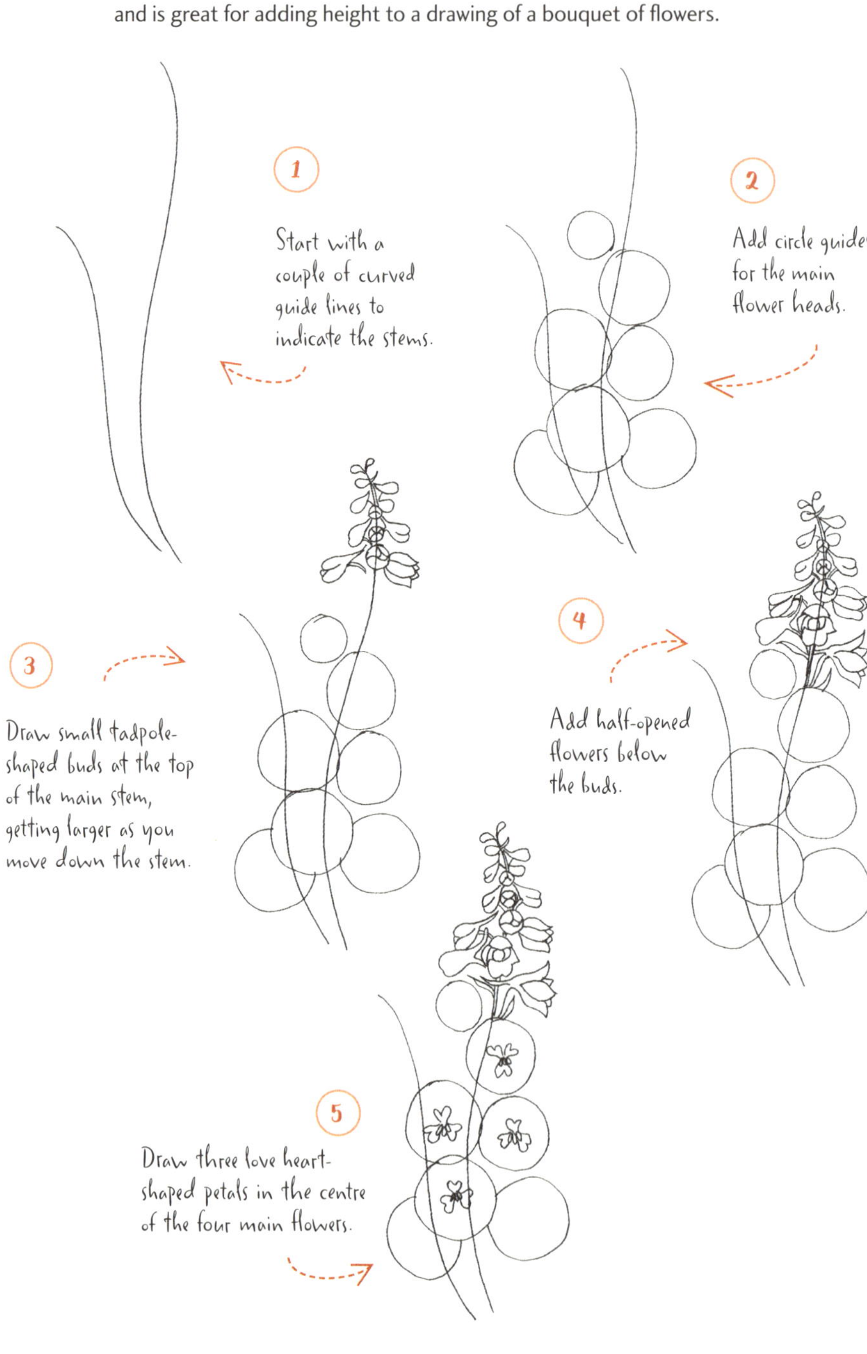

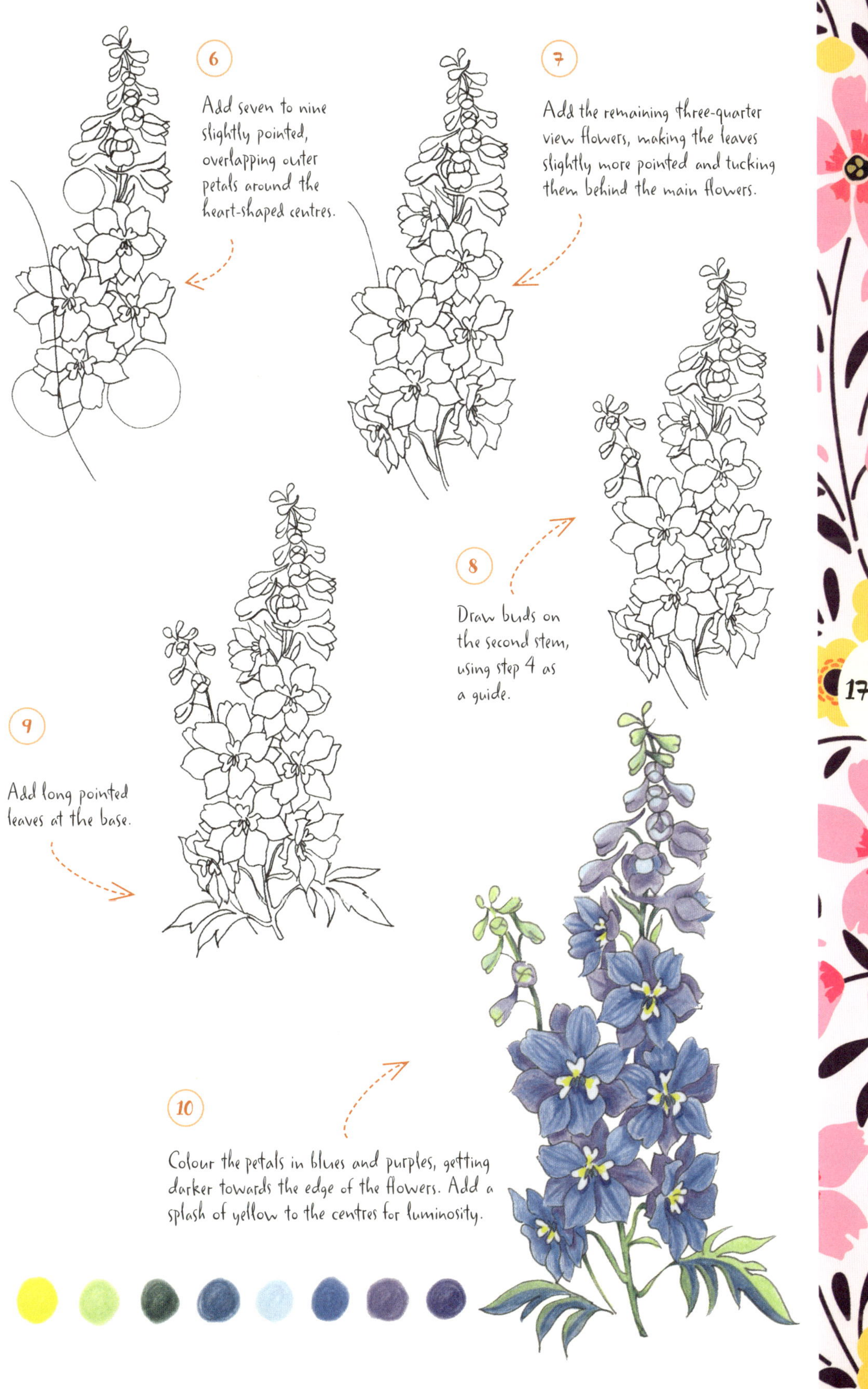

6

Add seven to nine slightly pointed, overlapping outer petals around the heart-shaped centres.

7

Add the remaining three-quarter view flowers, making the leaves slightly more pointed and tucking them behind the main flowers.

8

Draw buds on the second stem, using step 4 as a guide.

9

Add long pointed leaves at the base.

10

Colour the petals in blues and purples, getting darker towards the edge of the flowers. Add a splash of yellow to the centres for luminosity.

Crocus

This pretty perennial from the iris family comes in shades of pinks and purples, so is a lovely spring flower to brighten up any drawing.

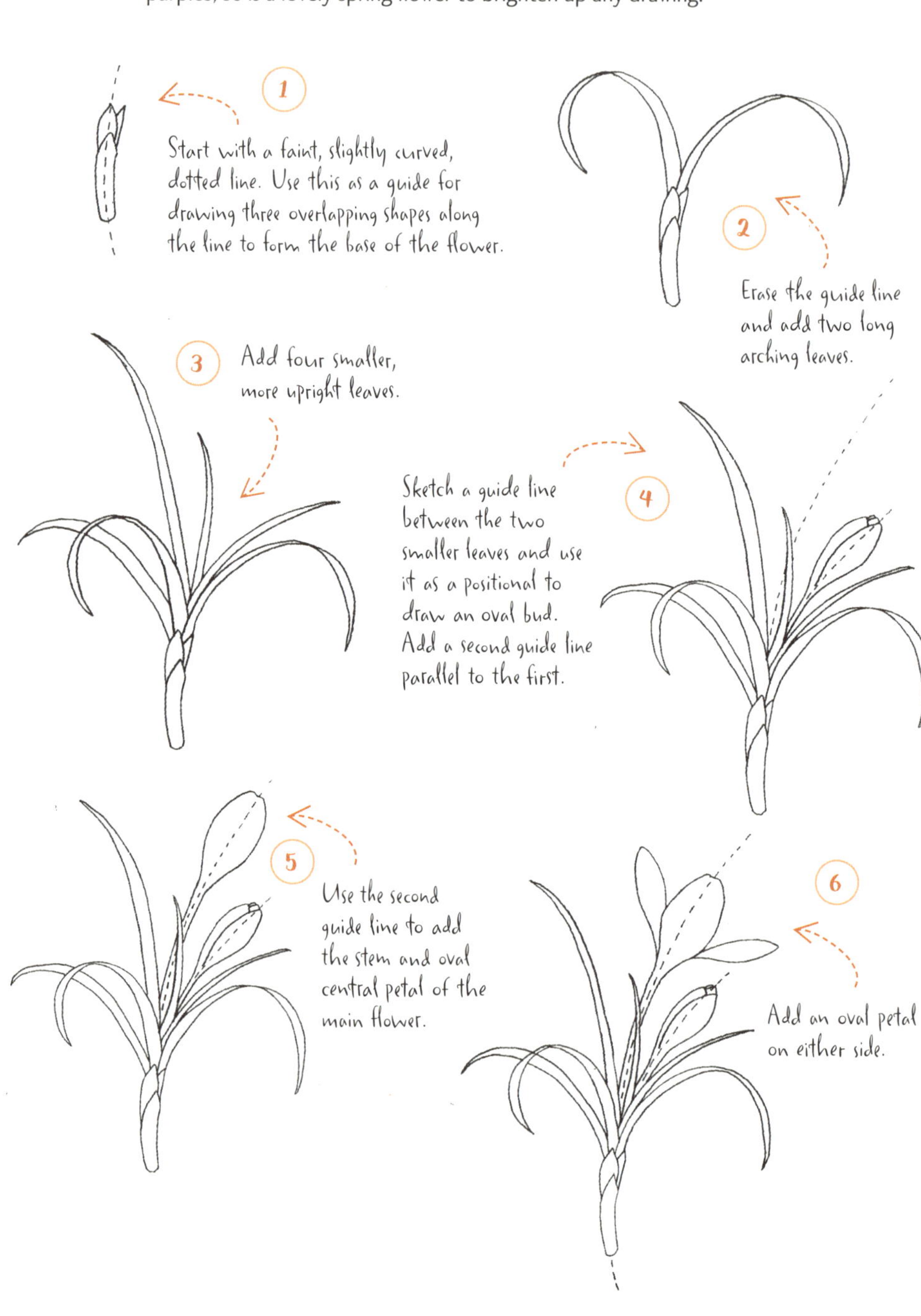

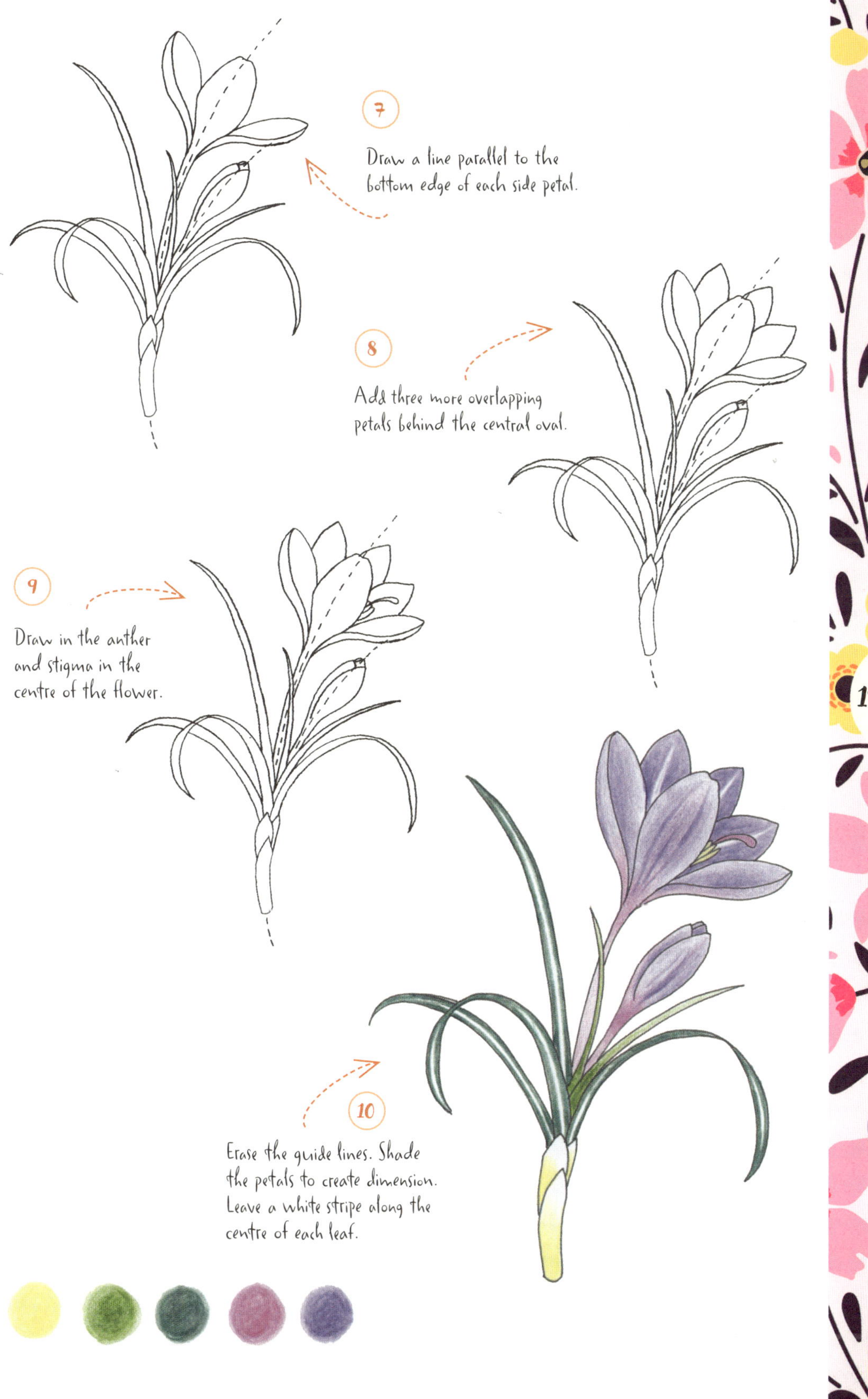
7
Draw a line parallel to the bottom edge of each side petal.
8
Add three more overlapping petals behind the central oval.
9
Draw in the anther and stigma in the centre of the flower.
10
Erase the guide lines. Shade the petals to create dimension. Leave a white stripe along the centre of each leaf.

Lily

Lilies are tall perennial plants with leafy stems. The flowers can be white or pink and have a strong scent.

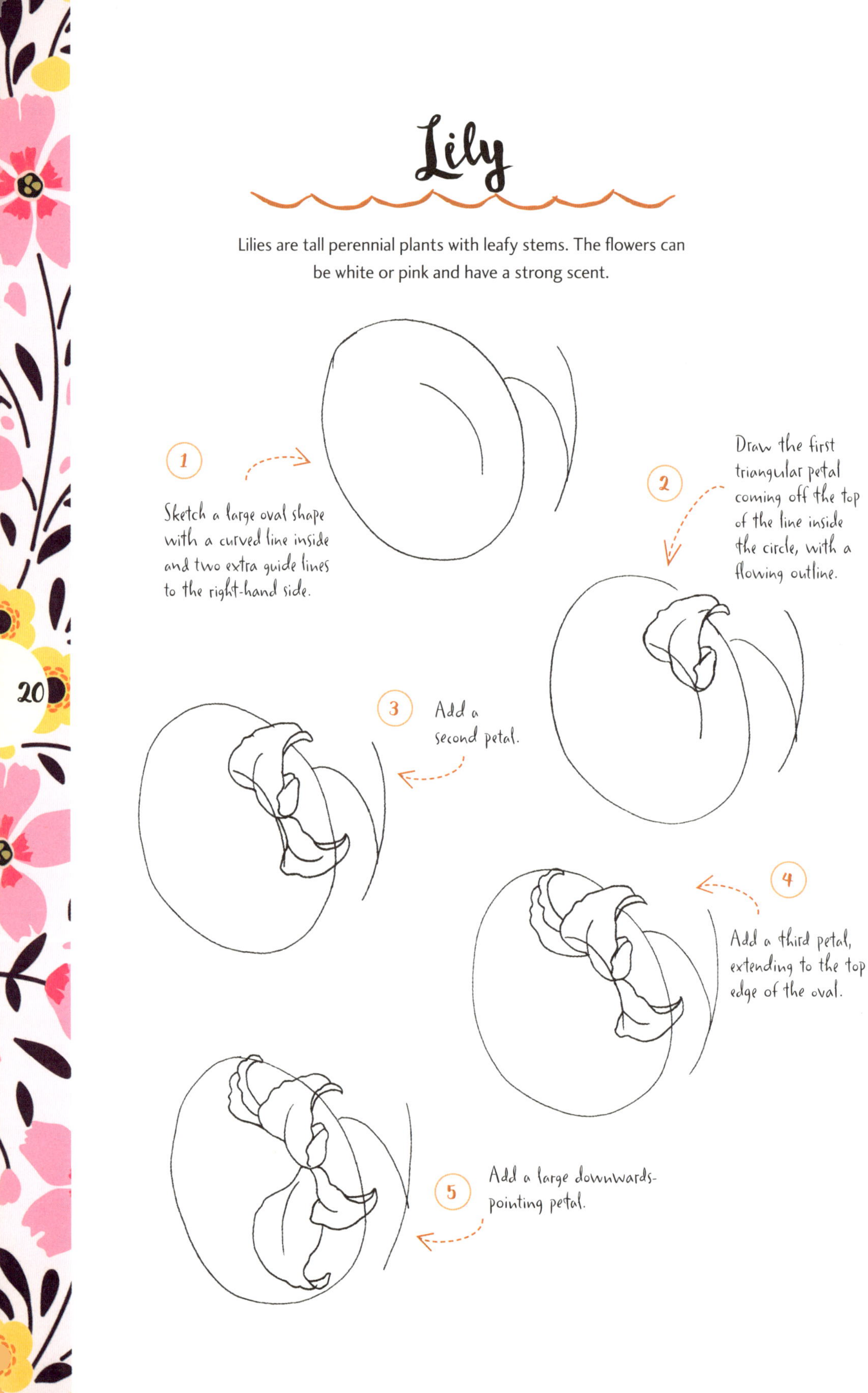

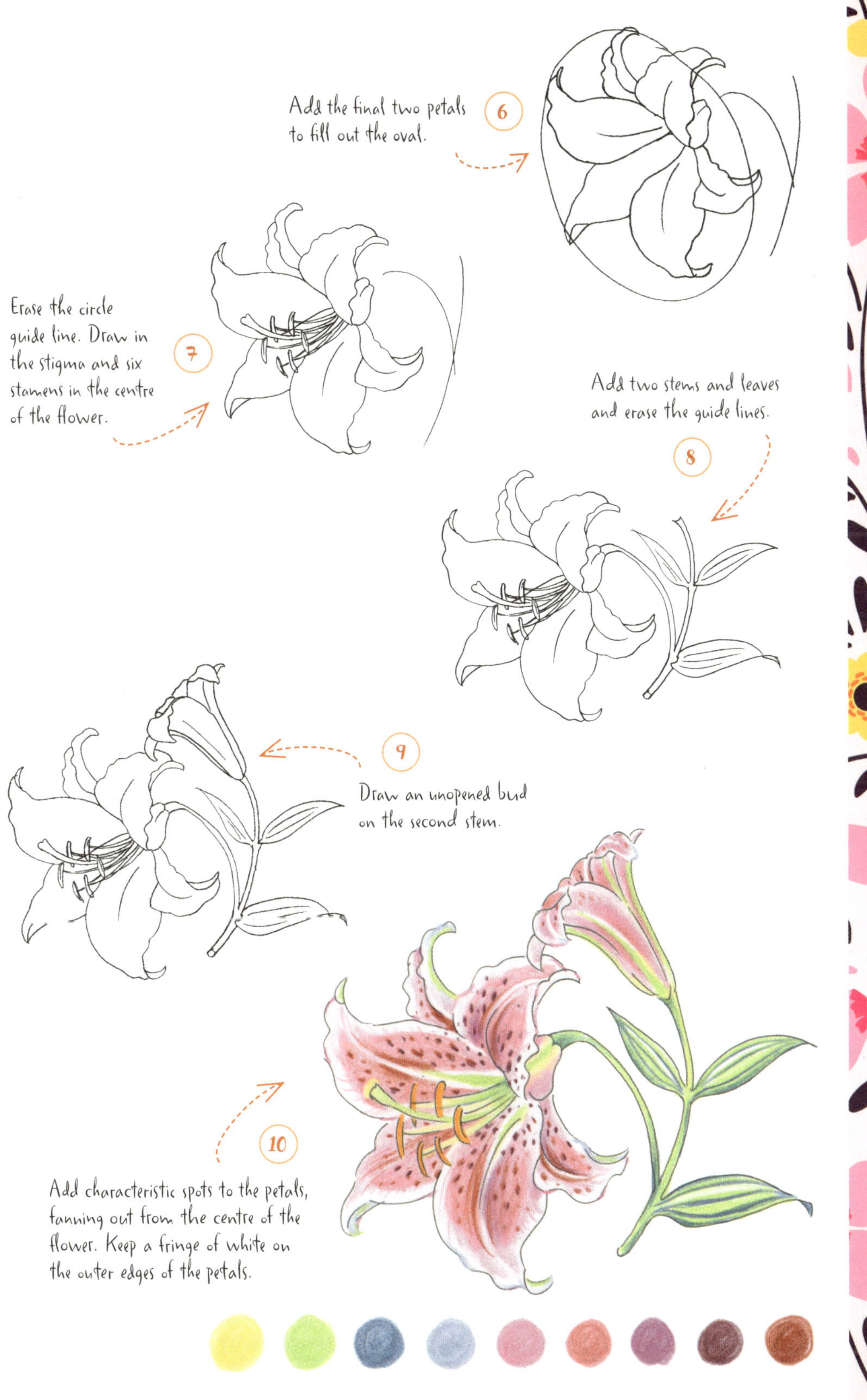
6
Add the final two petals to fill out the oval.
7
Erase the circle guide line. Draw in the stigma and six stamens in the centre of the flower.
8
Add two stems and leaves and erase the guide lines.
9
Draw an unopened bud on the second stem.
10
Add characteristic spots to the petals, fanning out from the centre of the flower. Keep a fringe of white on the outer edges of the petals.

Snowdrop

This delicate flower has a beautiful drooping shape and a clean white colour. Practise blending different greens on the leaves to accentuate freshness.

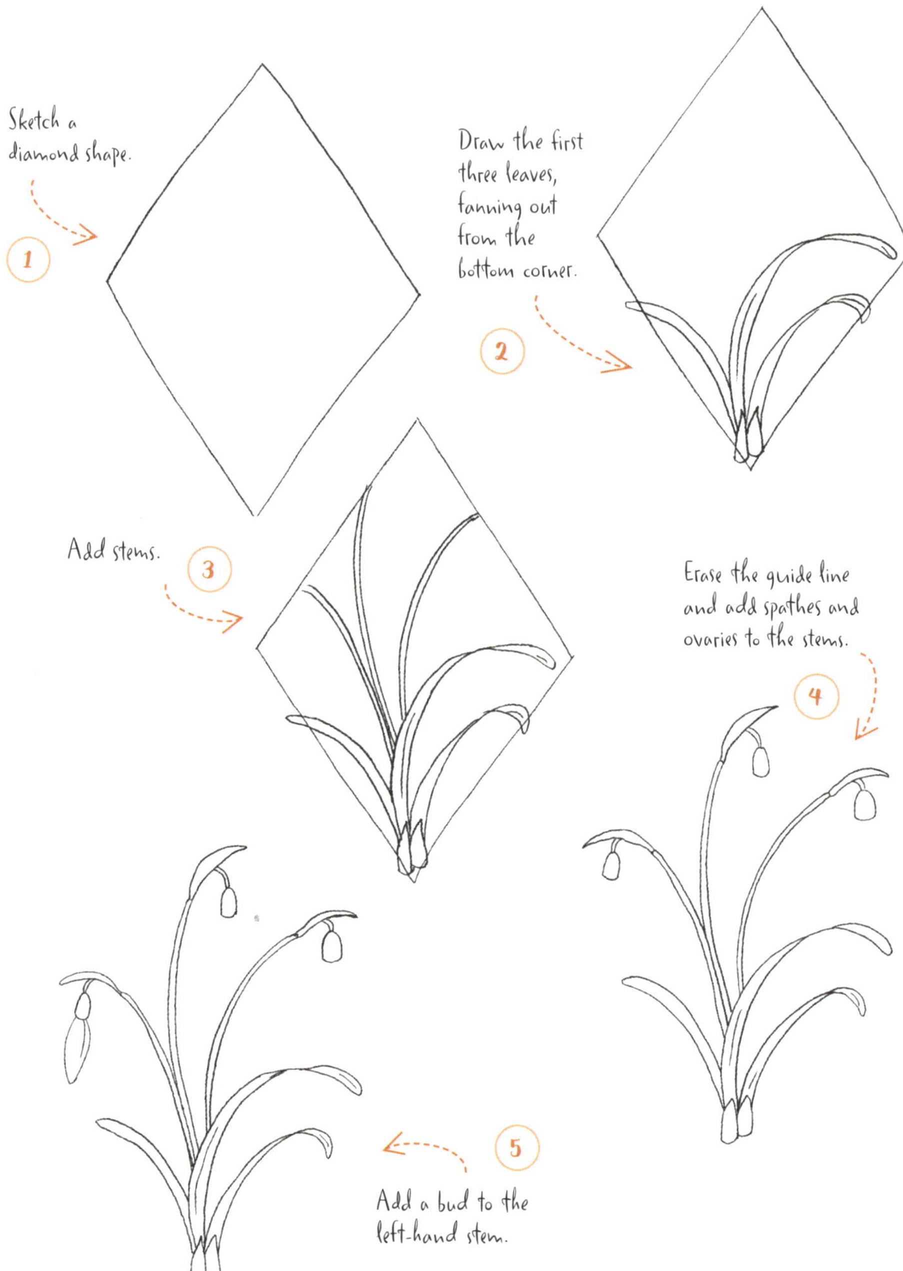

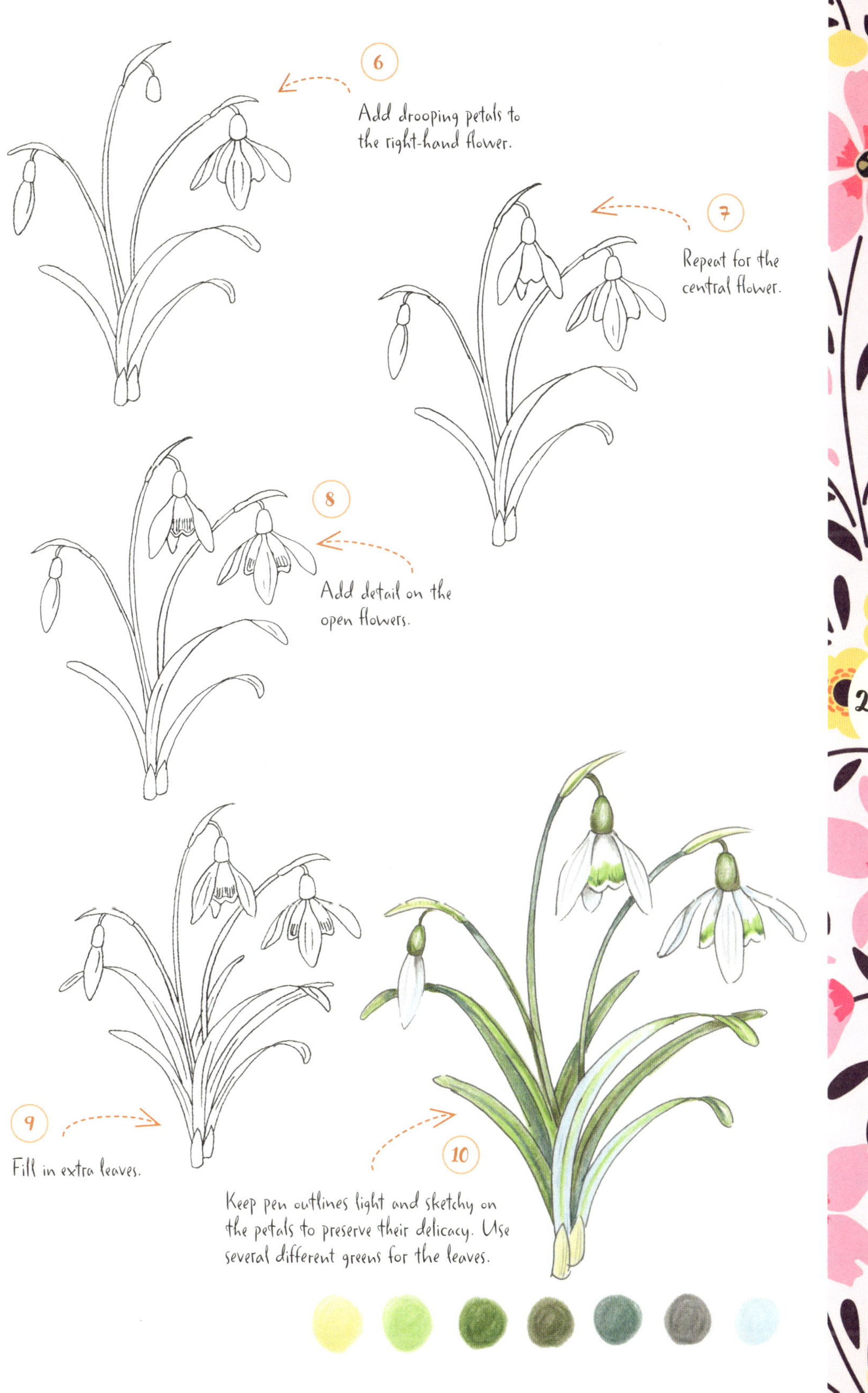
6
Add drooping petals to the right-hand flower.
7
Repeat for the central flower.
8
Add detail on the open flowers.
9
Fill in extra leaves.
10
Keep pen outlines light and sketchy on the petals to preserve their delicacy. Use several different greens for the leaves.

Bird of Paradise

This exotic flower cuts quite a striking design. It is slightly more complex than other illustrations, so follow each stage of the instructions carefully.

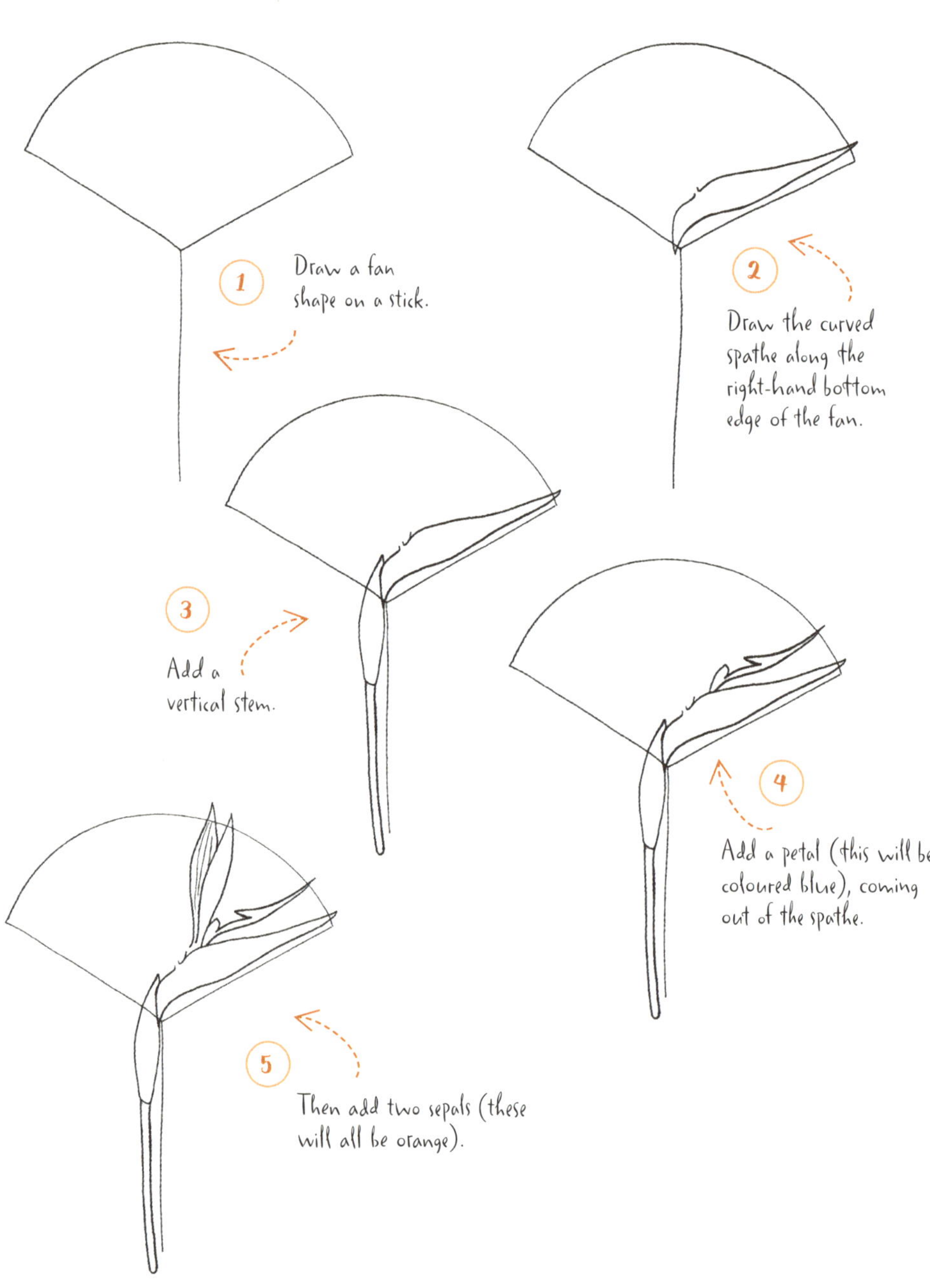

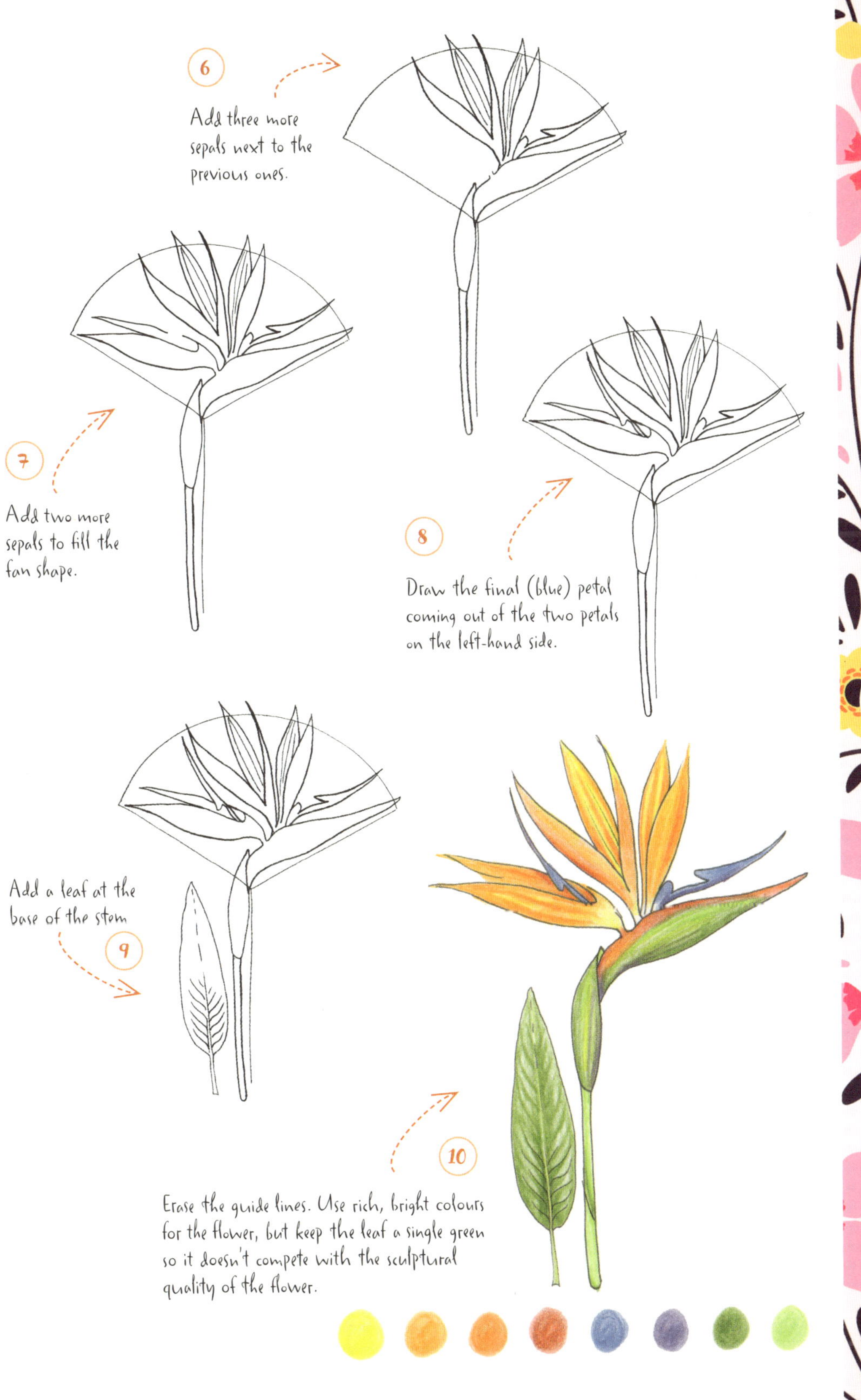
6
Add three more sepals next to the previous ones.
7
Add two more sepals to fill the fan shape.
8
Draw the final (blue) petal coming out of the two petals on the left-hand side.
Add a leaf at the base of the stem
9
10
Erase the guide lines. Use rich, bright colours for the flower, but keep the leaf a single green so it doesn't compete with the sculptural quality of the flower.

Calla

Follow the long lines to create this elegant design that can then be coloured pink, as below, or white or deep purple as other varieties appear.

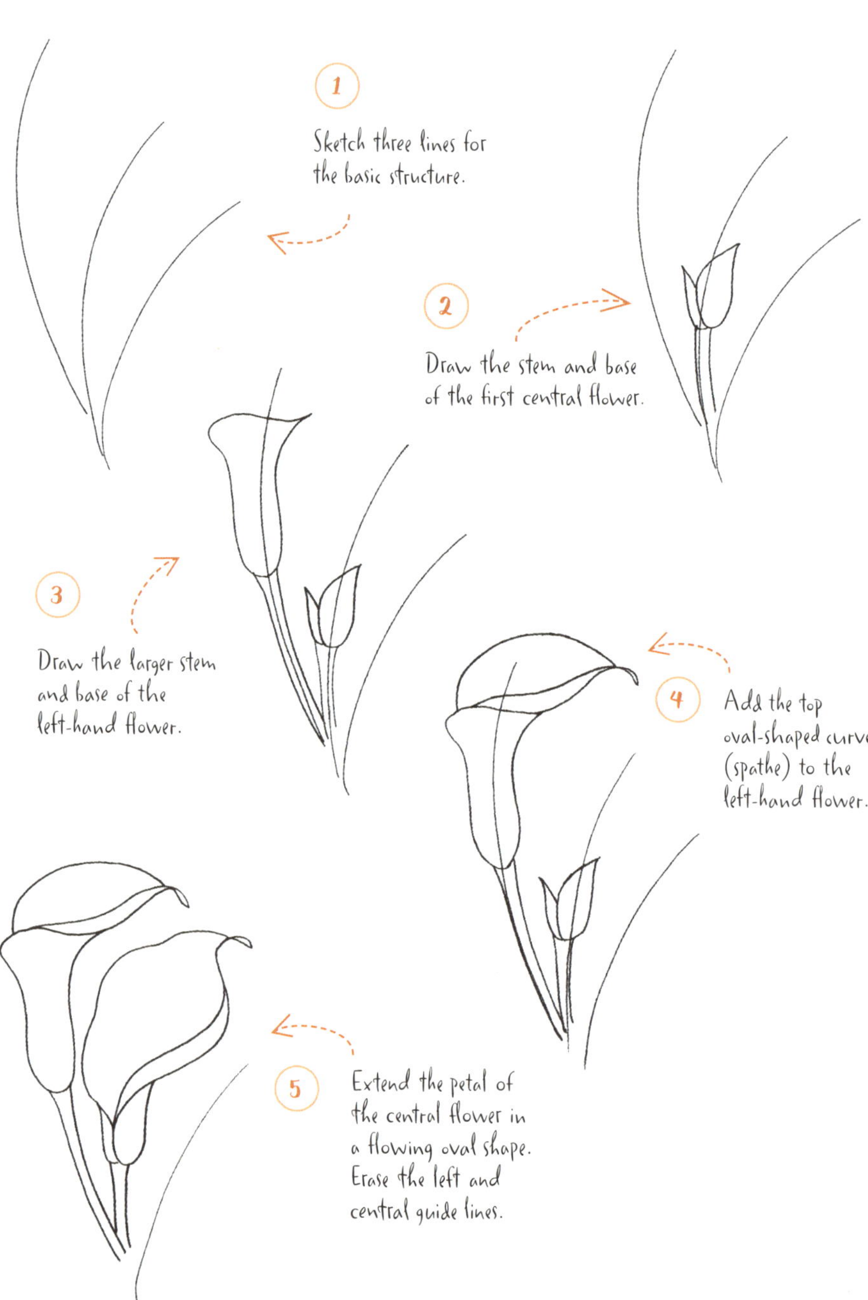

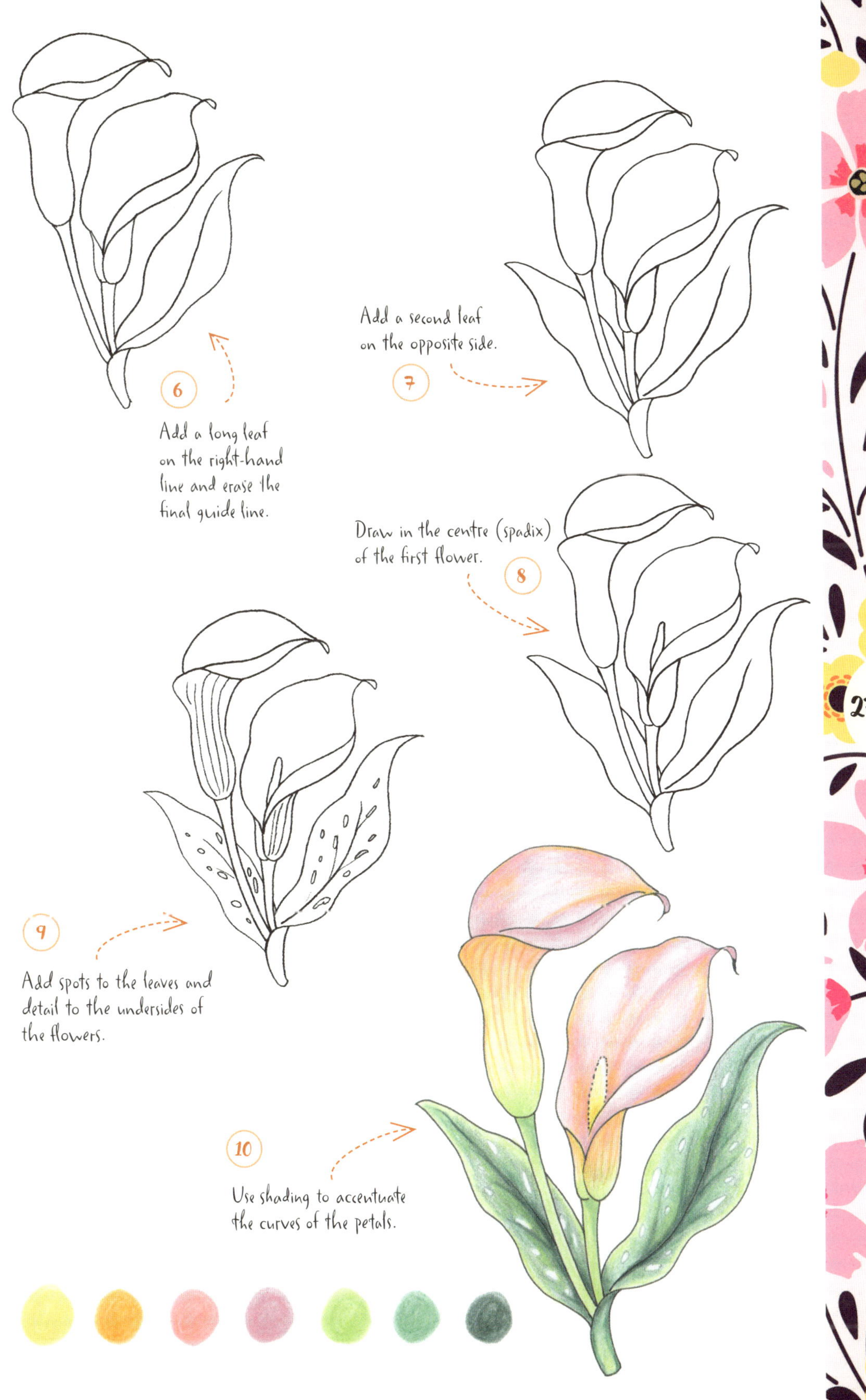
6
Add a long leaf on the right-hand line and erase the final guide line.
Add a second leaf on the opposite side.
7
Draw in the centre (spadix) of the first flower.
8
9
Add spots to the leaves and detail to the undersides of the flowers.
10
Use shading to accentuate the curves of the petals.

Foxglove

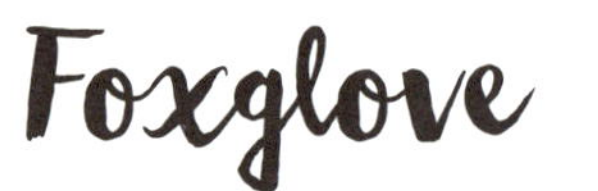

This pretty plant has many bell-shaped flowers along a central stem, which will add a splash of colour to any drawing.

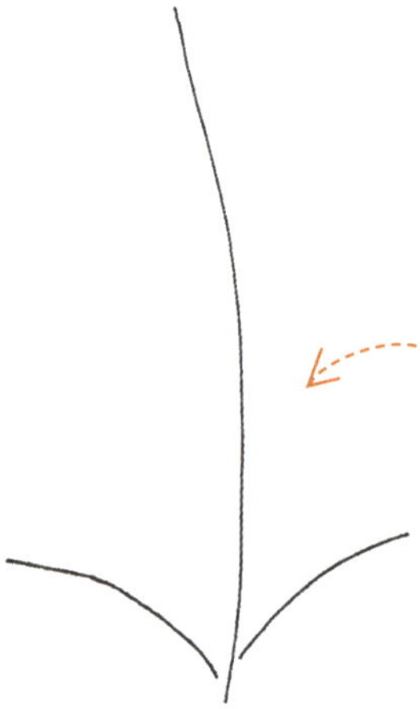

1 Draw the guide lines for the stem and leaves.

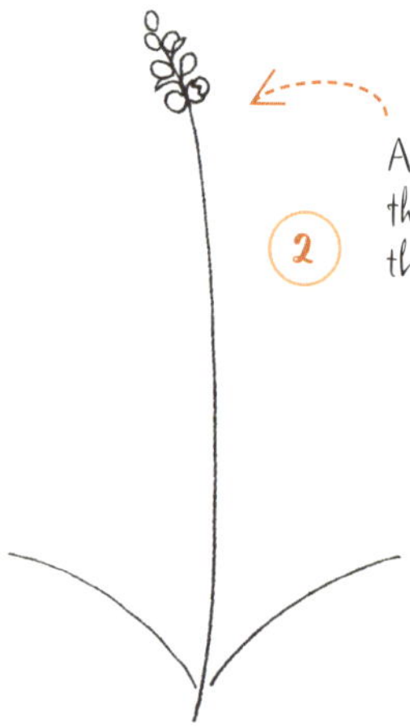

2 Add buds at the top of the stem.

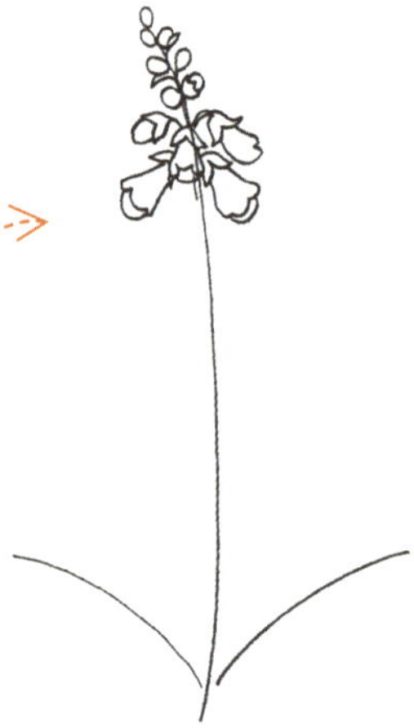

3 Draw a cluster of five semi-open buds underneath.

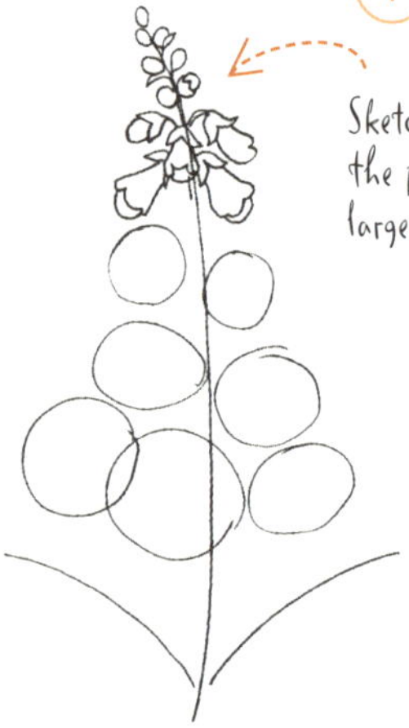

4 Sketch guide circles for the position of seven larger flower heads.

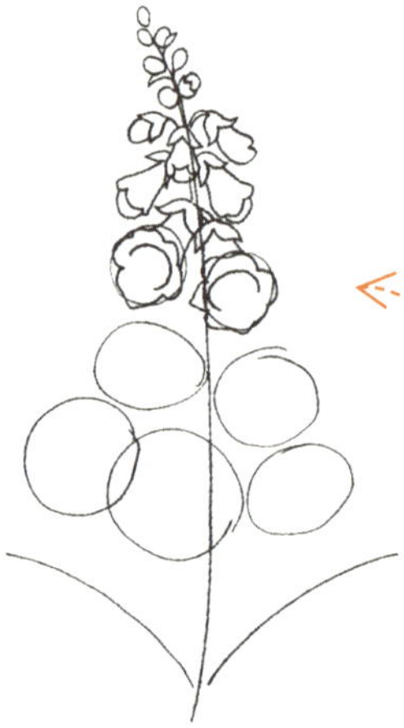

5 Draw in the first two flowers using the circles as a guide and adding a frilly edge.

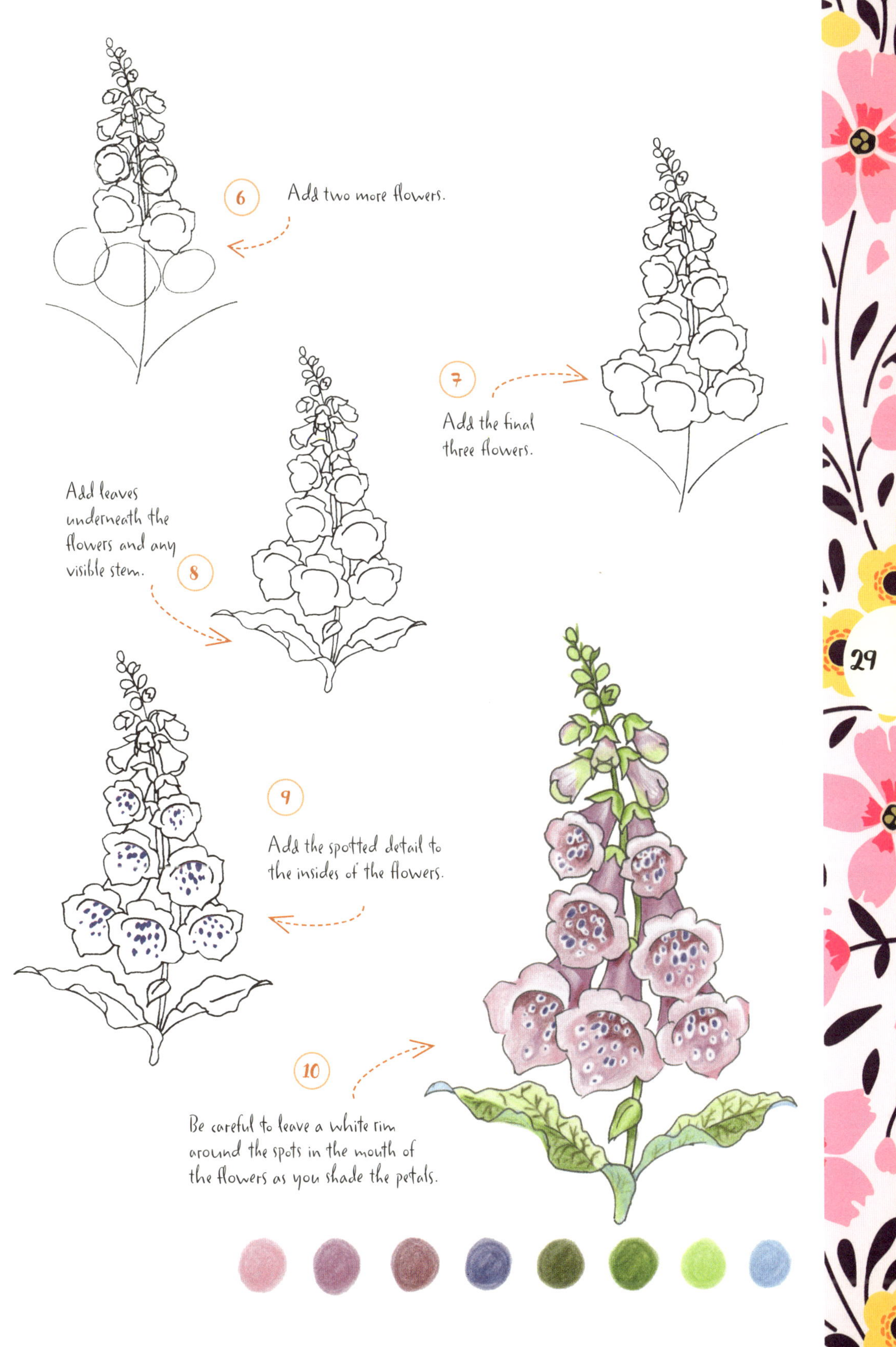
6
Add two more flowers.
7
Add the final three flowers.
Add leaves underneath the flowers and any visible stem.
8
9
Add the spotted detail to the insides of the flowers.
10
Be careful to leave a white rim around the spots in the mouth of the flowers as you shade the petals.

Water Lily

This pretty floating flower lives on water. It has large rounded leaves and comes in a lovely selection of colours, from oranges to whites and pinks.

1 Draw a bowl-shaped outline.

2 Draw five pointed petals along the front edge.

3 Add the spiky stamens in the centre.

4 Add three petals to the back rim and erase the guide lines.

5 Draw two oval guide lines around the main flower.

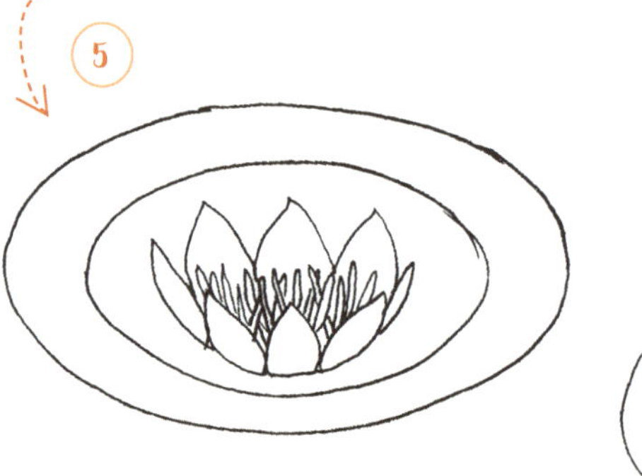

6 Fill the first oval with petals.

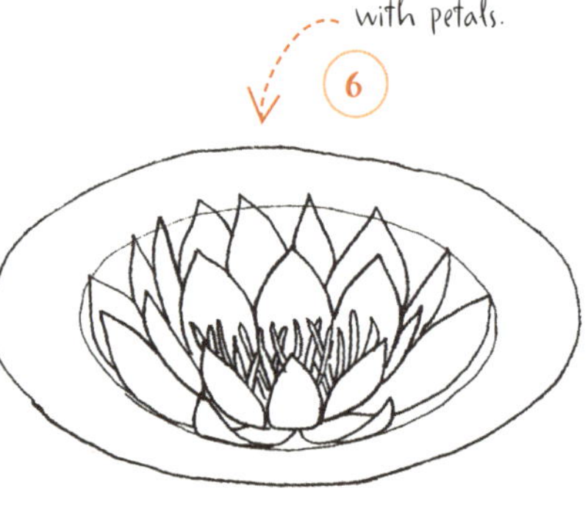

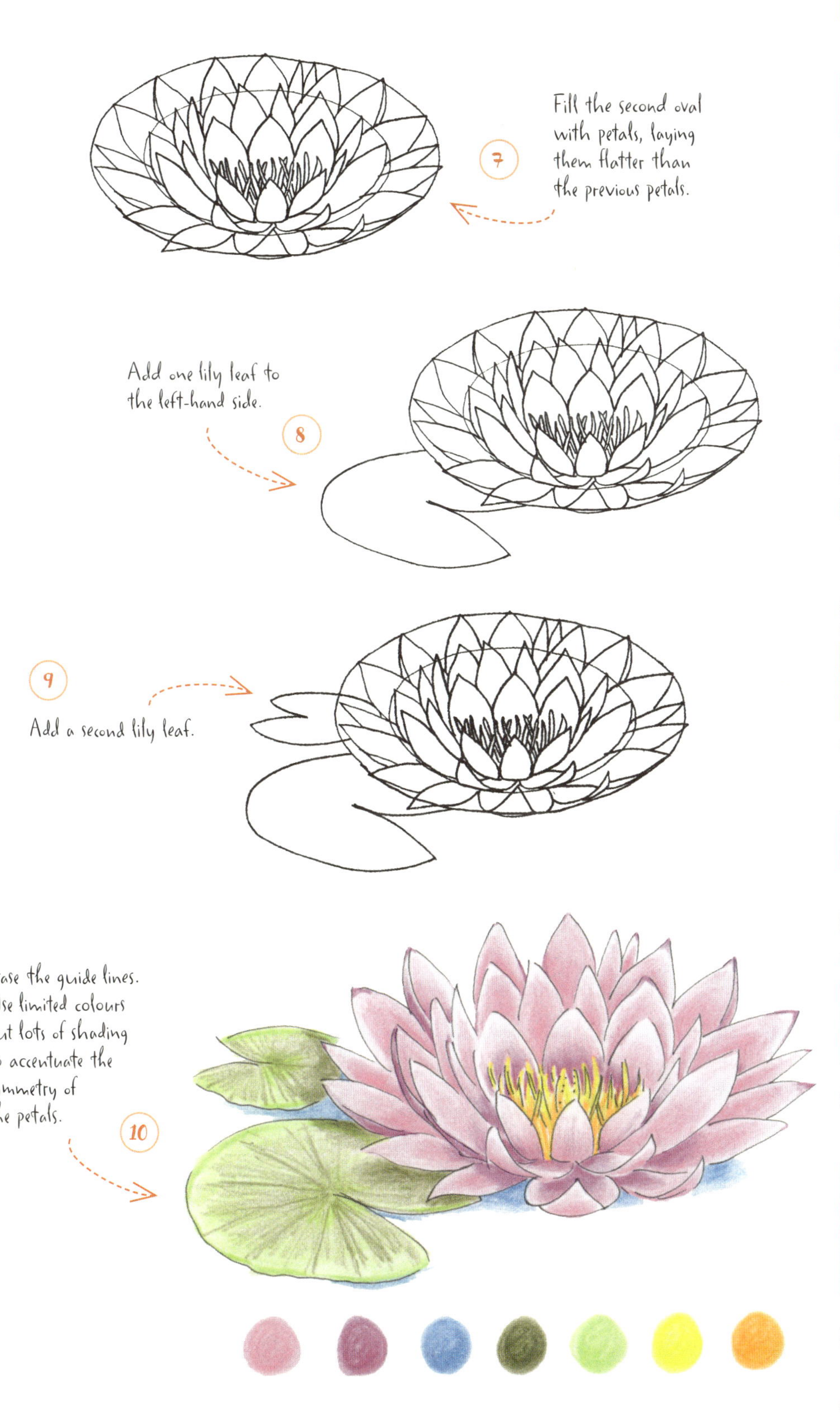
7
Fill the second oval with petals, laying them flatter than the previous petals.
Add one lily leaf to the left-hand side.
8
9
Add a second lily leaf.
Erase the guide lines. Use limited colours but lots of shading to accentuate the symmetry of the petals.
10

Tulip

These large, brightly coloured flowers generally appear in red, yellow or pink, but can come in other colours too. They have tightly packed petals that open up to a larger, more blousy shape.

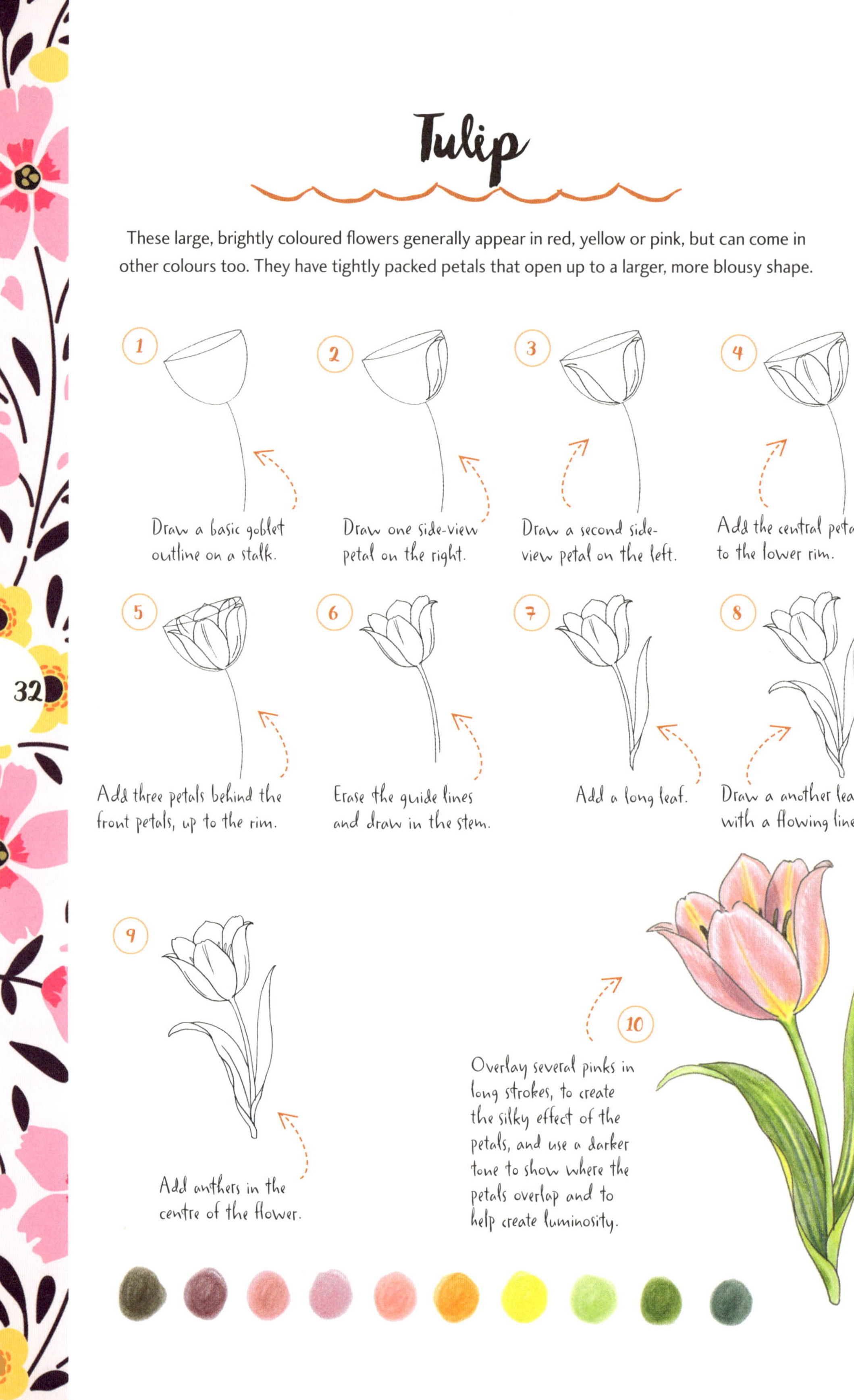

Gerbera

These full and sturdy flowers add a bright shock of colour to any bouquet. Experiment with colours and try these in yellows, reds and pinks too.

1

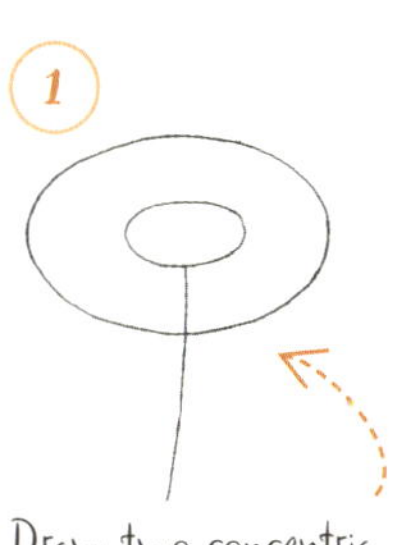

Draw two concentric ovals on a stick.

2

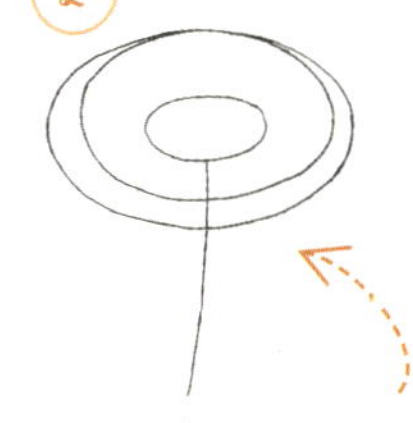

Draw a third oval in between the first two.

3

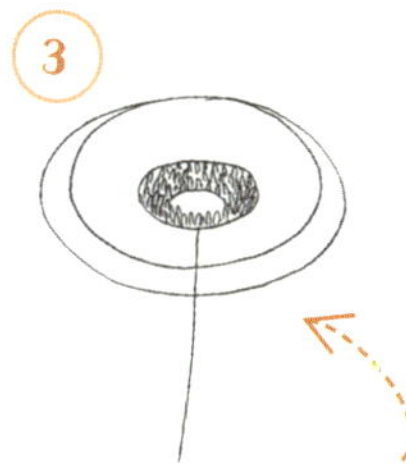

Draw in the centre of the flower.

4

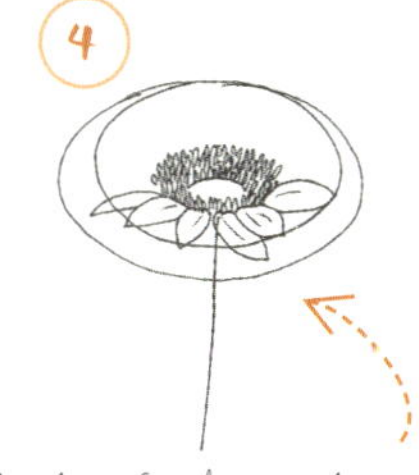

Add six foreshortened petals coming from centre.

5

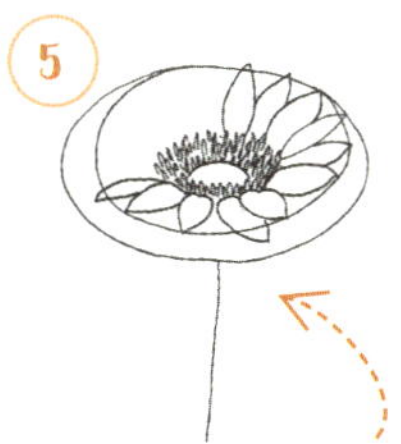

Fill the top right of the internal oval with petals.

6

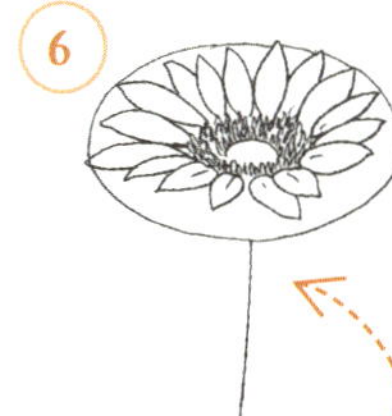

Repeat with the top left side.

7

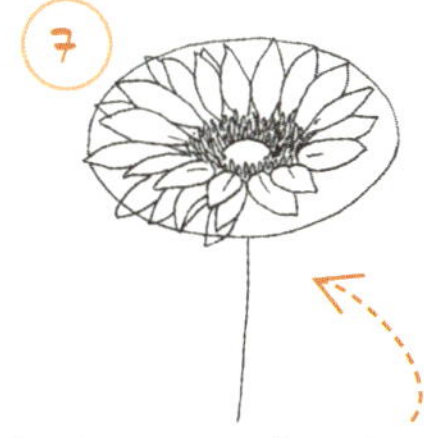

Add a lower row of petals in the left-hand quarter of the outer oval.

8

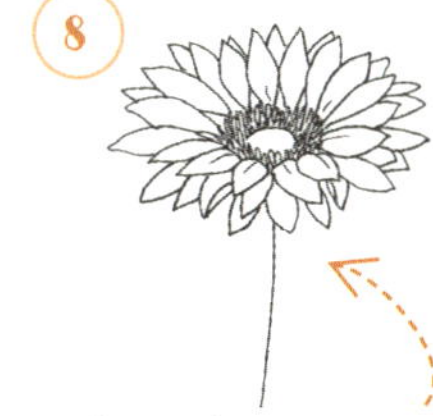

Fill the oval by adding petals underneath and between the first layer of petals. Erase the circular guide.

9

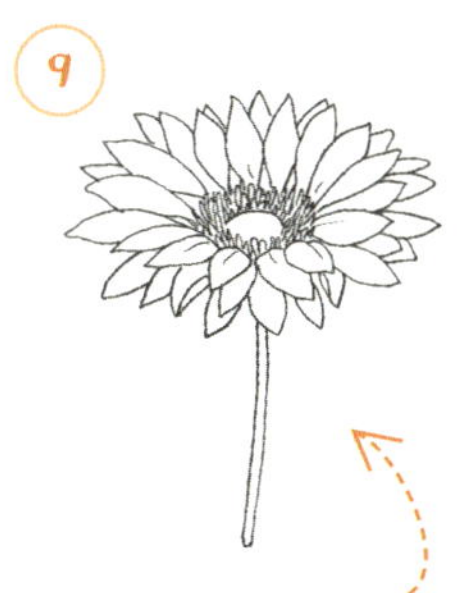

Draw in the stem.

10

Keep the centre dark and leave some white striations/stripes on the petals to keep them fresh looking.

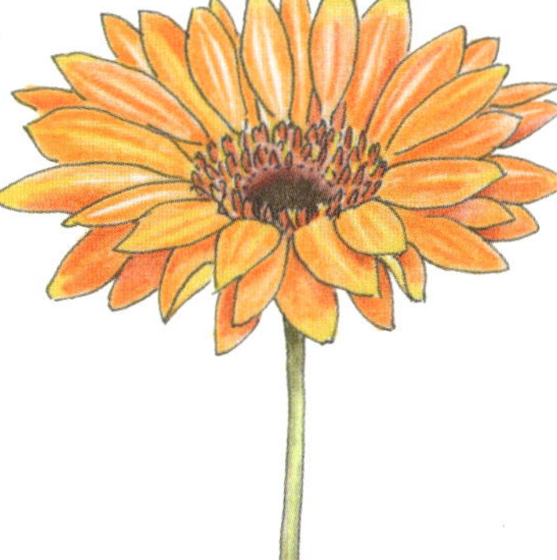

Sweet Pea

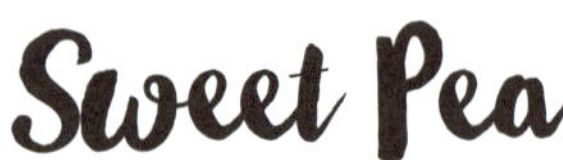

Sweet peas are an annual climbing plant and come in a lovely array of reds, pinks, purples and blues. This is a great flower to practise blending and shading with.

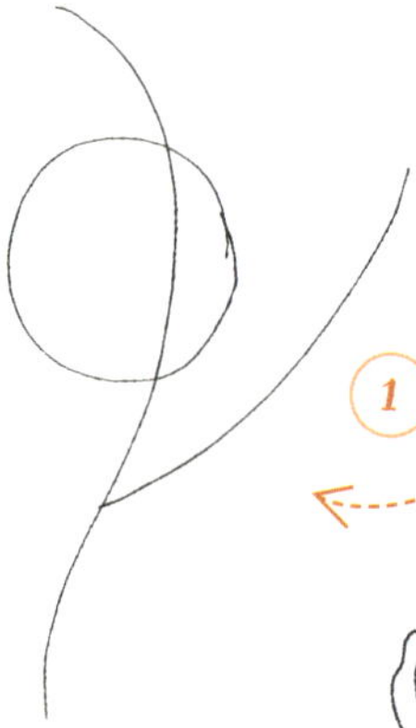

1 Sketch the basic stem lines and a guide circle for the central flower.

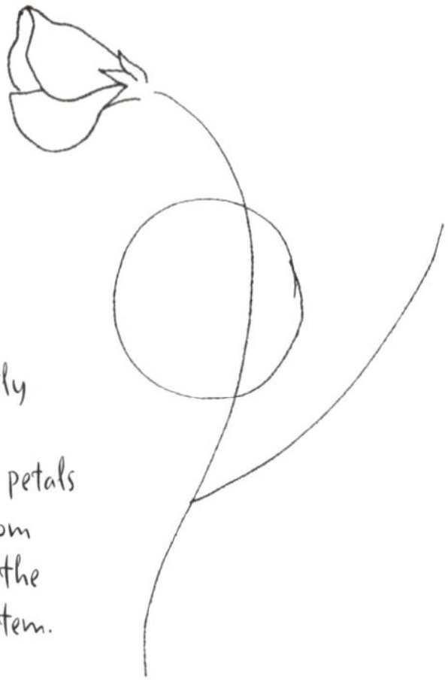

2 Draw slightly closed and overlapping petals emerging from the end of the left-hand stem.

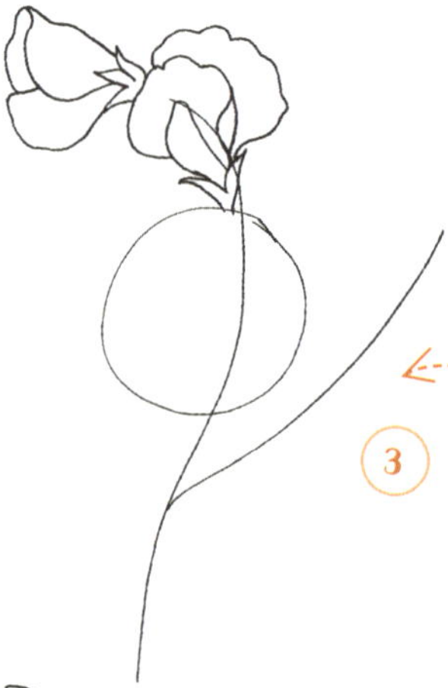

3 Working down the stem, add the next flower with rounded, open petals.

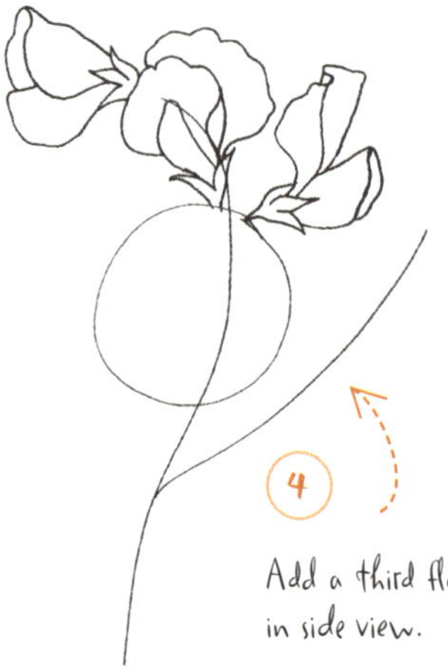

4 Add a third flower in side view.

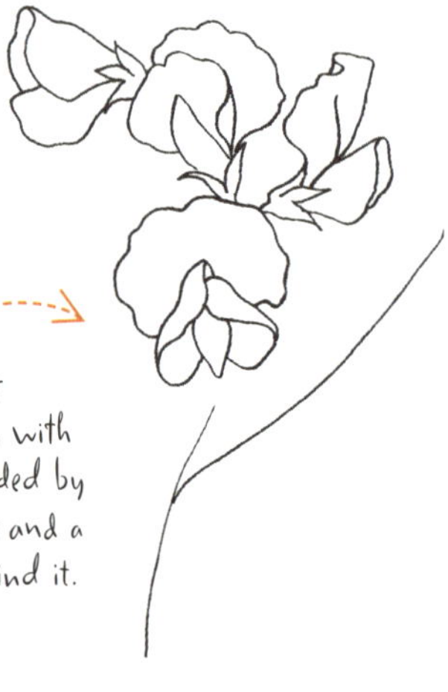

5 Draw the next flower within the guide circle, with a central bud, surrounded by two overlapping petals and a semi-circular petal behind it. Erase the guide circle.

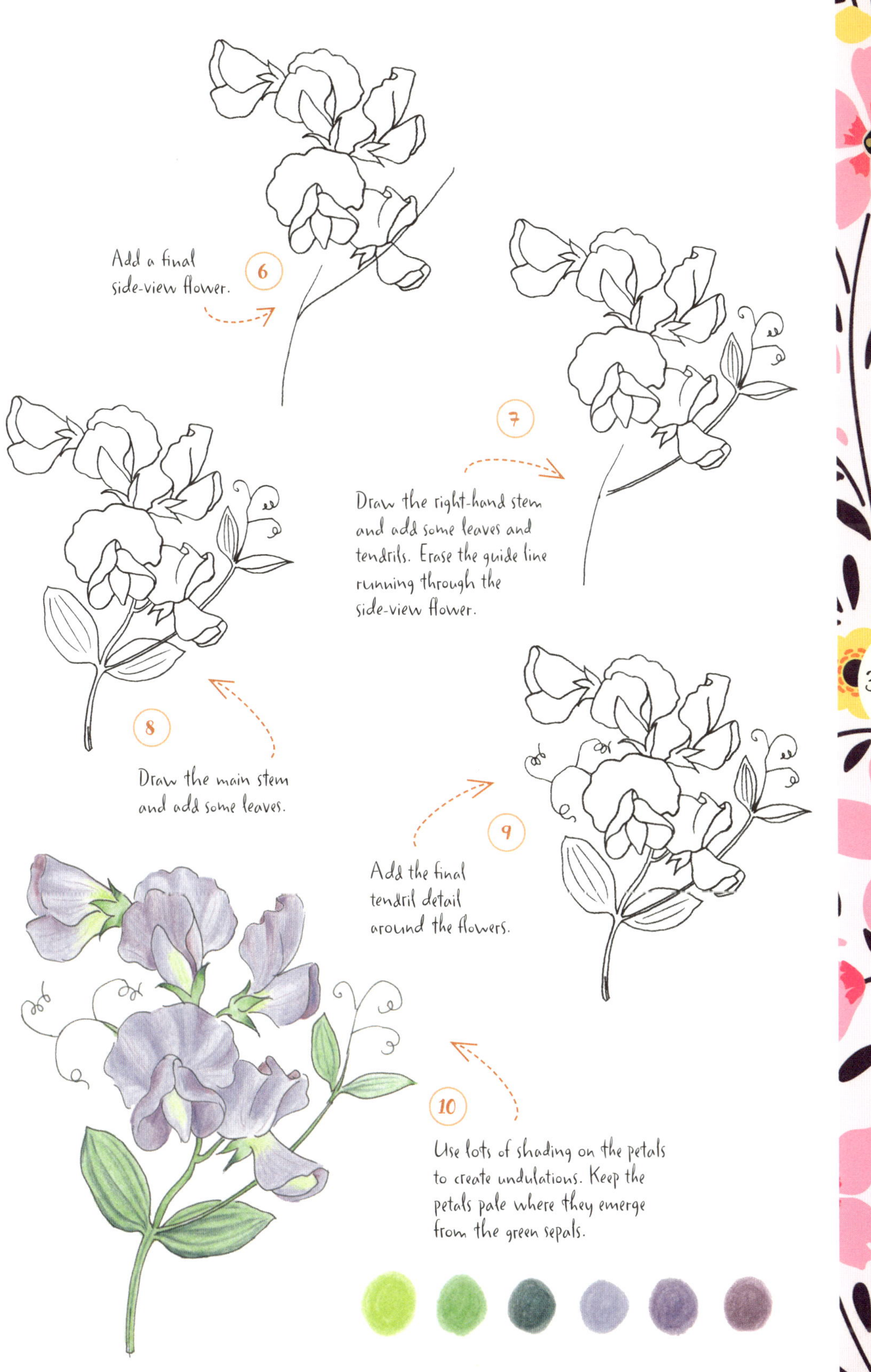
6
Add a final side-view flower.
7
Draw the right-hand stem and add some leaves and tendrils. Erase the guide line running through the side-view flower.
8
Draw the main stem and add some leaves.
9
Add the final tendril detail around the flowers.
10
Use lots of shading on the petals to create undulations. Keep the petals pale where they emerge from the green sepals.

Lavender

This fragrant plant has a multitude of uses, from its ability to attract bees to the garden to its applications in beauty and health remedies. The spiky flowers should be easy to master with these instructions.

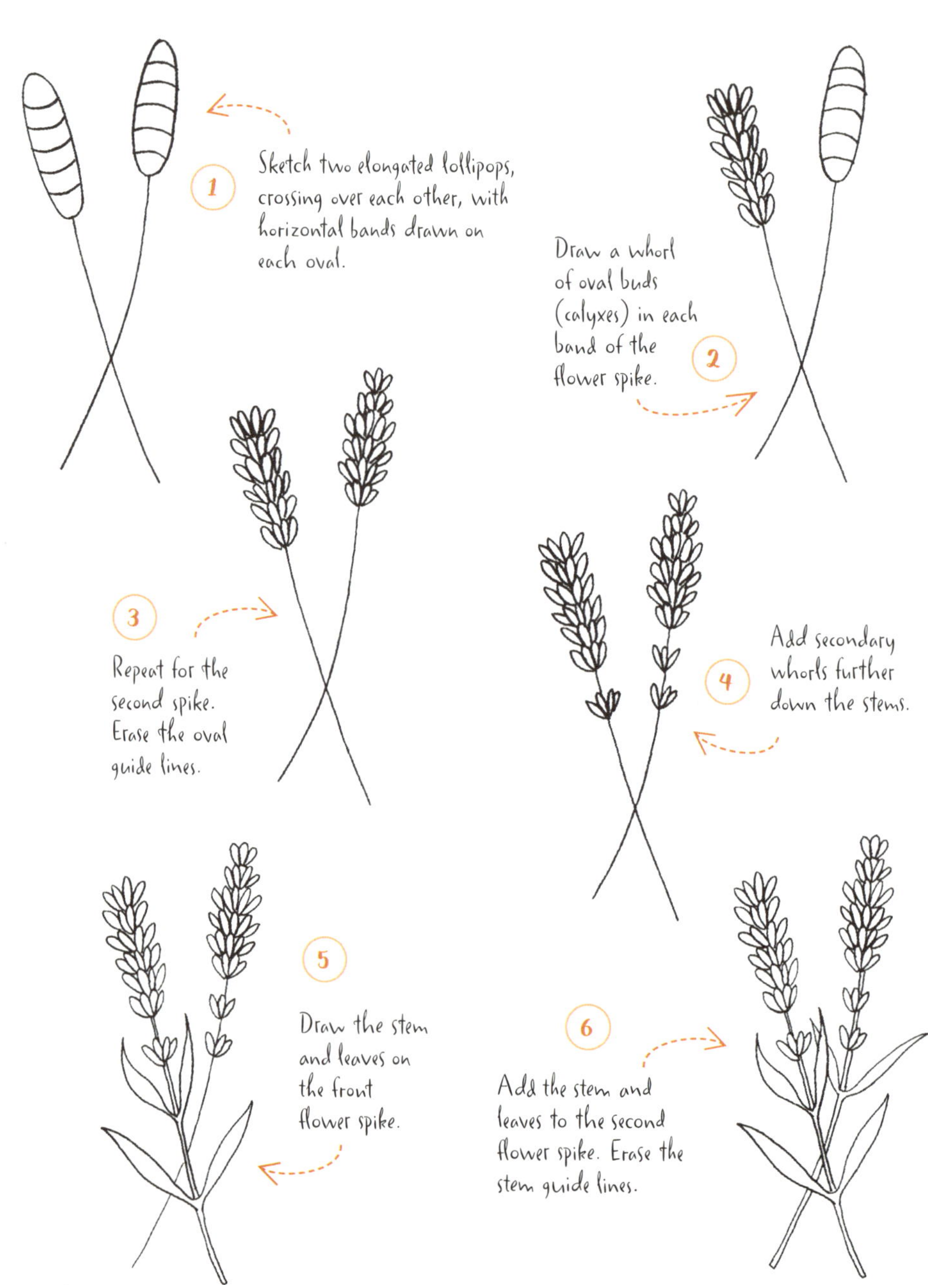

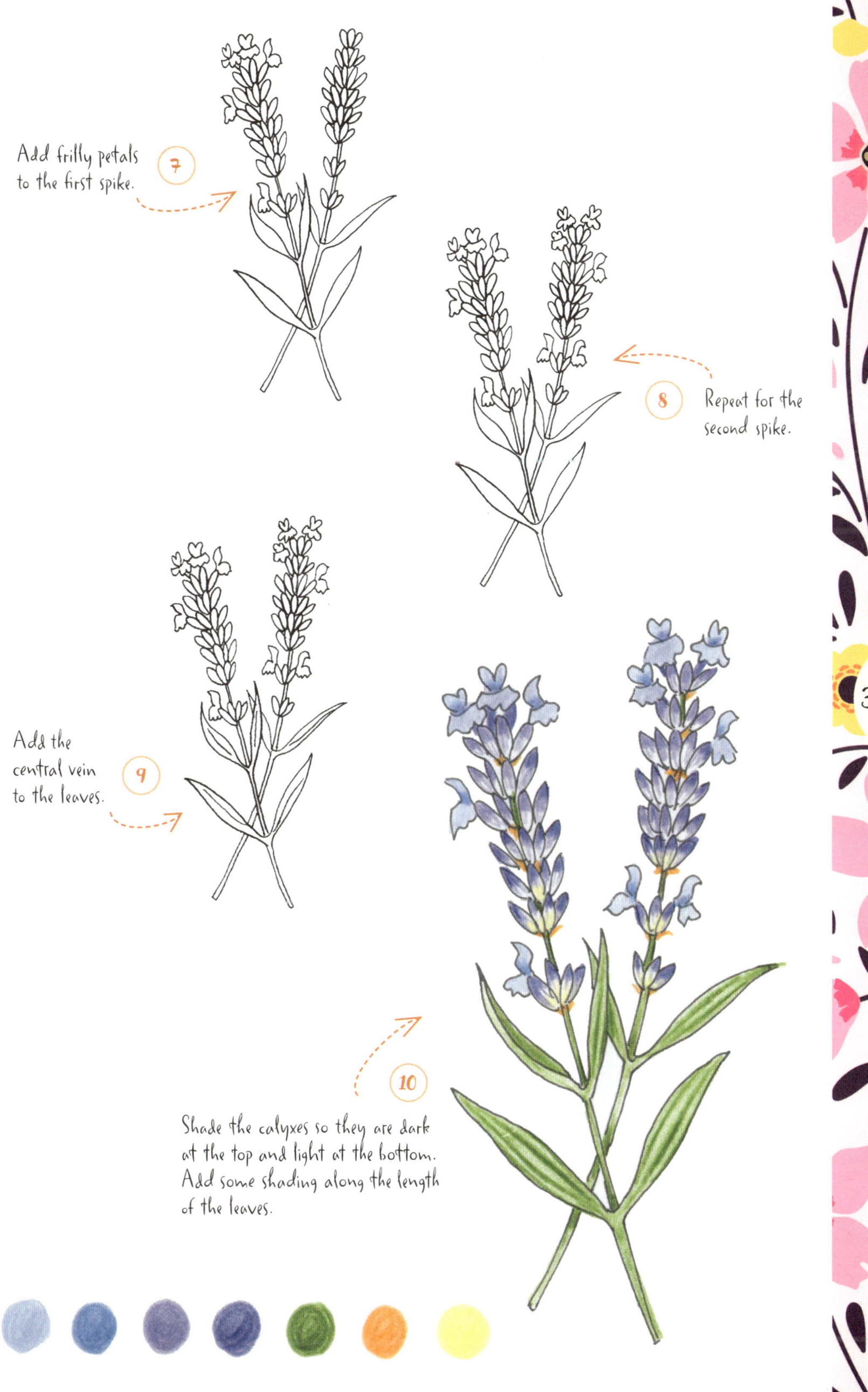
Add frilly petals to the first spike.
7
8
Repeat for the second spike.
Add the central vein to the leaves.
9
10
Shade the calyxes so they are dark at the top and light at the bottom. Add some shading along the length of the leaves.

Passion Flower

The passion flower is an evergreen climbing plant, so once you have mastered one of these unusual looking flowers, you could progress to a fuller climbing design.

1 Begin with the stigmas and ovary in the centre of the flower.

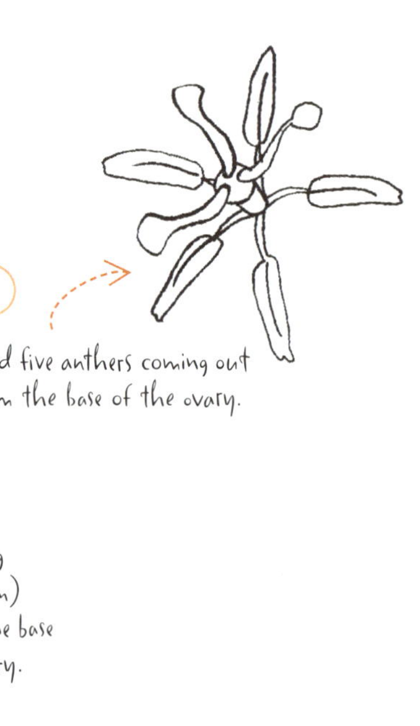

2 Add five anthers coming out from the base of the ovary.

3 Add a ring (operculum) around the base of the ovary.

4 Sketch two, slightly off-centre, circles.

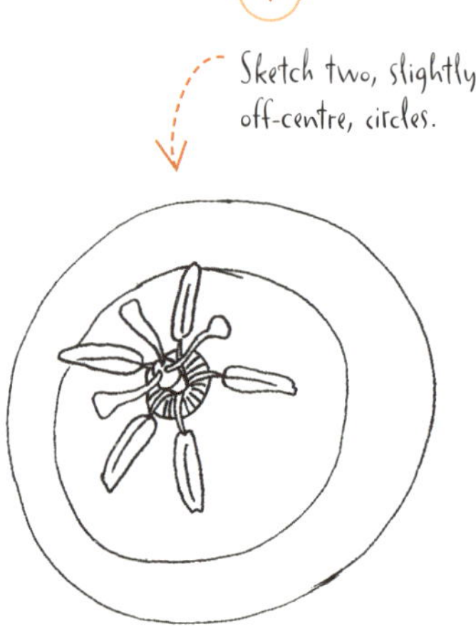

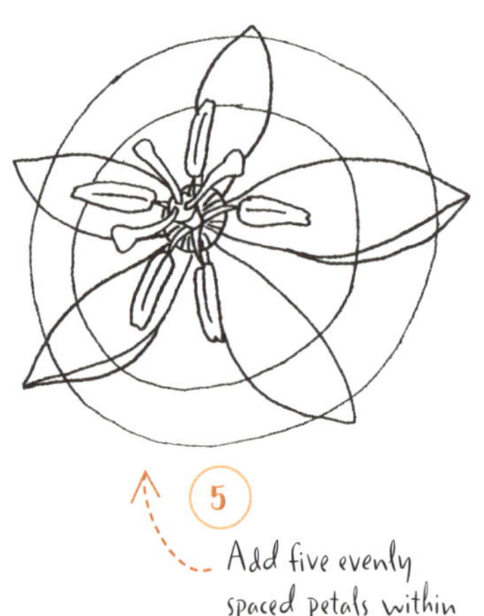

5 Add five evenly spaced petals within the larger circle.

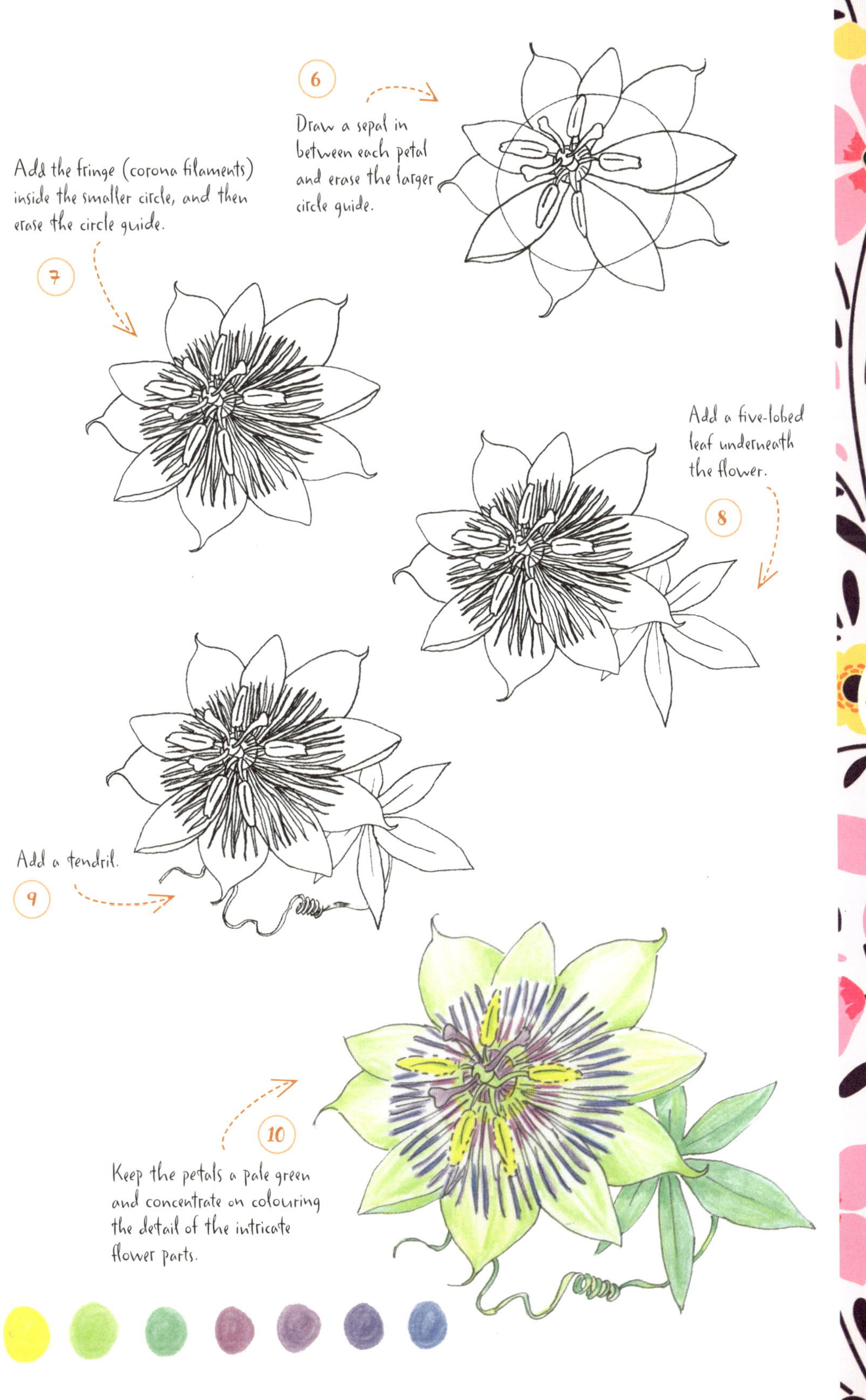
6
Draw a sepal in between each petal and erase the larger circle guide.
7
Add the fringe (corona filaments) inside the smaller circle, and then erase the circle guide.
8
Add a five-lobed leaf underneath the flower.
9
Add a tendril.
10
Keep the petals a pale green and concentrate on colouring the detail of the intricate flower parts.

Poppy

Poppies are a wonderful rich red colour and create quite a striking image, whether a single flower or a whole spread of poppies in a field.

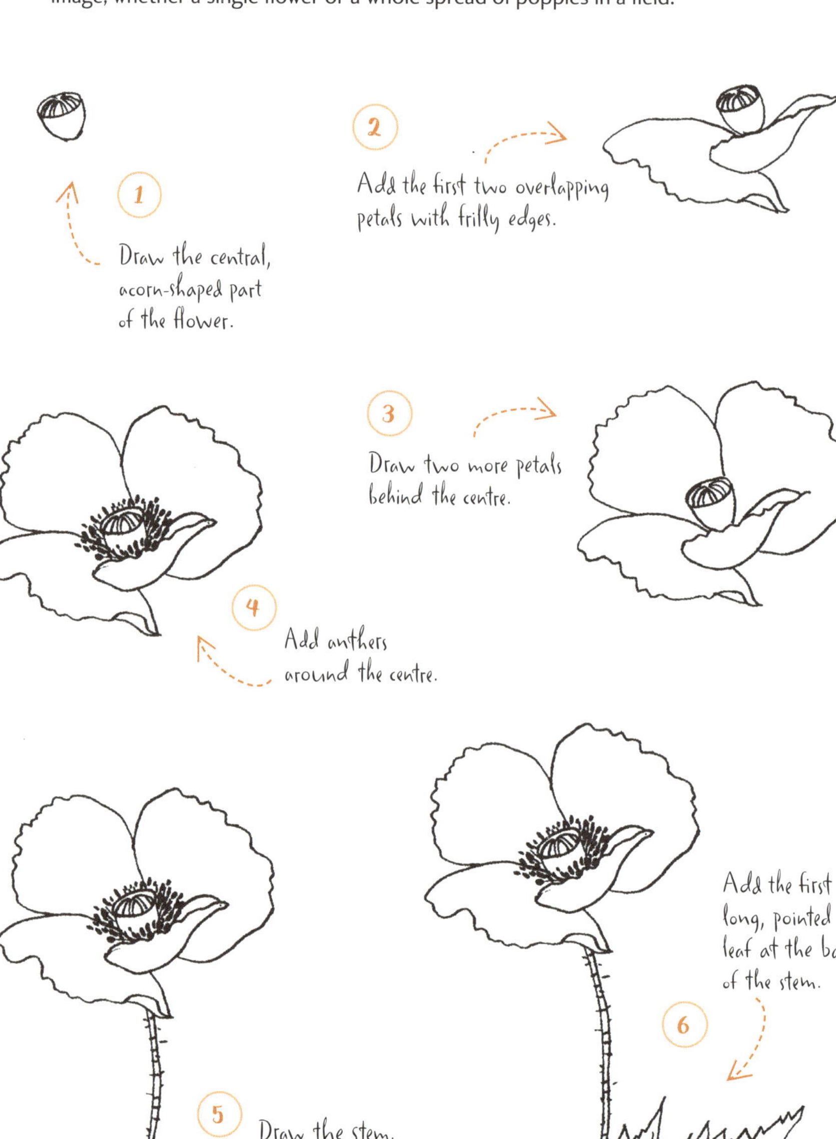

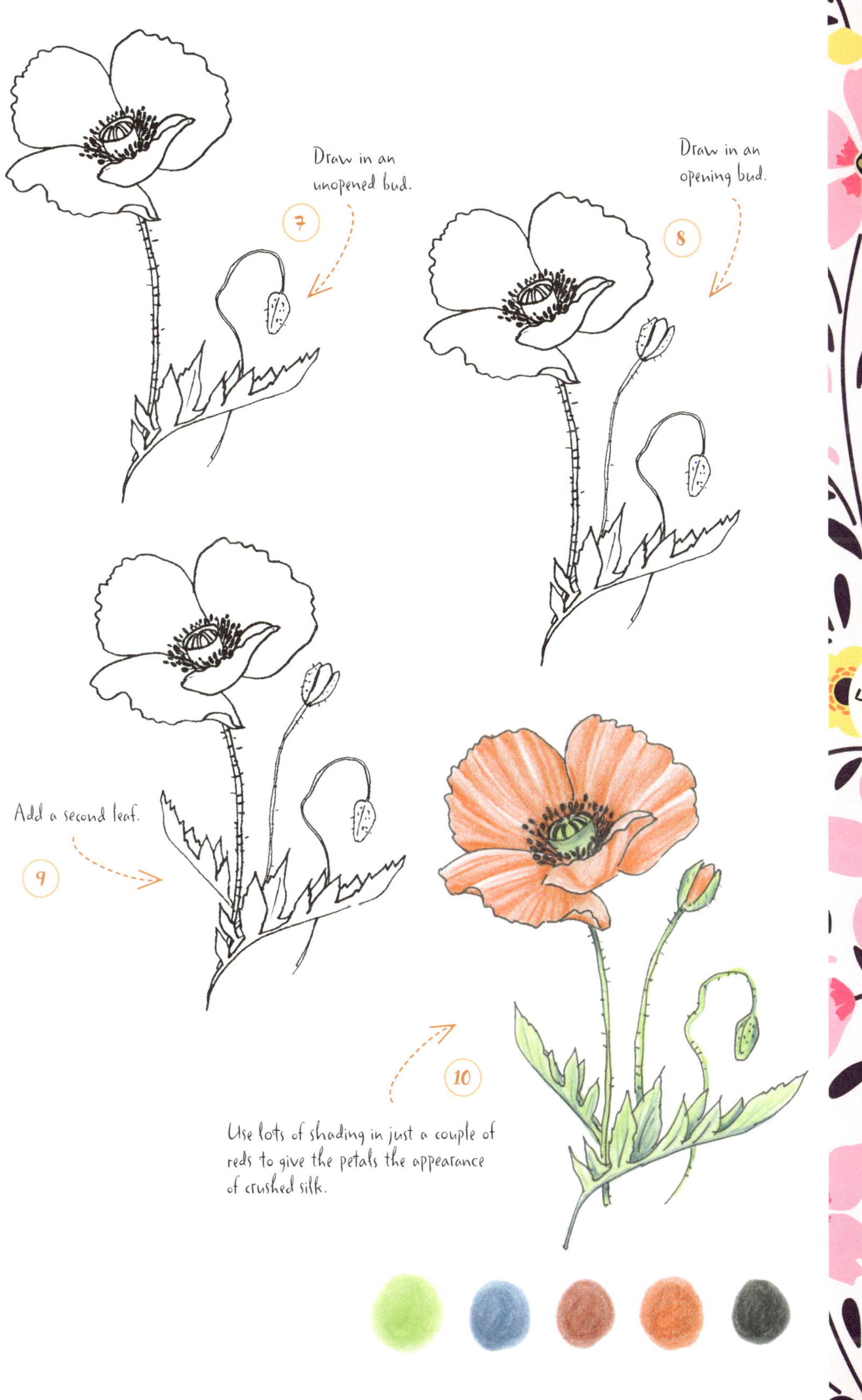
Draw in an unopened bud.
7
Draw in an opening bud.
8
Add a second leaf.
9
10
Use lots of shading in just a couple of reds to give the petals the appearance of crushed silk.

Bluebell

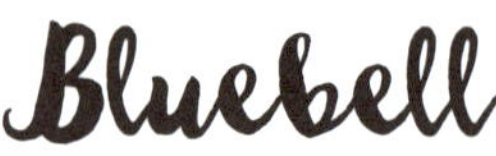

Bluebells are an iconic wild flower, well known for growing in their masses in wooded areas. Sketch a mass of these blue-tinged wonders for a carpet of colour.

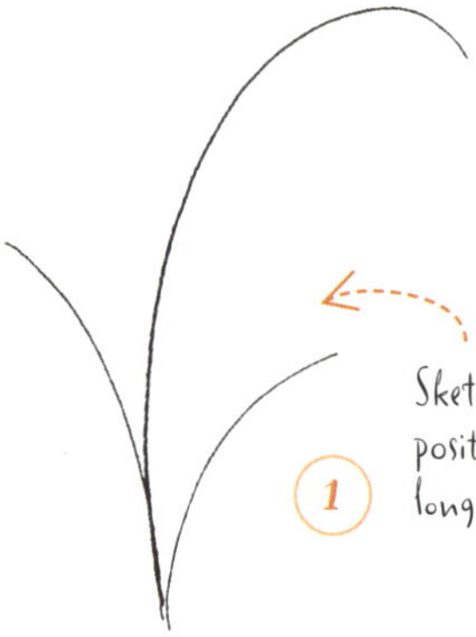

1 Sketch stem and leaf positions with three long flowing lines.

2 Add eight flower stalks along the middle line.

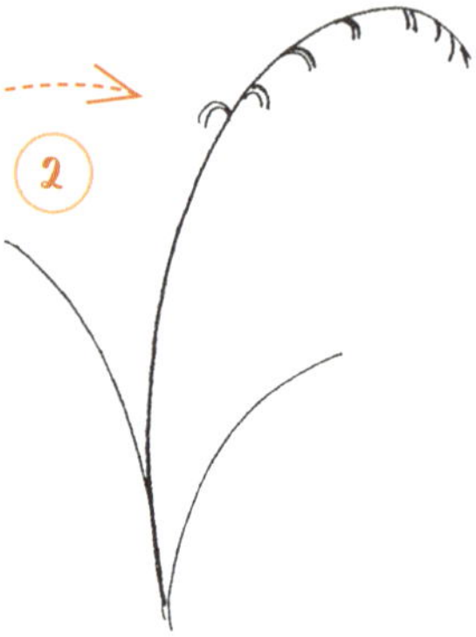

3 Sketch a simple bell shape for the first flower.

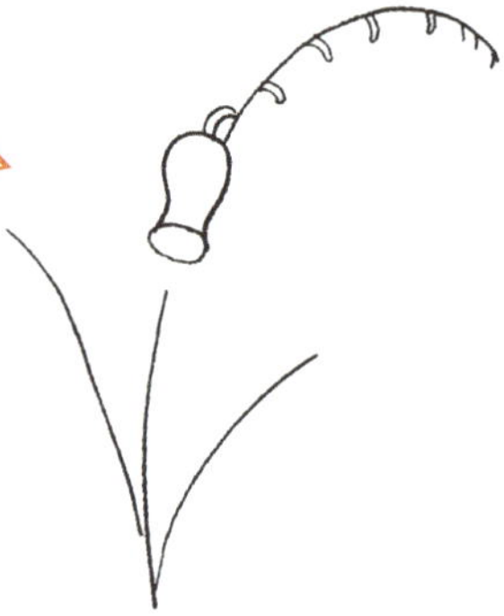

Add the upturned petals around the rim of the bell shape. 4

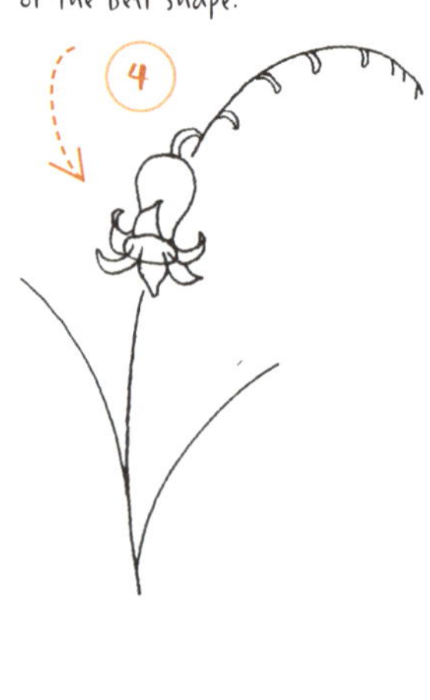

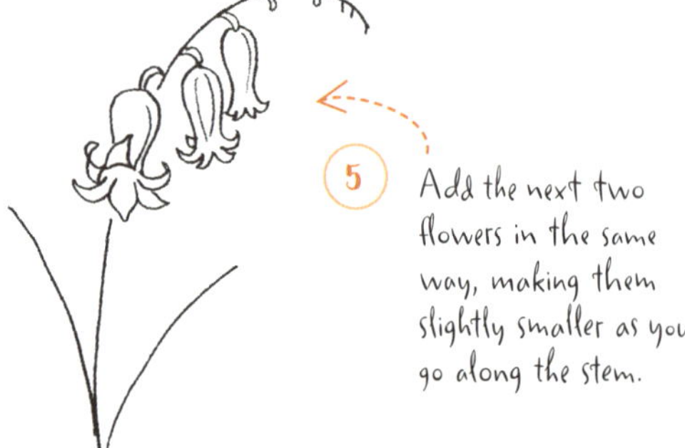

5 Add the next two flowers in the same way, making them slightly smaller as you go along the stem.

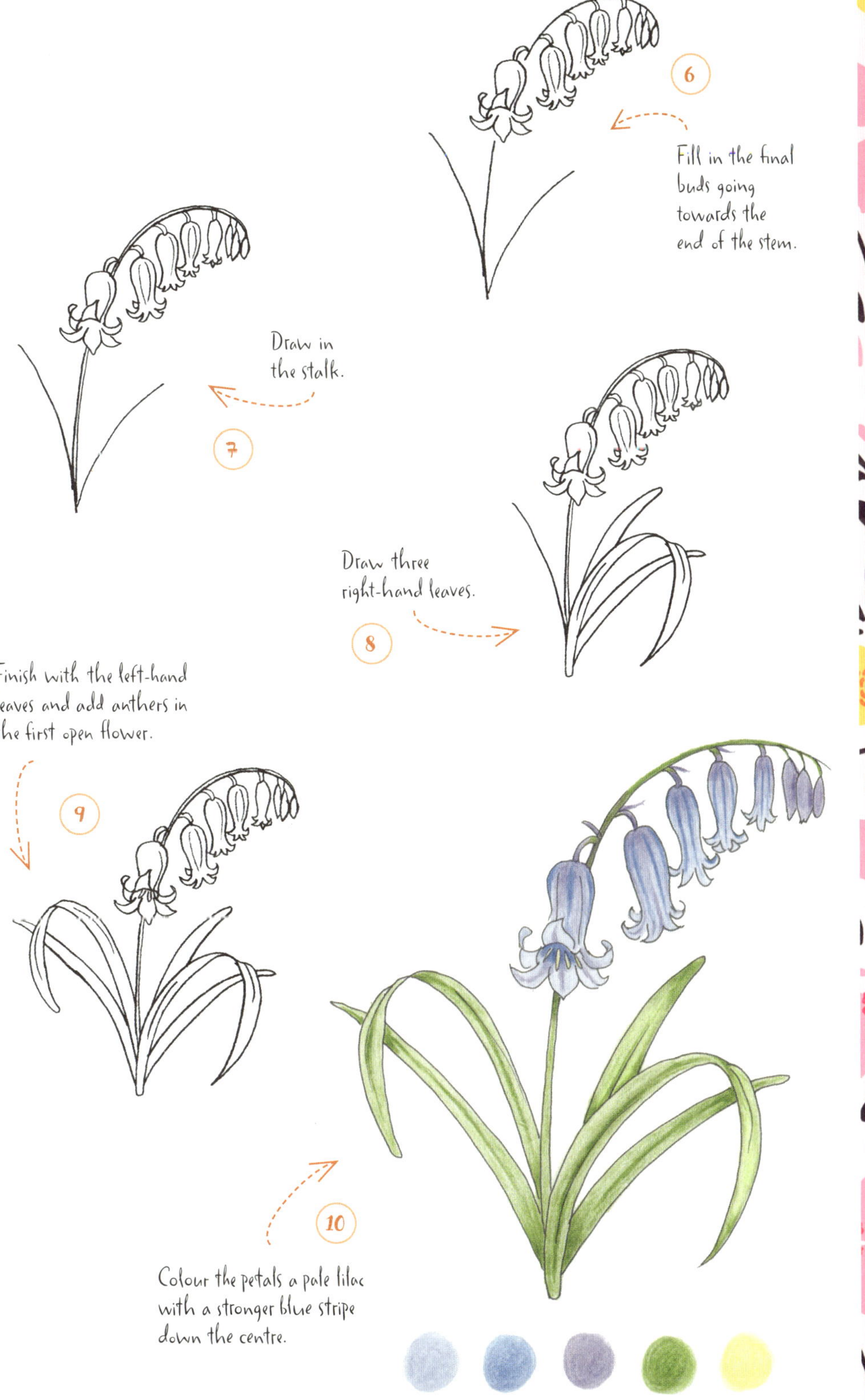
6
Fill in the final buds going towards the end of the stem.
Draw in the stalk.
7
Draw three right-hand leaves.
8
Finish with the left-hand leaves and add anthers in the first open flower.
9
10
Colour the petals a pale lilac with a stronger blue stripe down the centre.

Sunflower

This bright and cheerful looking flower is a real sign of sunshine and happiness. The flower itself is quite big, so it presents plenty of opportunity for shading and adding detail.

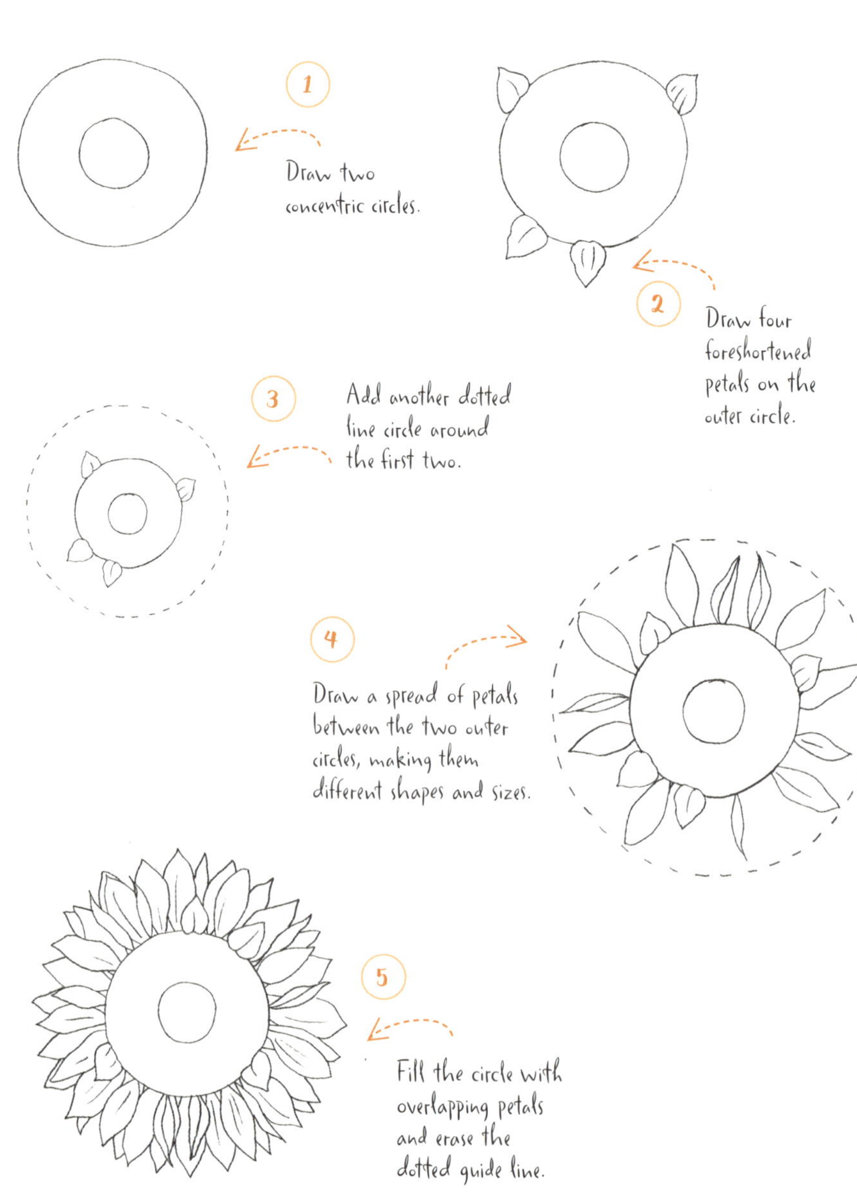

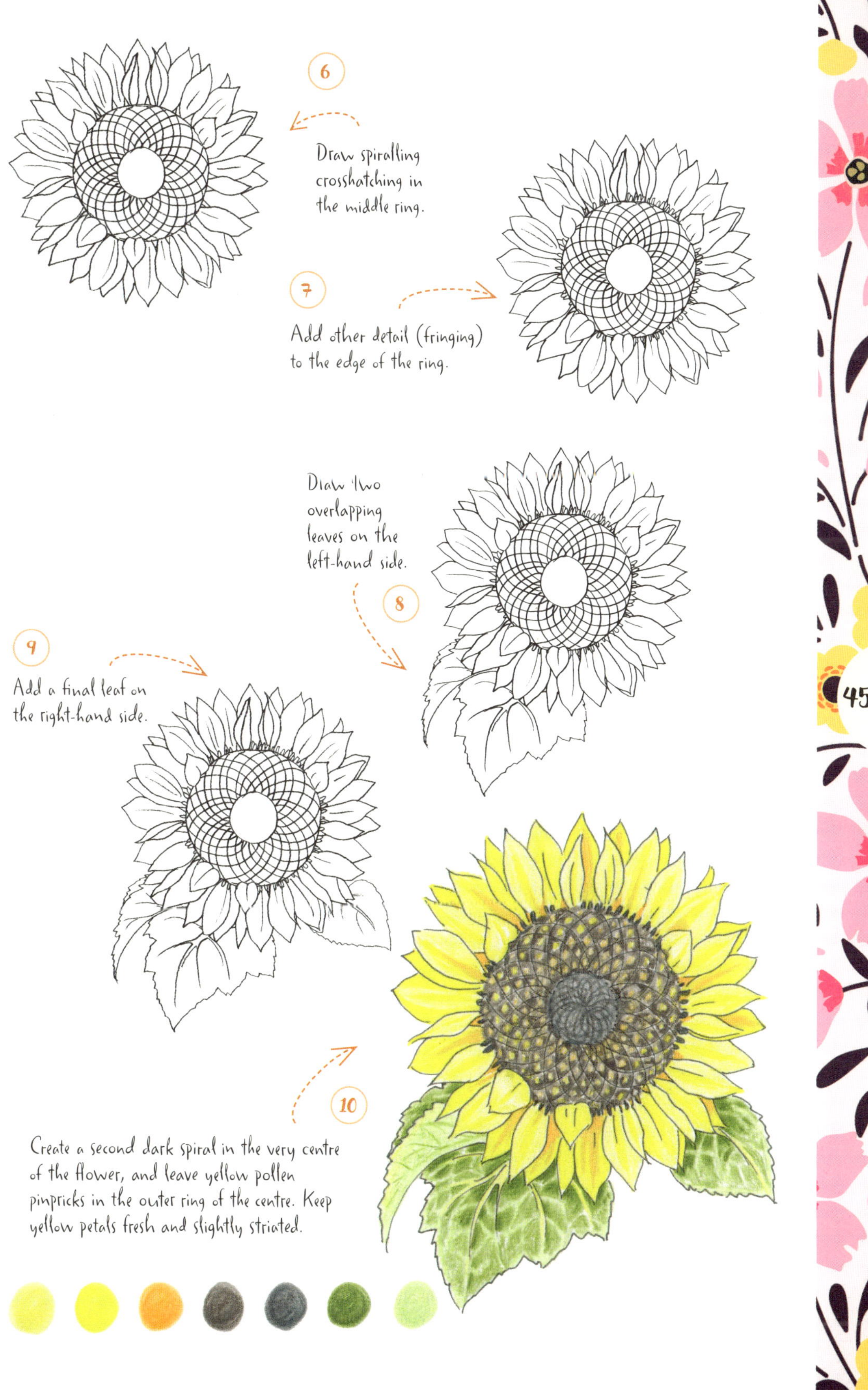
6
Draw spiralling crosshatching in the middle ring.
7
Add other detail (fringing) to the edge of the ring.
Draw two overlapping leaves on the left-hand side.
8
9
Add a final leaf on the right-hand side.
10
Create a second dark spiral in the very centre of the flower, and leave yellow pollen pinpricks in the outer ring of the centre. Keep yellow petals fresh and slightly striated.

Hibiscus

This large, beautiful flower really has some impact and would be a dramatic accent to any drawing.

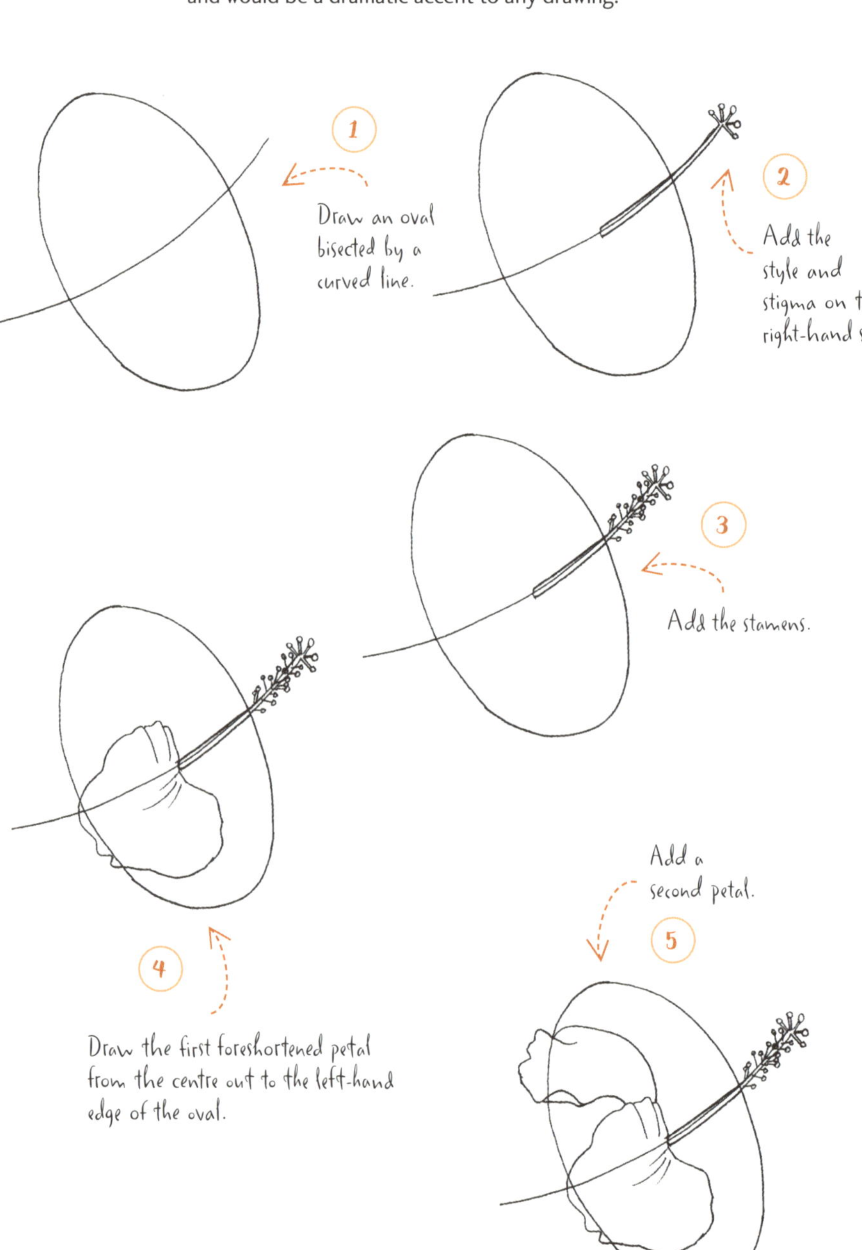

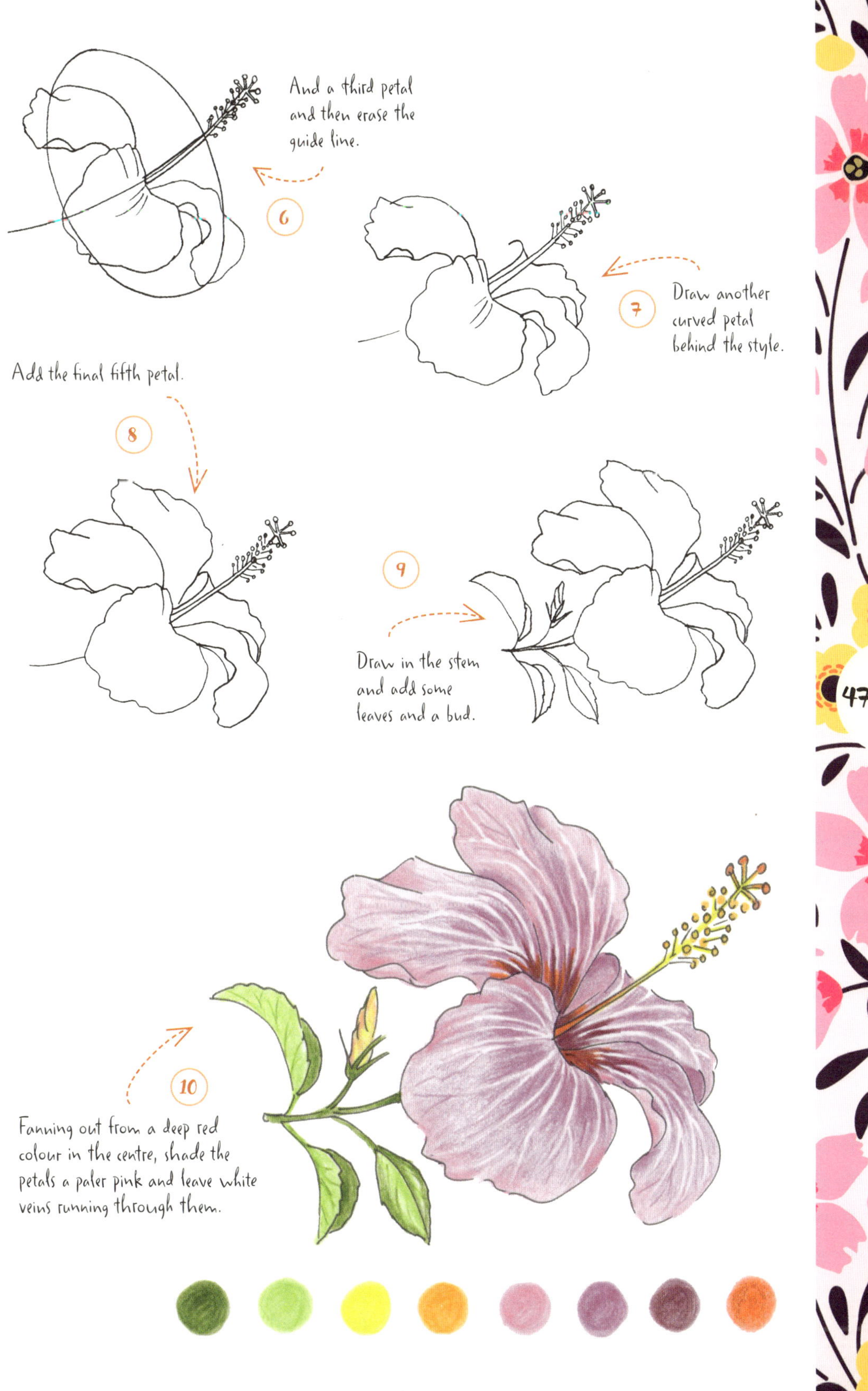
And a third petal
and then erase the
guide line.
6
7
Draw another
curved petal
behind the style.
Add the final fifth petal.
8
9
Draw in the stem
and add some
leaves and a bud.
10
Fanning out from a deep red
colour in the centre, shade the
petals a paler pink and leave white
veins running through them.

Banana Flower

This tropical flower is a beautiful shade of purple and will bring a punch of sunshine to any drawing.

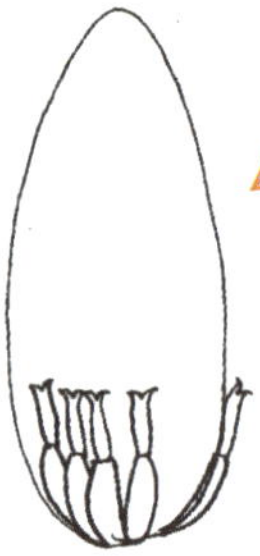

1

Sketch an elongated oval and draw five florets around the base.

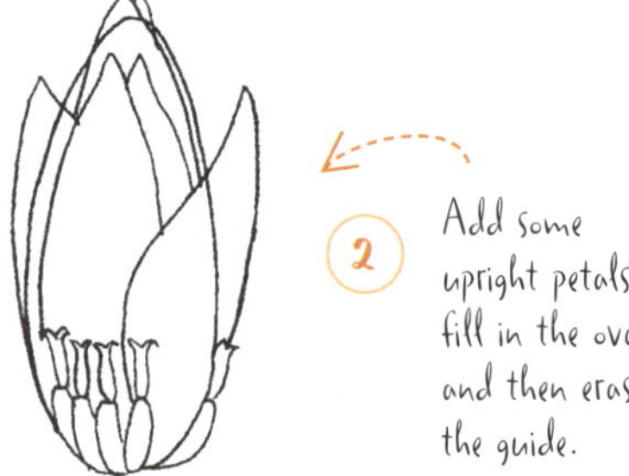

2

Add some upright petals to fill in the oval and then erase the guide.

Draw one main curled-over petal at the front of the flower.

3

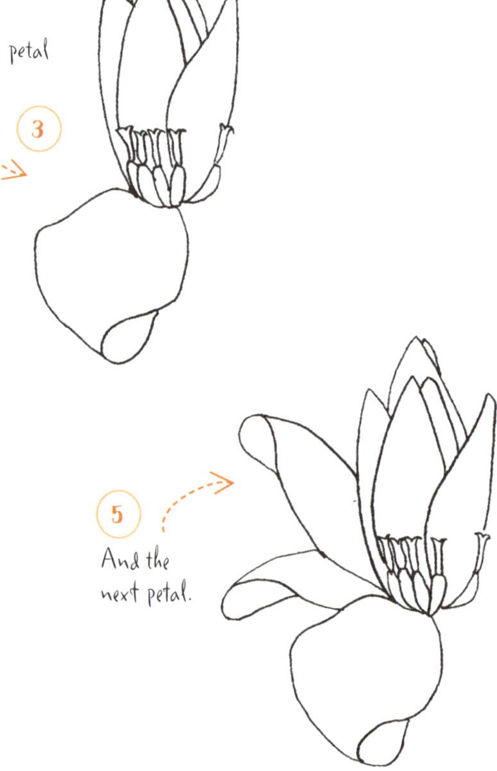

Working clockwise, add the next petal.

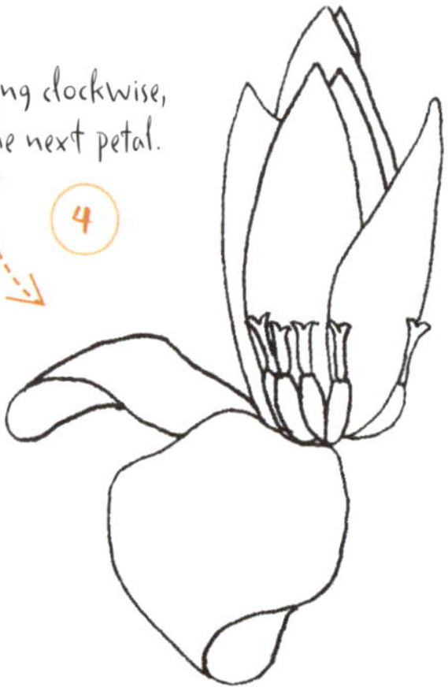

4

5

And the next petal.

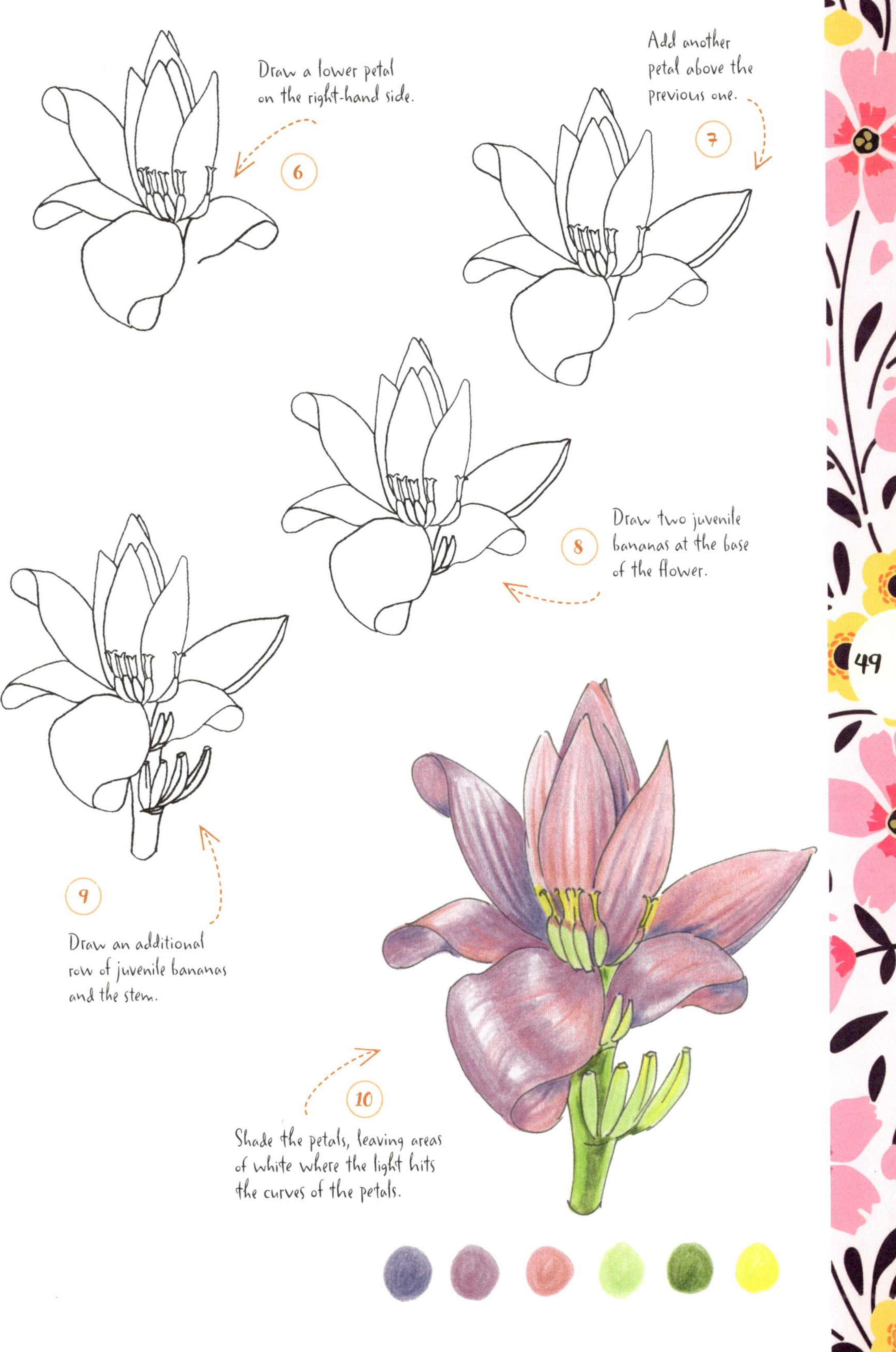
6
Draw a lower petal on the right-hand side.
7
Add another petal above the previous one.
8
Draw two juvenile bananas at the base of the flower.
9
Draw an additional row of juvenile bananas and the stem.
10
Shade the petals, leaving areas of white where the light hits the curves of the petals.

Hydrangea

The tight, compact flowers on a hydrangea offer a perfect opportunity to practise working in smaller detail.

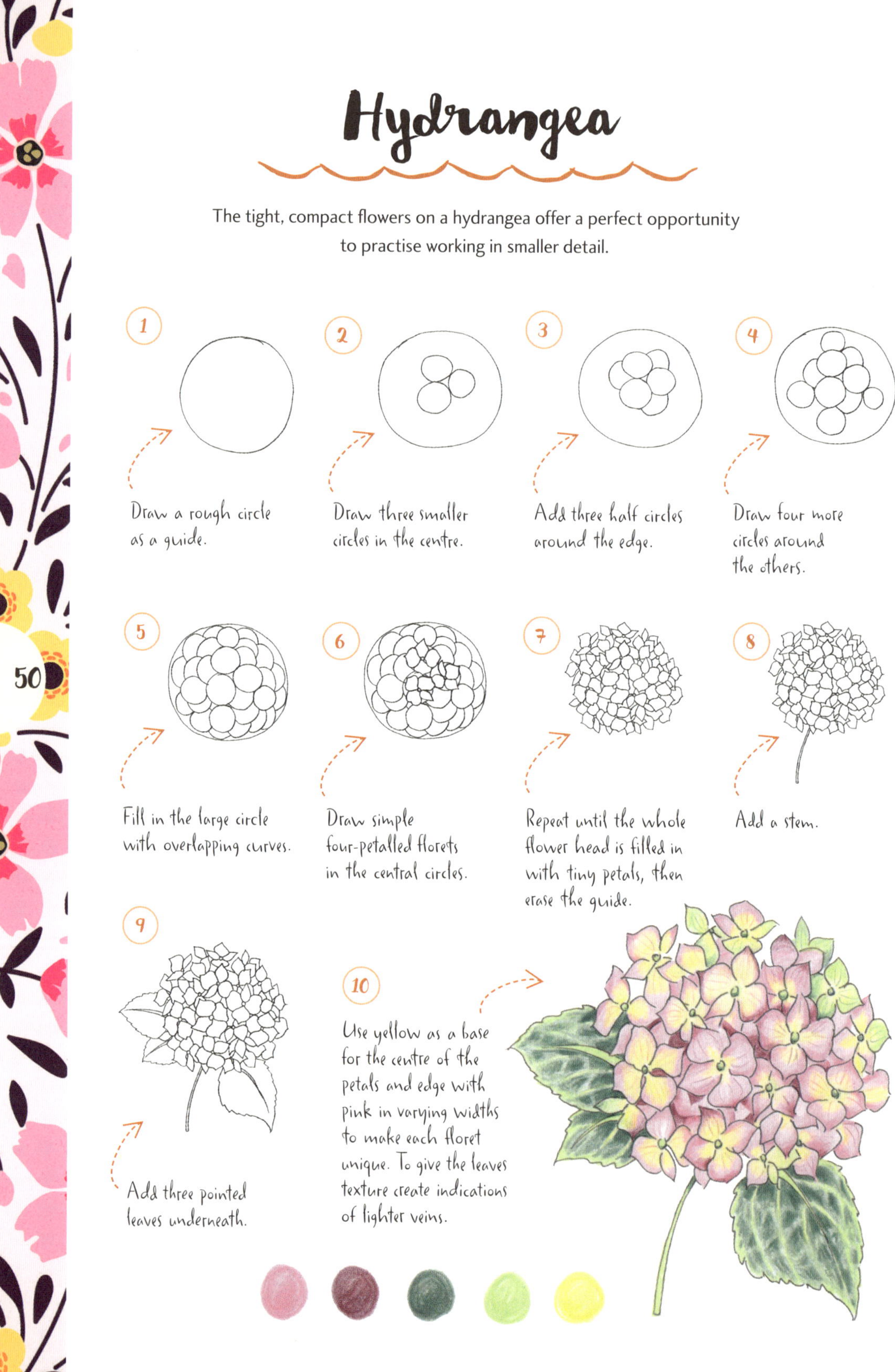

Daffodil

These spring flowers will bring a ray of sunshine to any drawing. Starting with the basic funnel shape will help you get the proportions right.

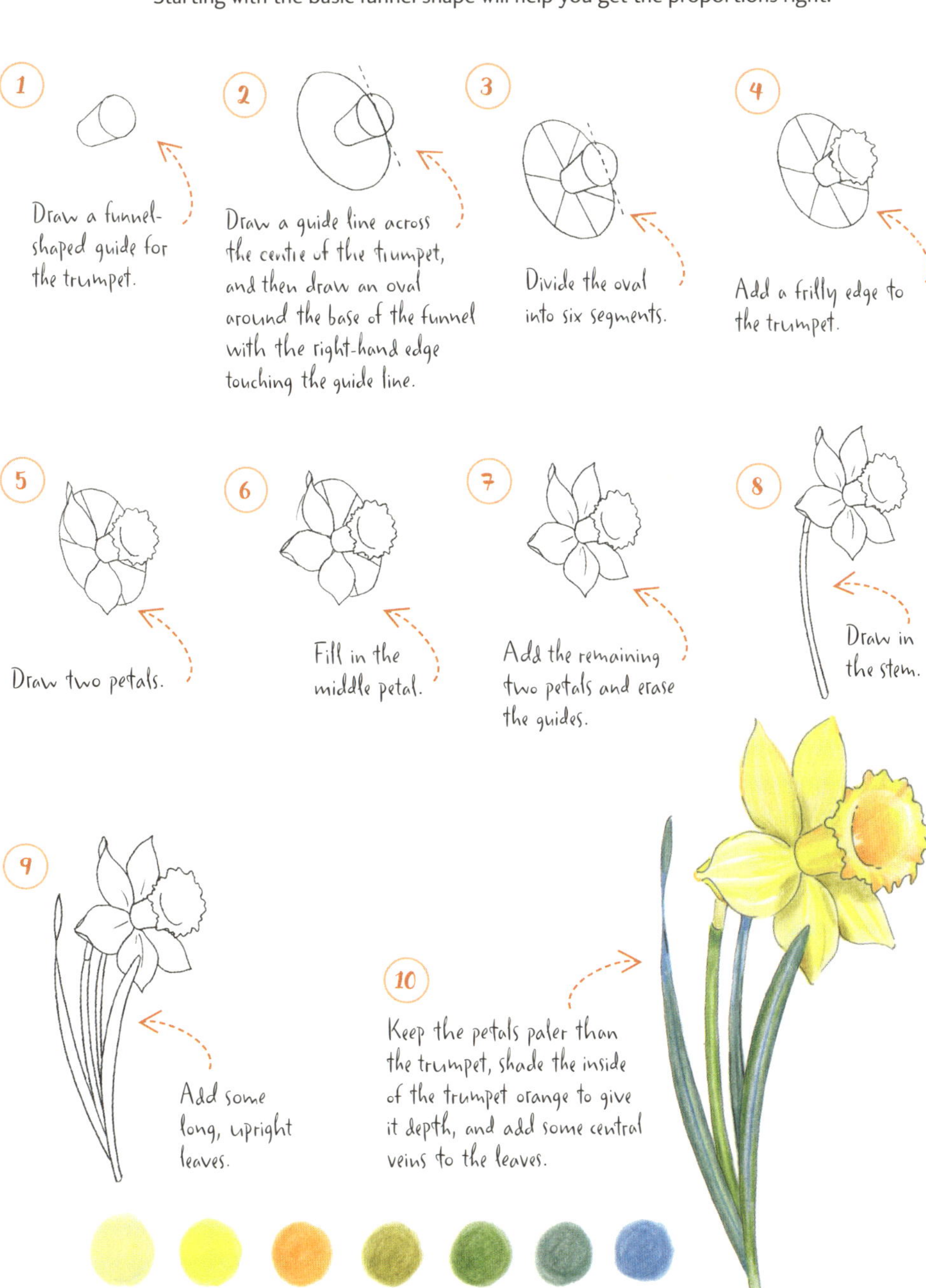

Pansy

The colours on the petals of a pansy will help you practise blending different colours, such as the blues, purples and yellows shown here.

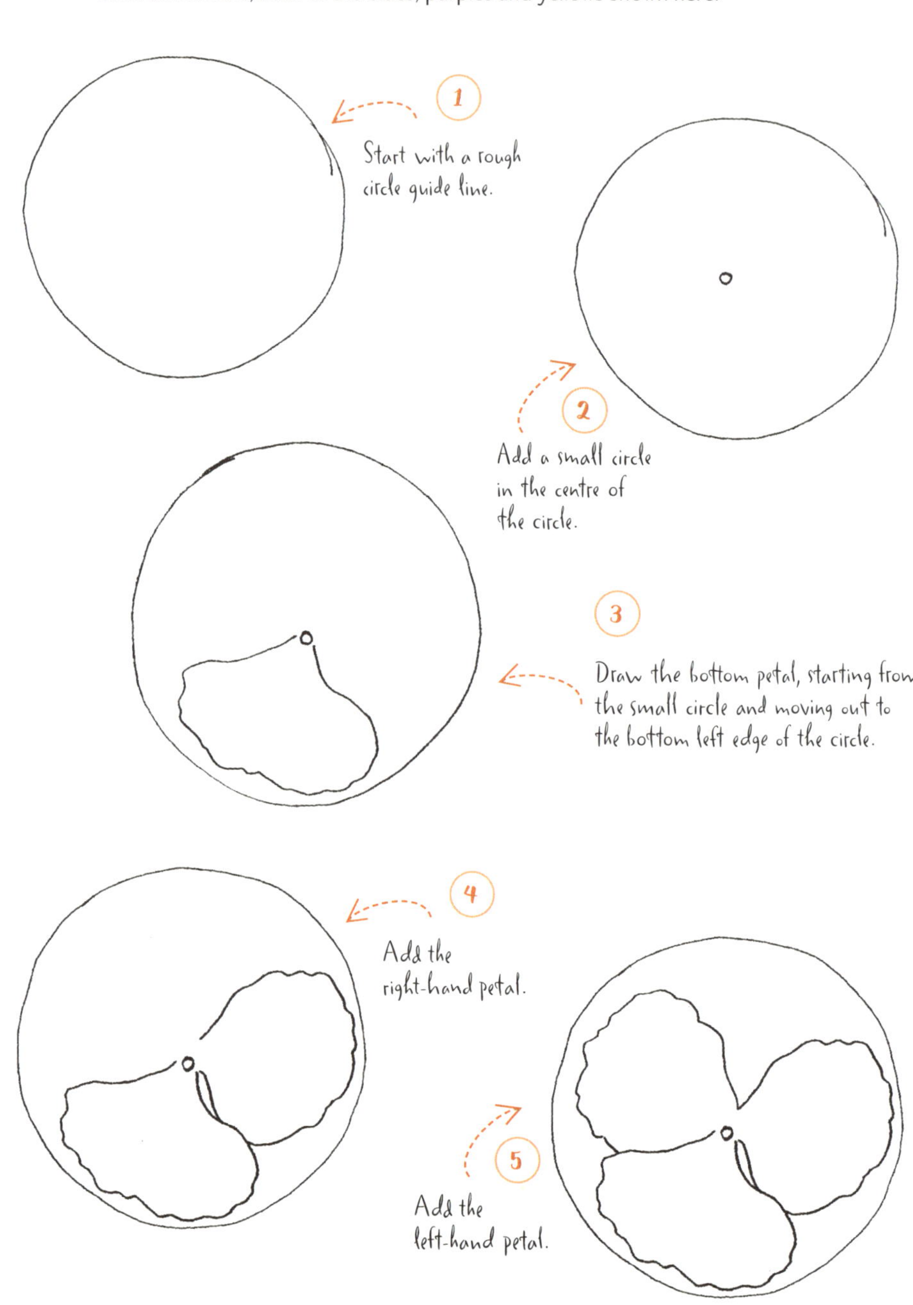

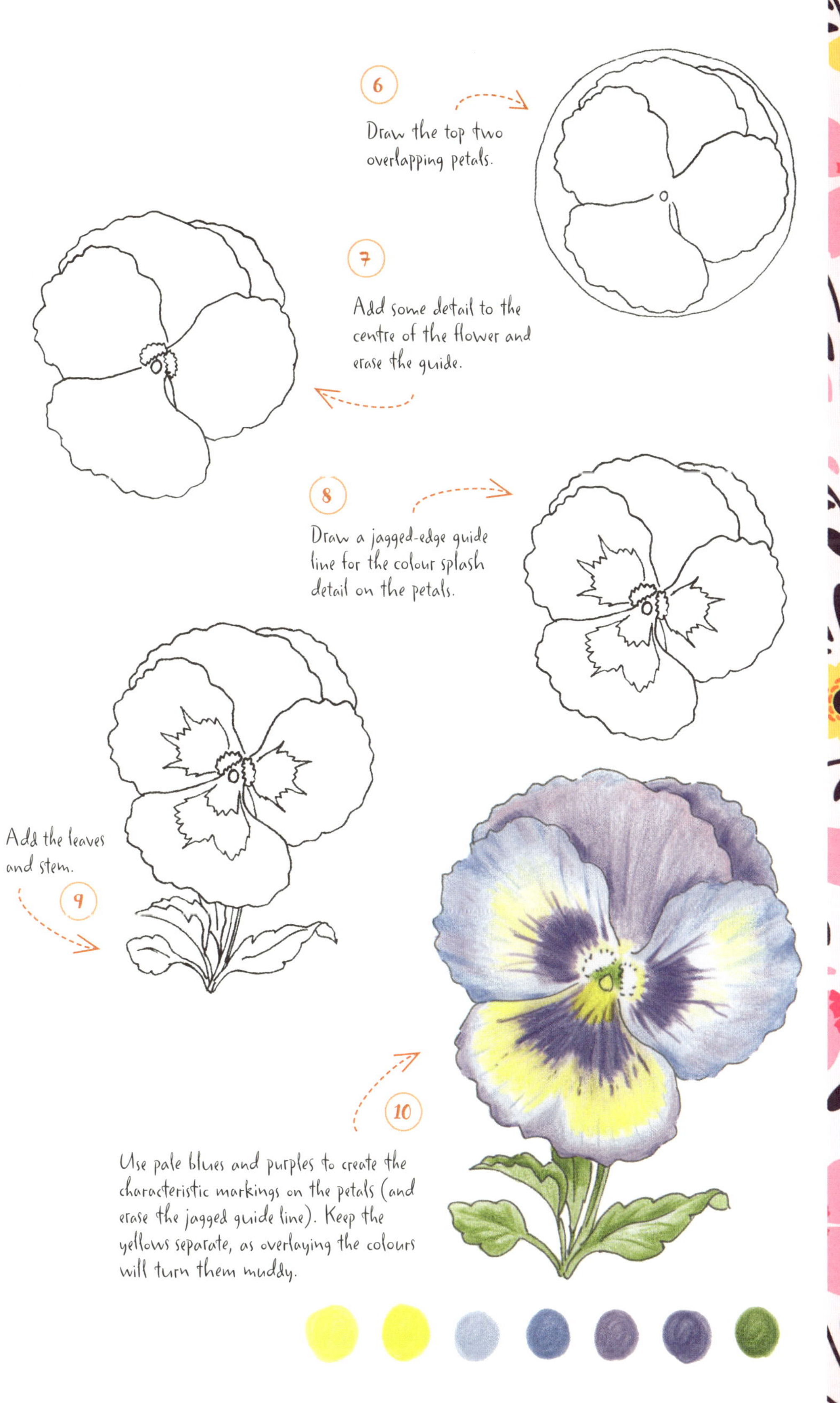
6
Draw the top two overlapping petals.
7
Add some detail to the centre of the flower and erase the guide.
8
Draw a jagged-edge guide line for the colour splash detail on the petals.
Add the leaves and stem.
9
10
Use pale blues and purples to create the characteristic markings on the petals (and erase the jagged guide line). Keep the yellows separate, as overlaying the colours will turn them muddy.

Peony

Peonies have a luscious, blousy shape full of large drooping petals. They are great for adding a richness and fullness to a bouquet drawing.

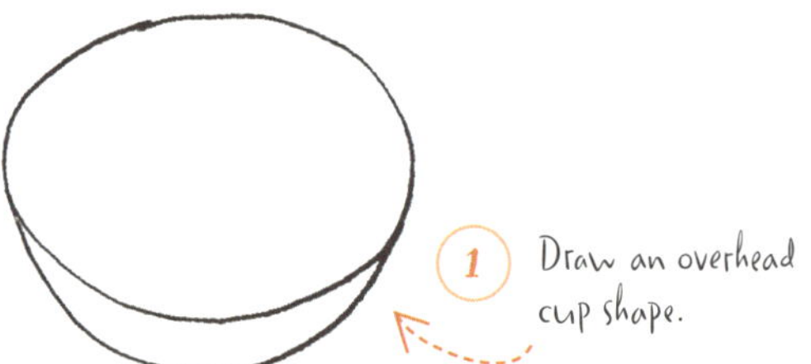

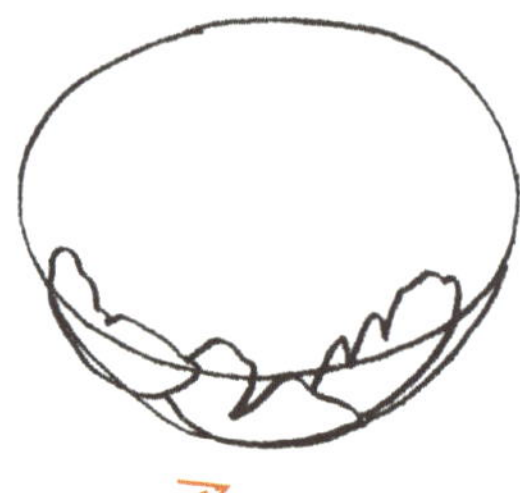

2

Draw three jagged petals across the front face of the cup.

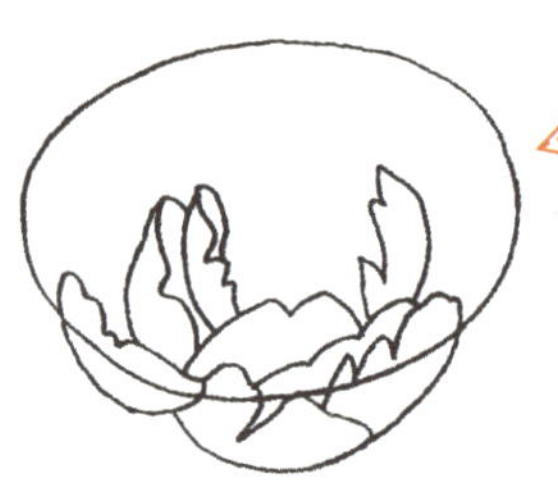

3

Add four more petals going in towards the centre of the flower.

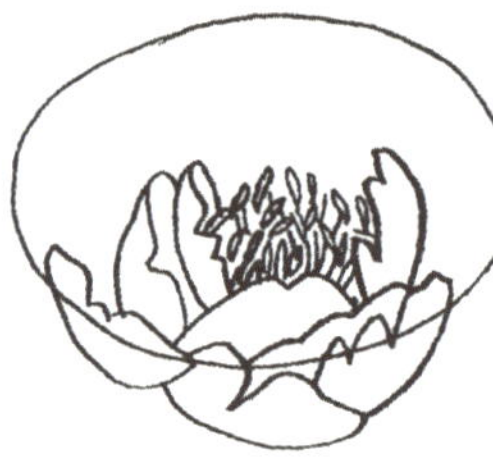

4

Fill in the anthers in the centre of the flower.

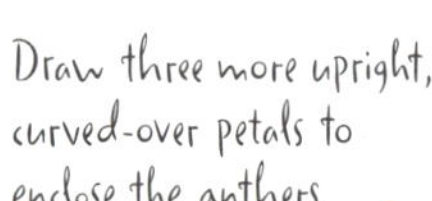

5

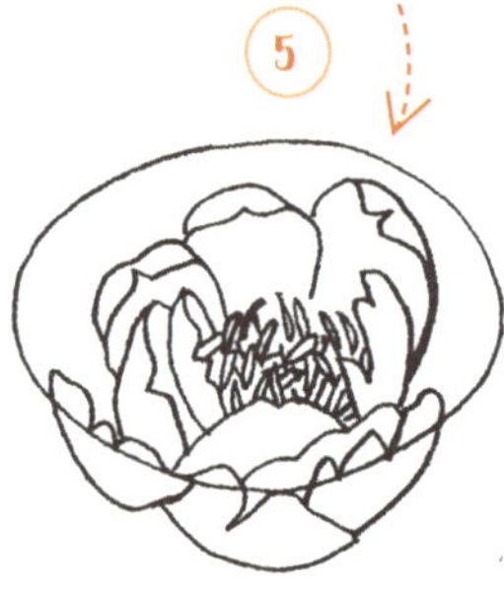

6

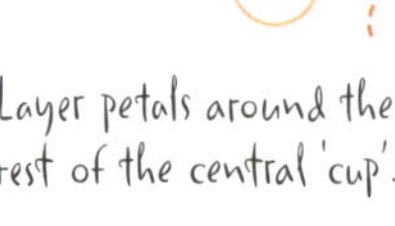

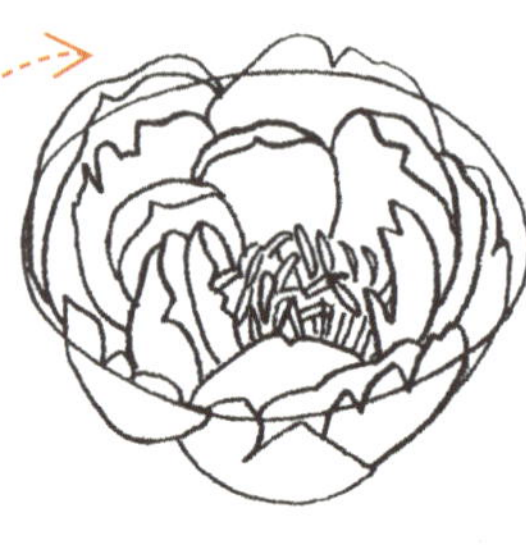

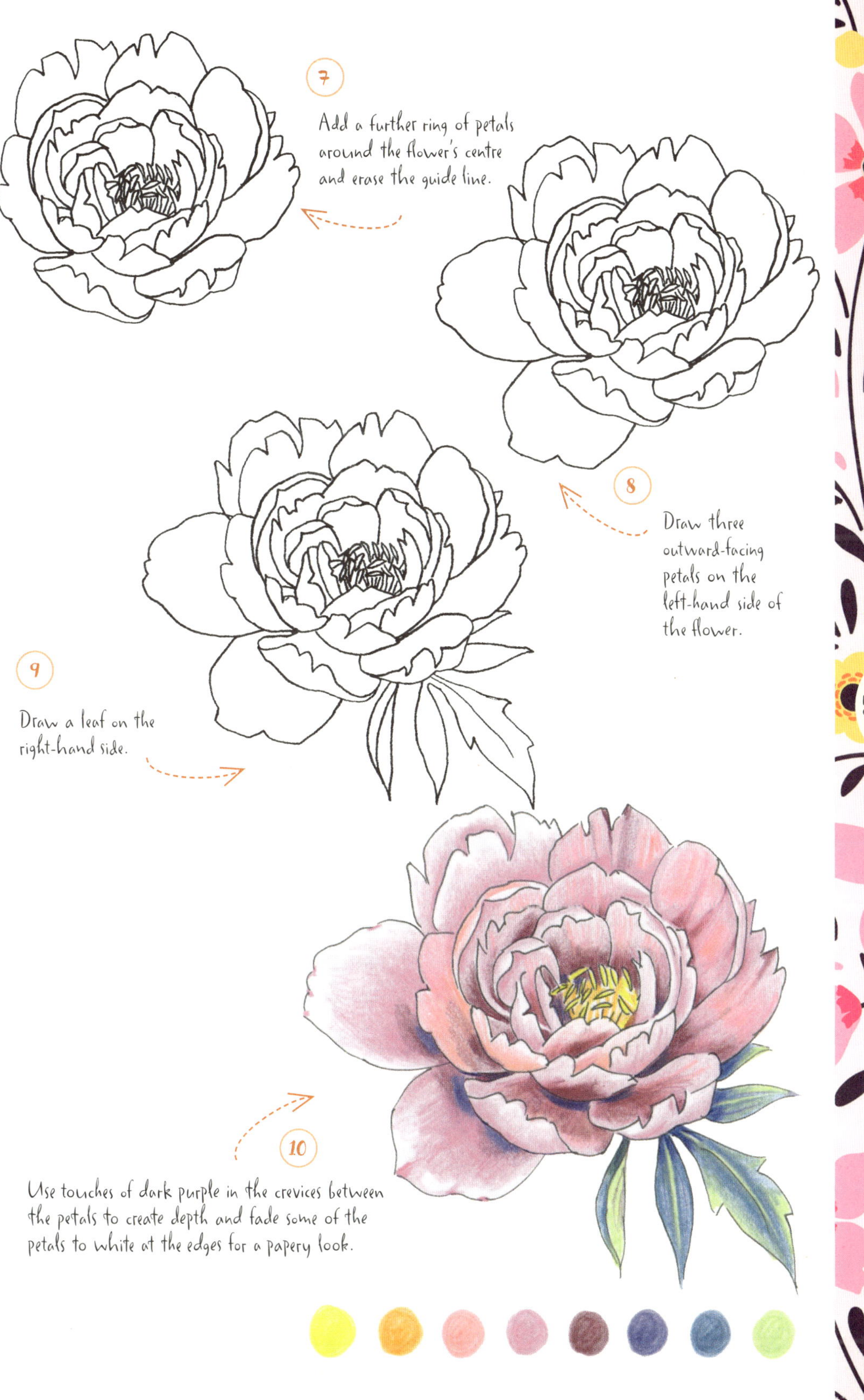
7
Add a further ring of petals around the flower's centre and erase the guide line.
8
Draw three outward-facing petals on the left-hand side of the flower.
9
Draw a leaf on the right-hand side.
10
Use touches of dark purple in the crevices between the petals to create depth and fade some of the petals to white at the edges for a papery look.

Carnation

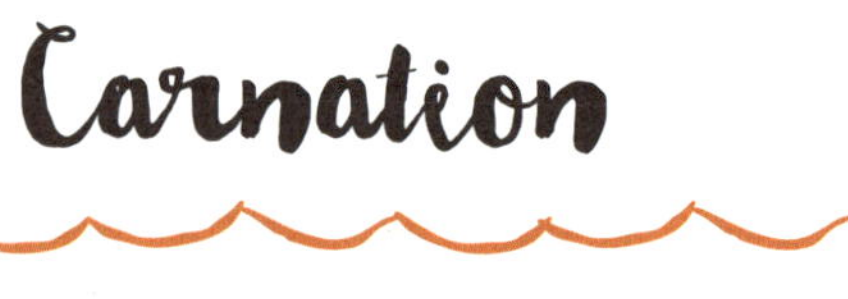

These pretty flowers are quite distinctive with their frilly edged petals and lovely shades of pink.

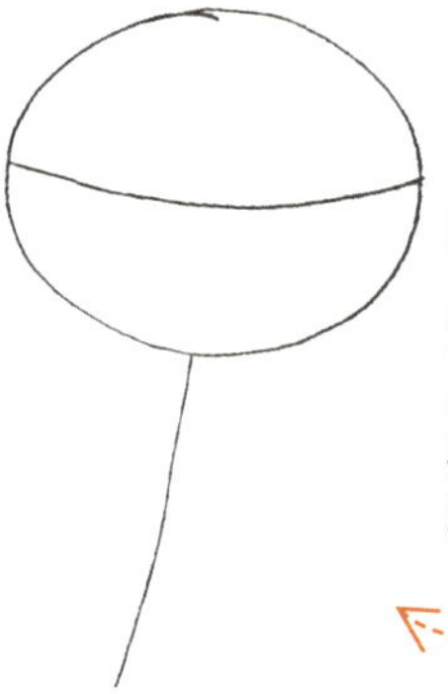

1 Sketch a squashed circle, with a horizontal central line, on a stick.

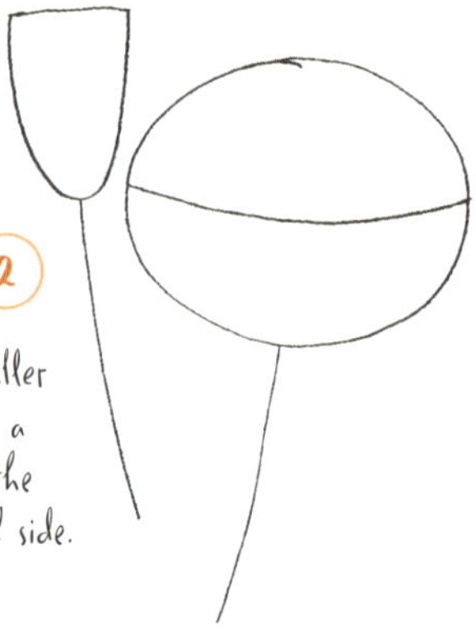

2 Add a taller goblet on a stick to the left-hand side.

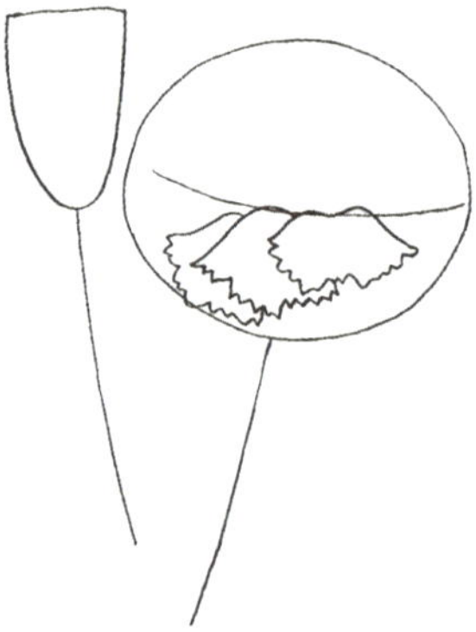

3 Draw three tooth-edged petals 'hanging' from the horizontal central line.

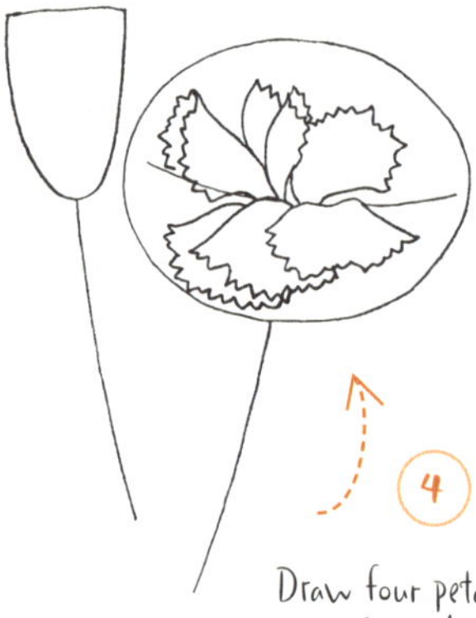

4 Draw four petals rising from the central line.

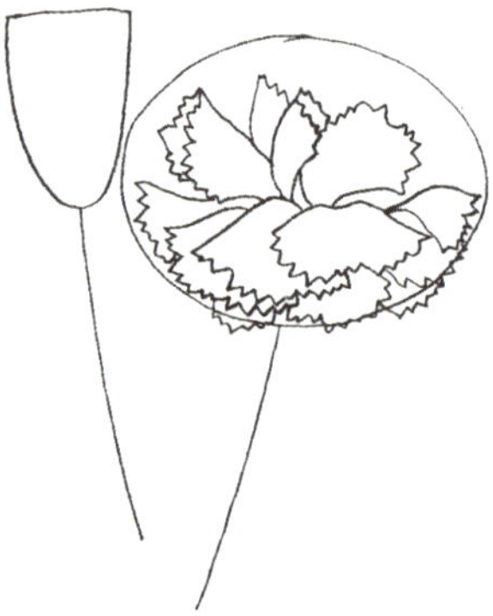

5 Fill in the lower half of the circle with more petals and frilly edges.

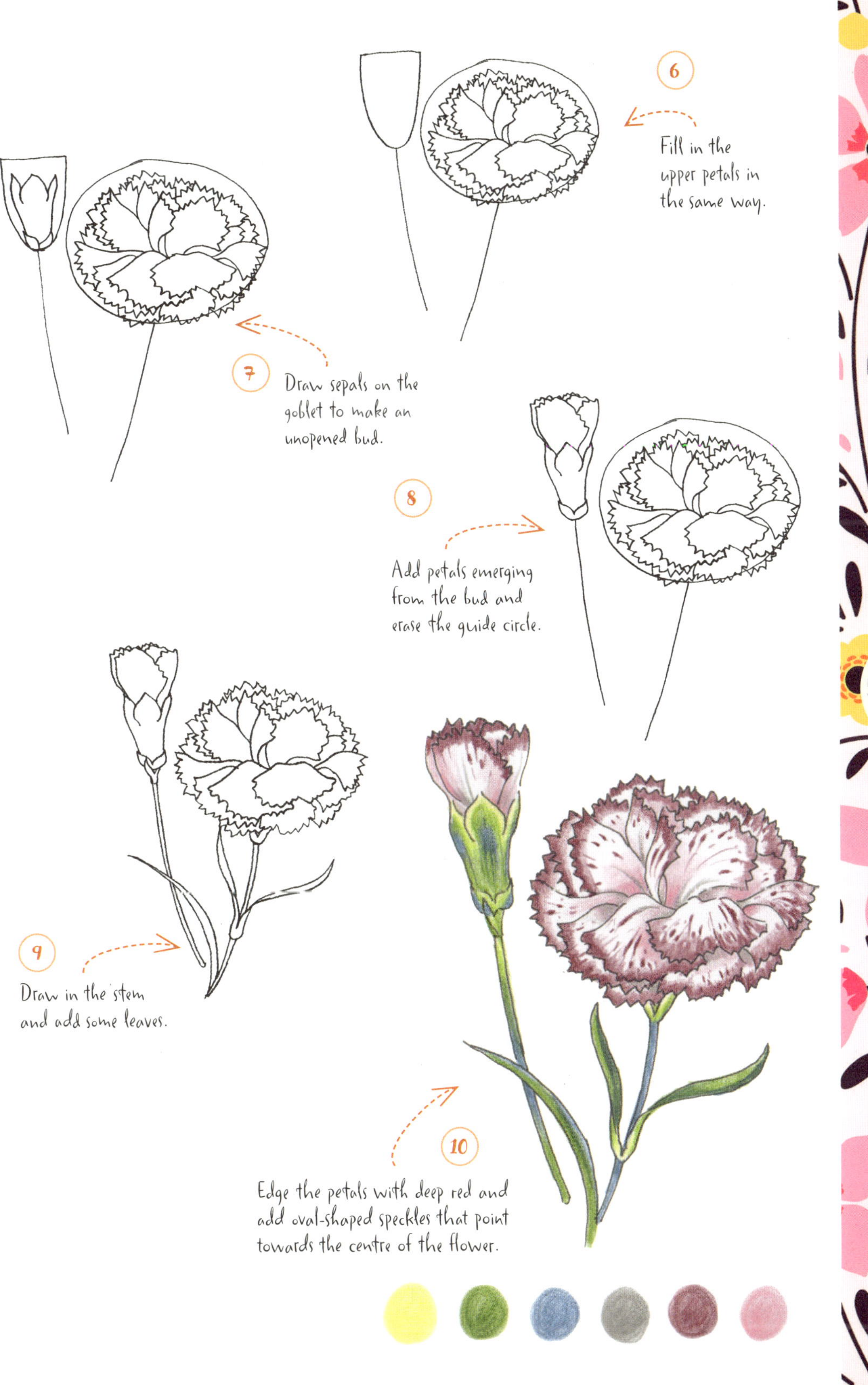
6
Fill in the upper petals in the same way.
7
Draw sepals on the goblet to make an unopened bud.
8
Add petals emerging from the bud and erase the guide circle.
9
Draw in the stem and add some leaves.
10
Edge the petals with deep red and add oval-shaped speckles that point towards the centre of the flower.

Forget-me-not

The tiny flowers on the stems of this pretty plant means that it almost creates its own spray bouquet on a single stem. It offers a good chance to practise working on a drawing with smaller details.

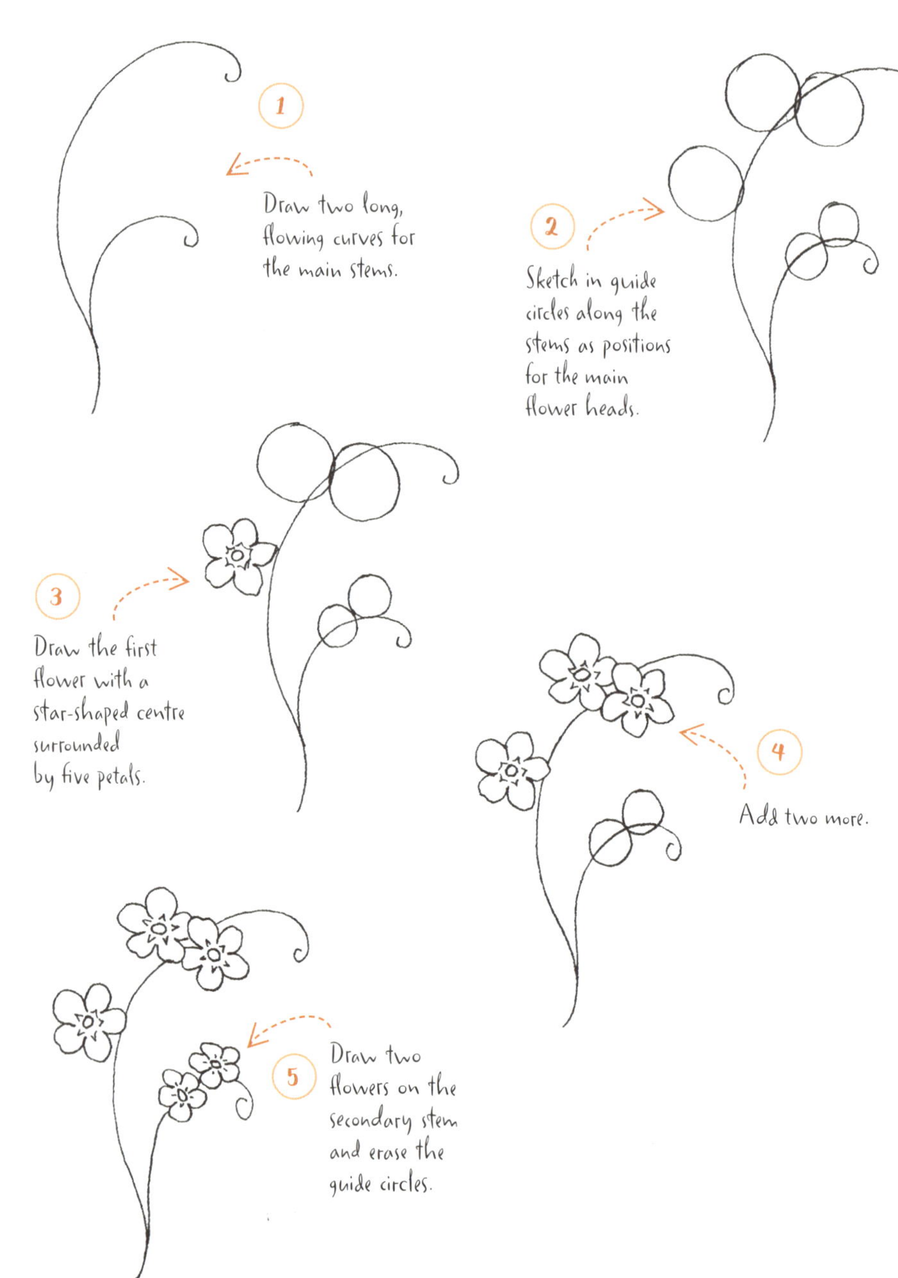

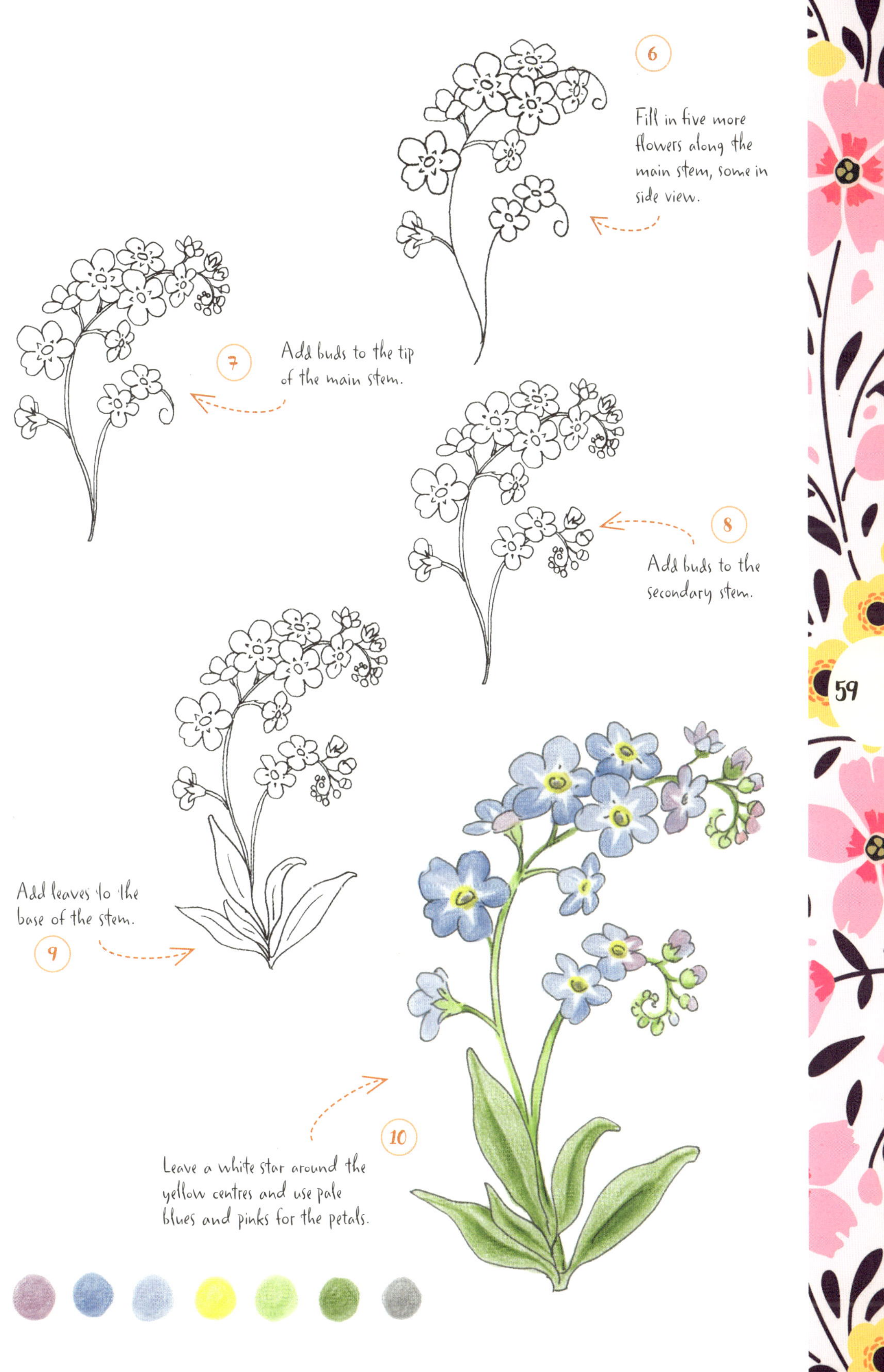
6
Fill in five more flowers along the main stem, some in side view.
7
Add buds to the tip of the main stem.
8
Add buds to the secondary stem.
Add leaves to the base of the stem.
9
10
Leave a white star around the yellow centres and use pale blues and pinks for the petals.

Sweet William

This is a traditional cottage plant with a dense clustering of flowers in pretty pinks, reds and purples.

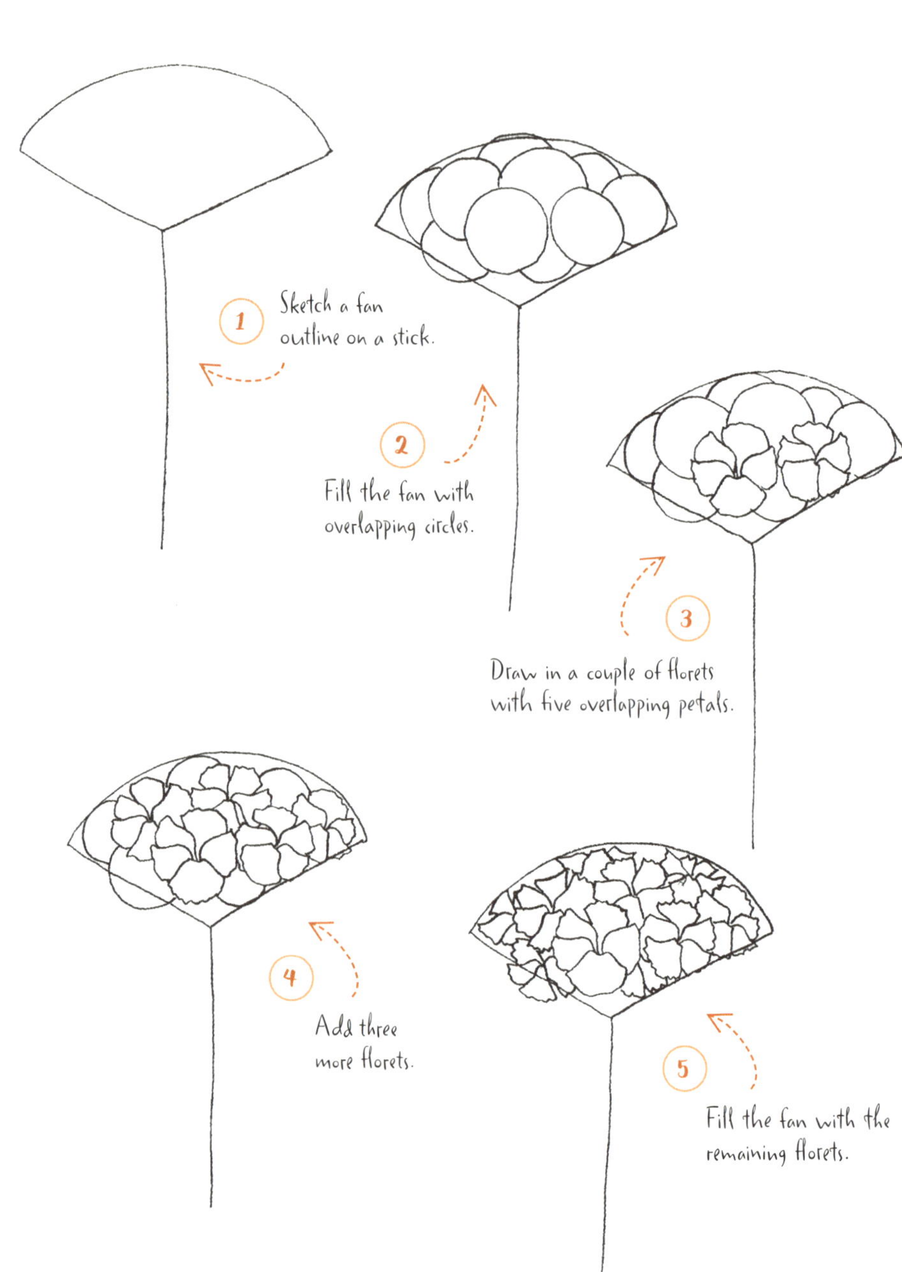

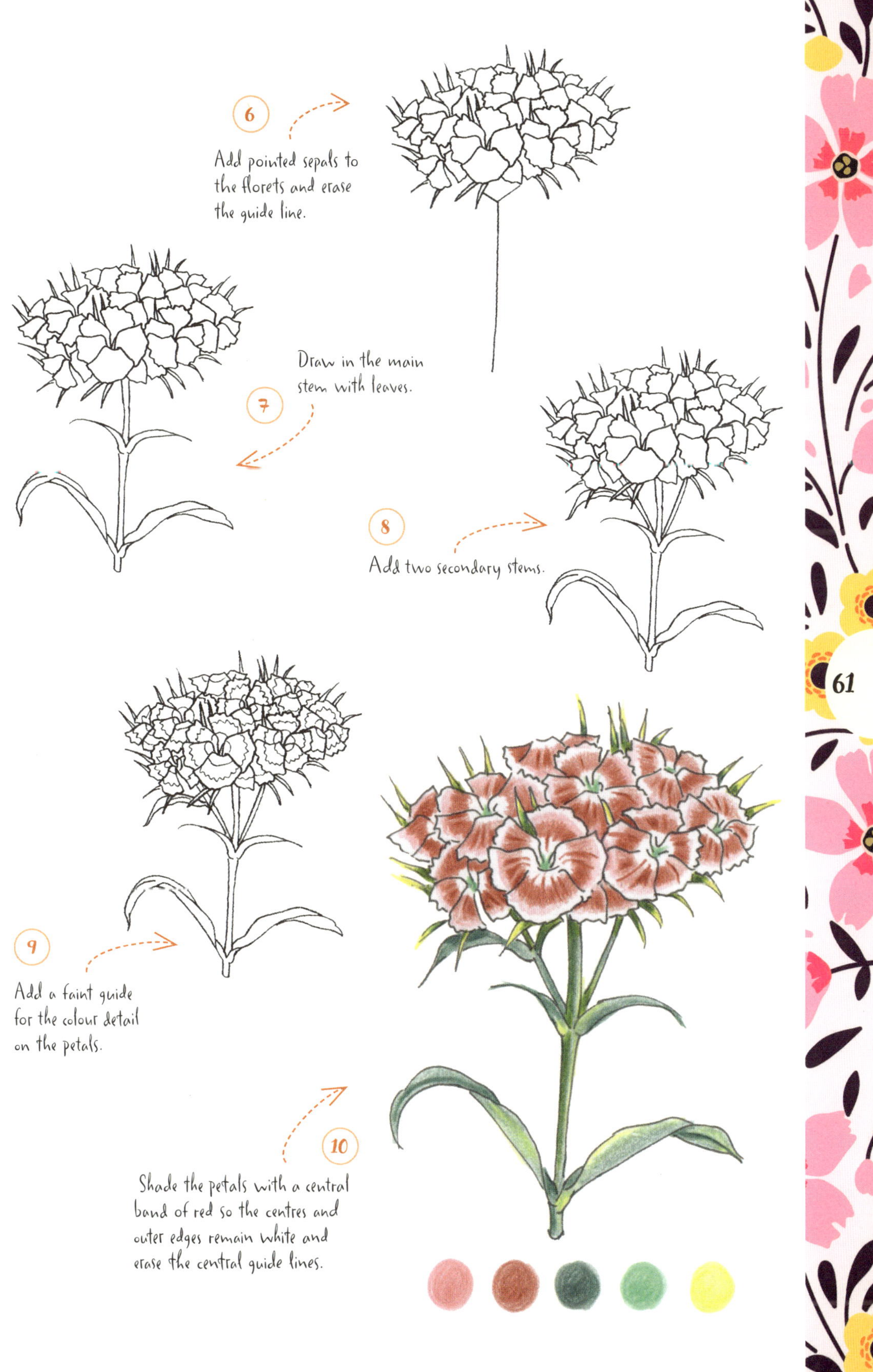
6
Add pointed sepals to the florets and erase the guide line.
7
Draw in the main stem with leaves.
8
Add two secondary stems.
9
Add a faint guide for the colour detail on the petals.
10
Shade the petals with a central band of red so the centres and outer edges remain white and erase the central guide lines.

Daisy

The simple daisy is a great shape to master as part of your flower tutorials.

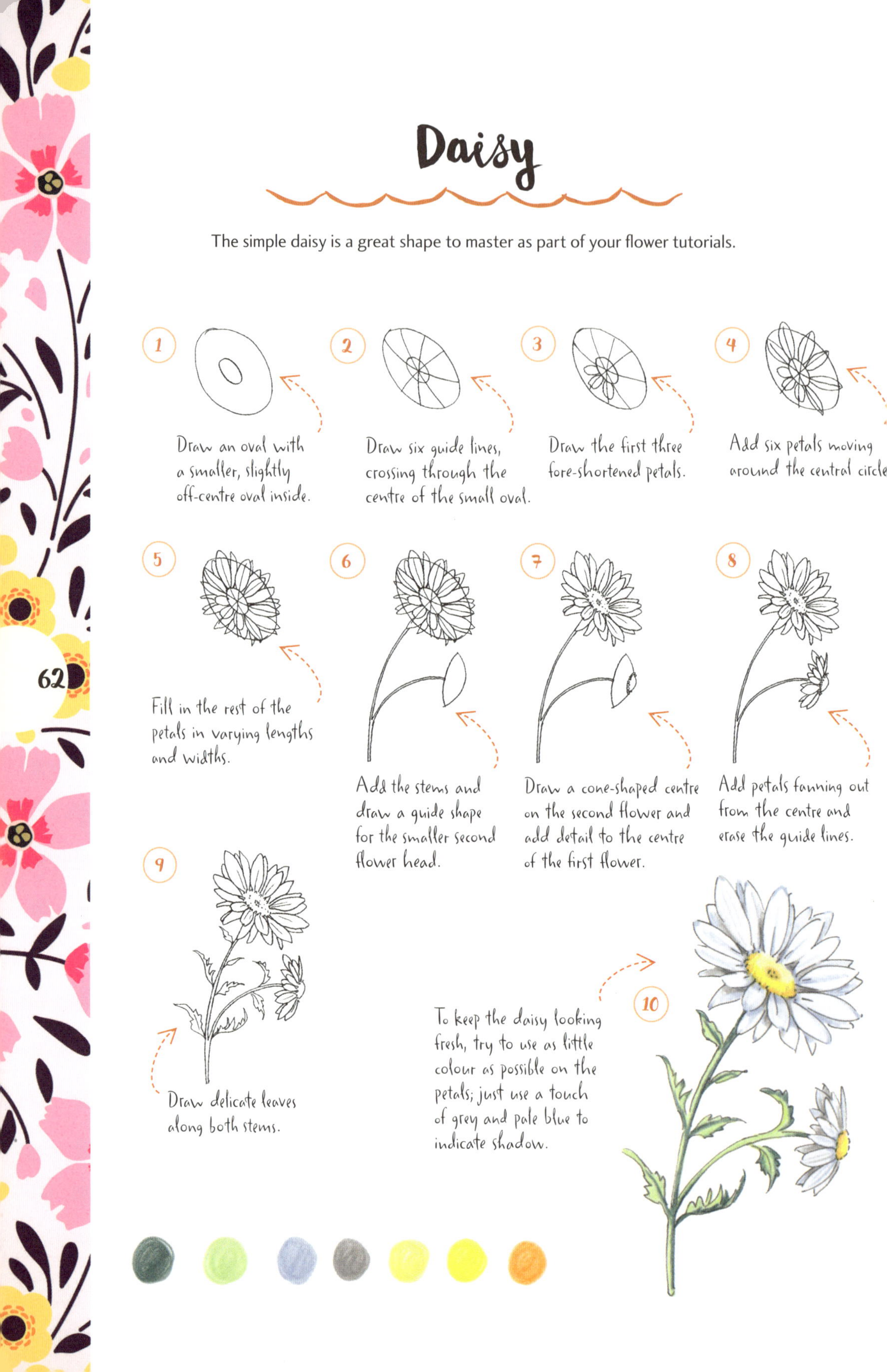

Orchid

These elegant oriental flowers may be difficult to look after in the flesh, but needn't be difficult to draw with this easy step-by-step guide.

1

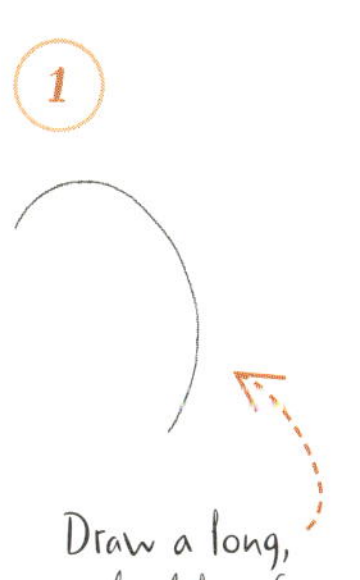

Draw a long, arched line for the stem.

2

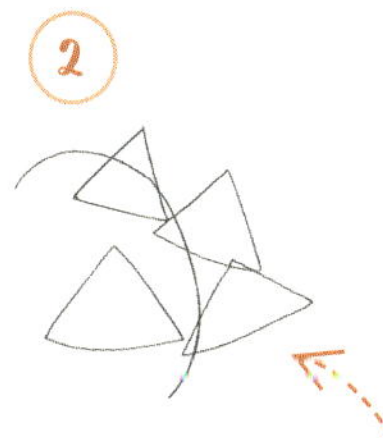

Sketch four triangle outlines along the stem.

3

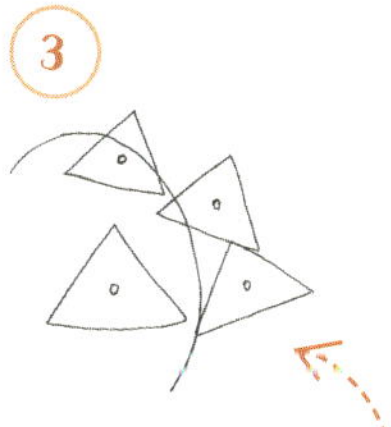

Draw a small circle in the middle of each triangle.

4

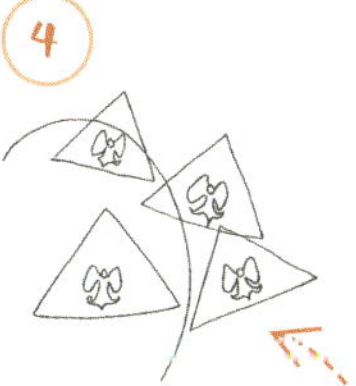

Add the central petals.

5

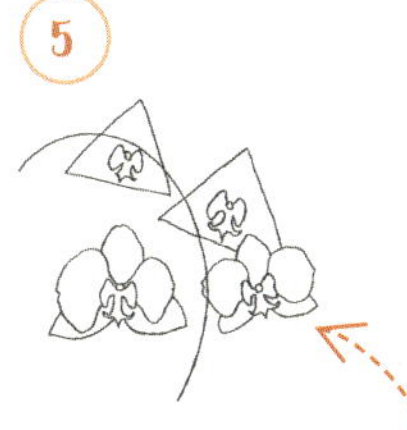

Draw the petals of the first two flowers. There should be five petals.

6

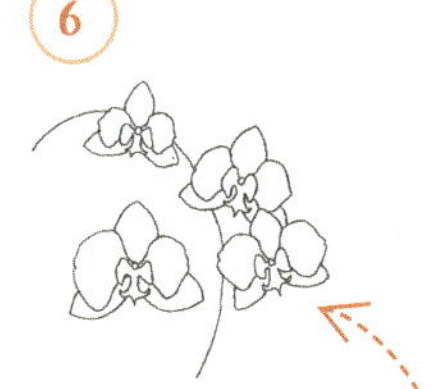

Repeat for the remaining flower and erase the guide triangles.

7

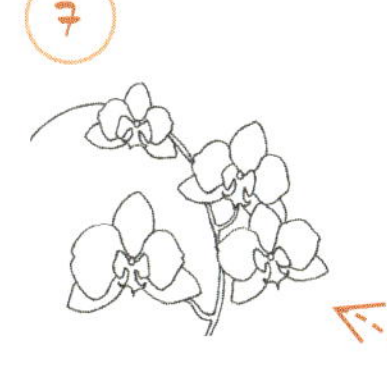

Draw in the stem.

8

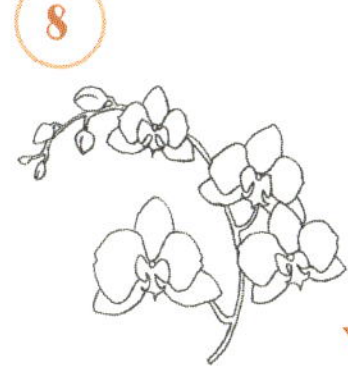

Add some smaller buds towards the end of the stem.

9

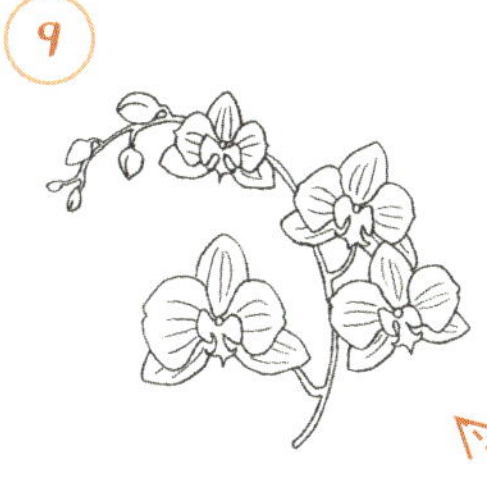

Add faint guide lines for the petal detail.

10

Keep the colours delicate and pretty. Use different shades of pink, fading towards the petal edges, which can be highlighted with pale blue.

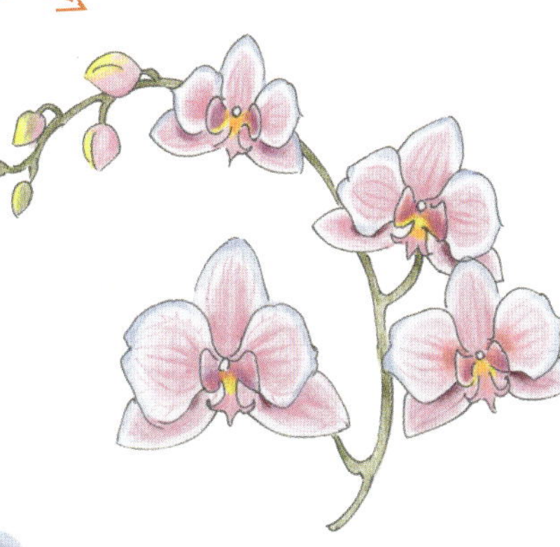

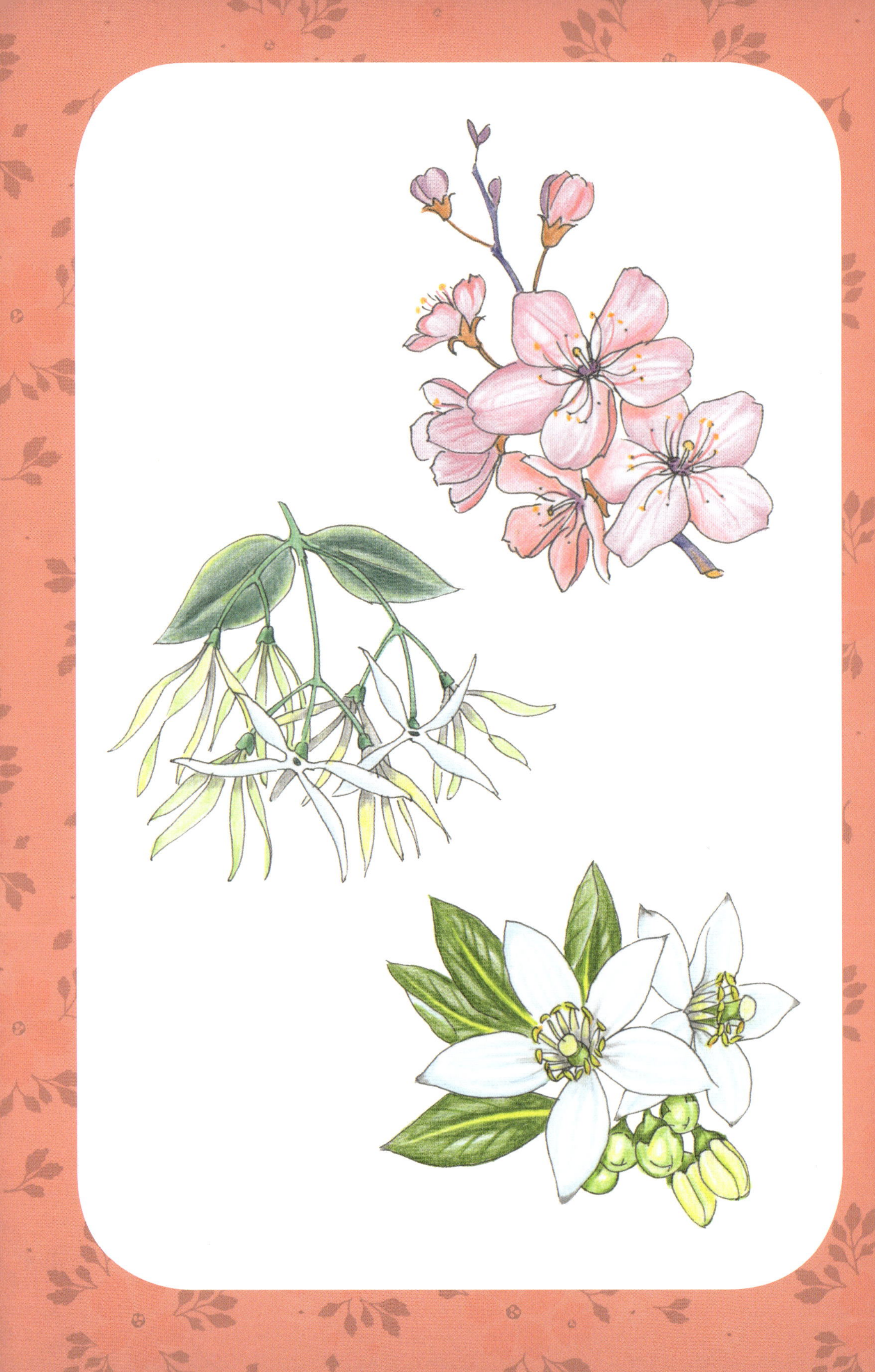

Blossoms

Magnolia

The distinctive white and pink flower of the magnolia tree signals the start of warmer weather.

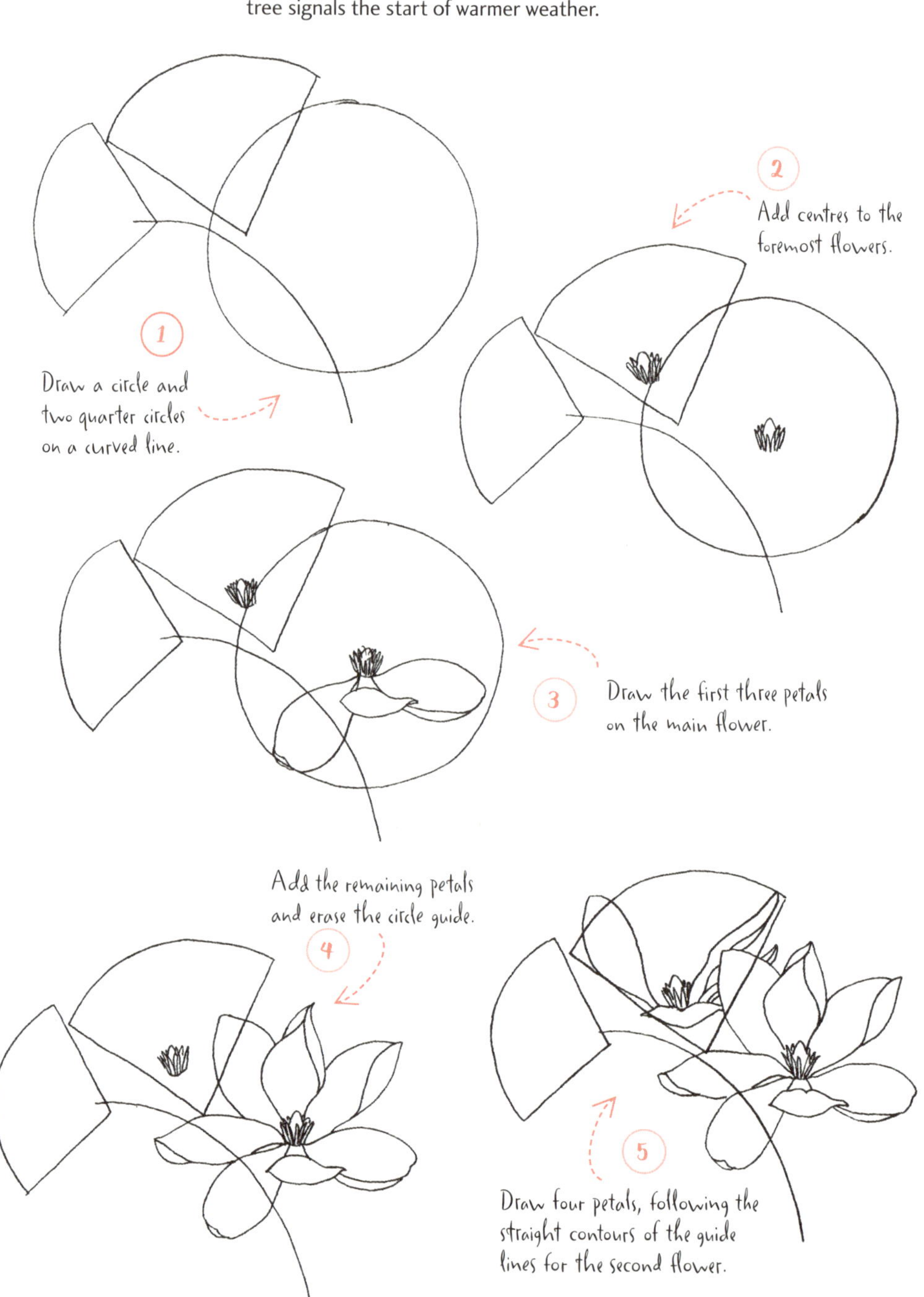

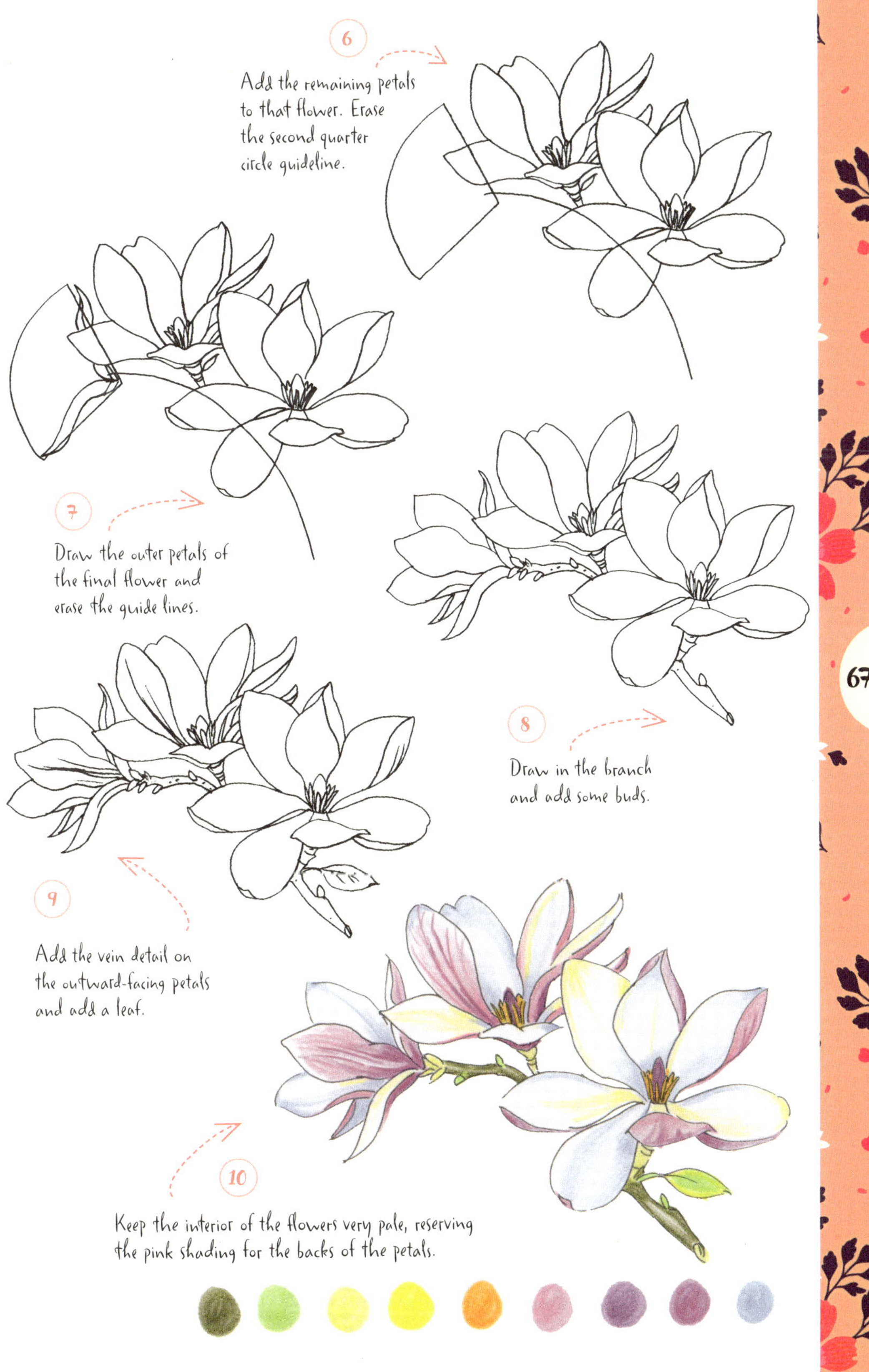

6

Add the remaining petals to that flower. Erase the second quarter circle guideline.

7

Draw the outer petals of the final flower and erase the guide lines.

8

Draw in the branch and add some buds.

9

Add the vein detail on the outward-facing petals and add a leaf.

10

Keep the interior of the flowers very pale, reserving the pink shading for the backs of the petals.

Oklahoma Redbud

The bright pink flowers and glossy leaves of this tree will add a fantastic splash of colour to any drawing.

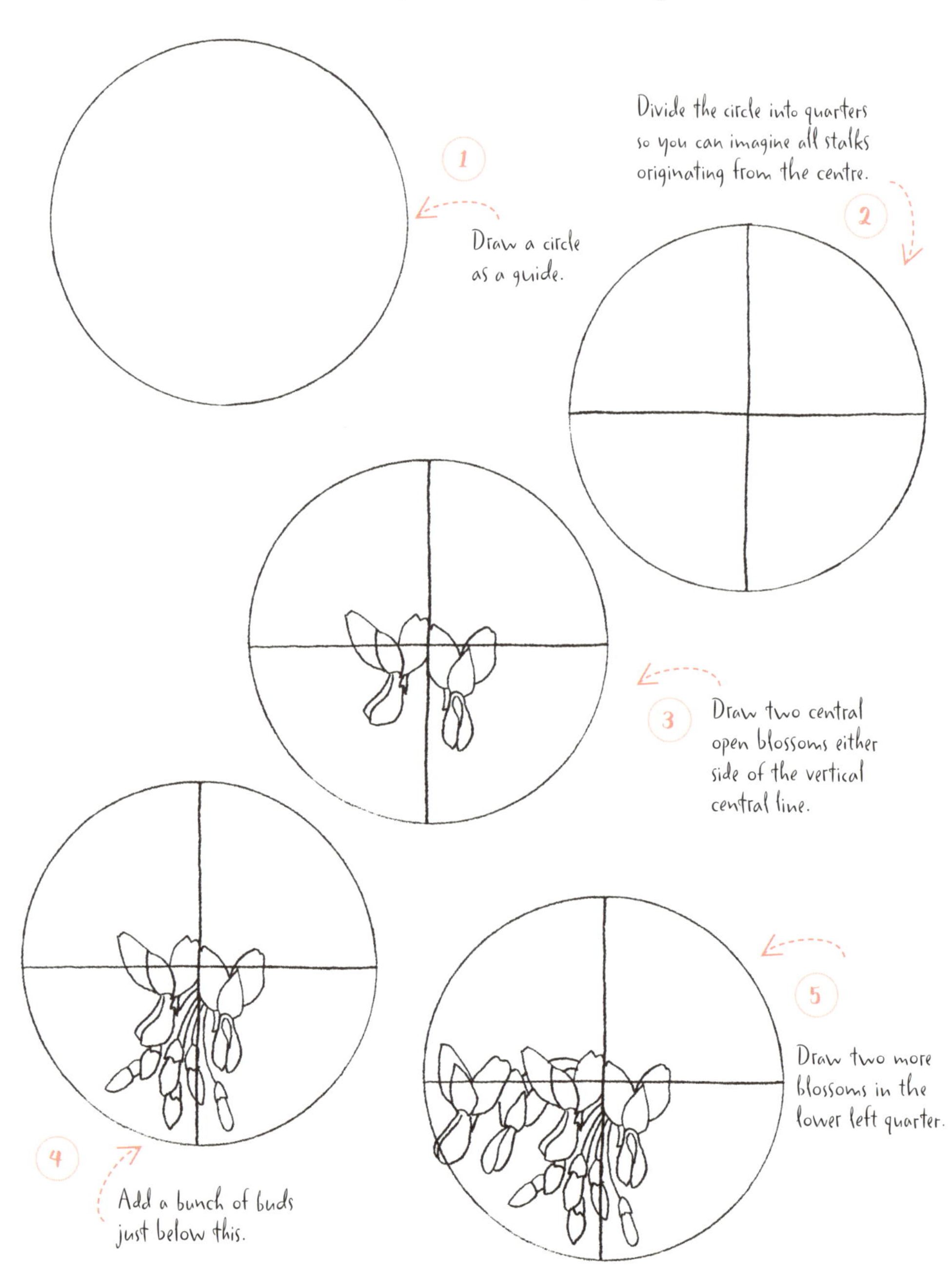

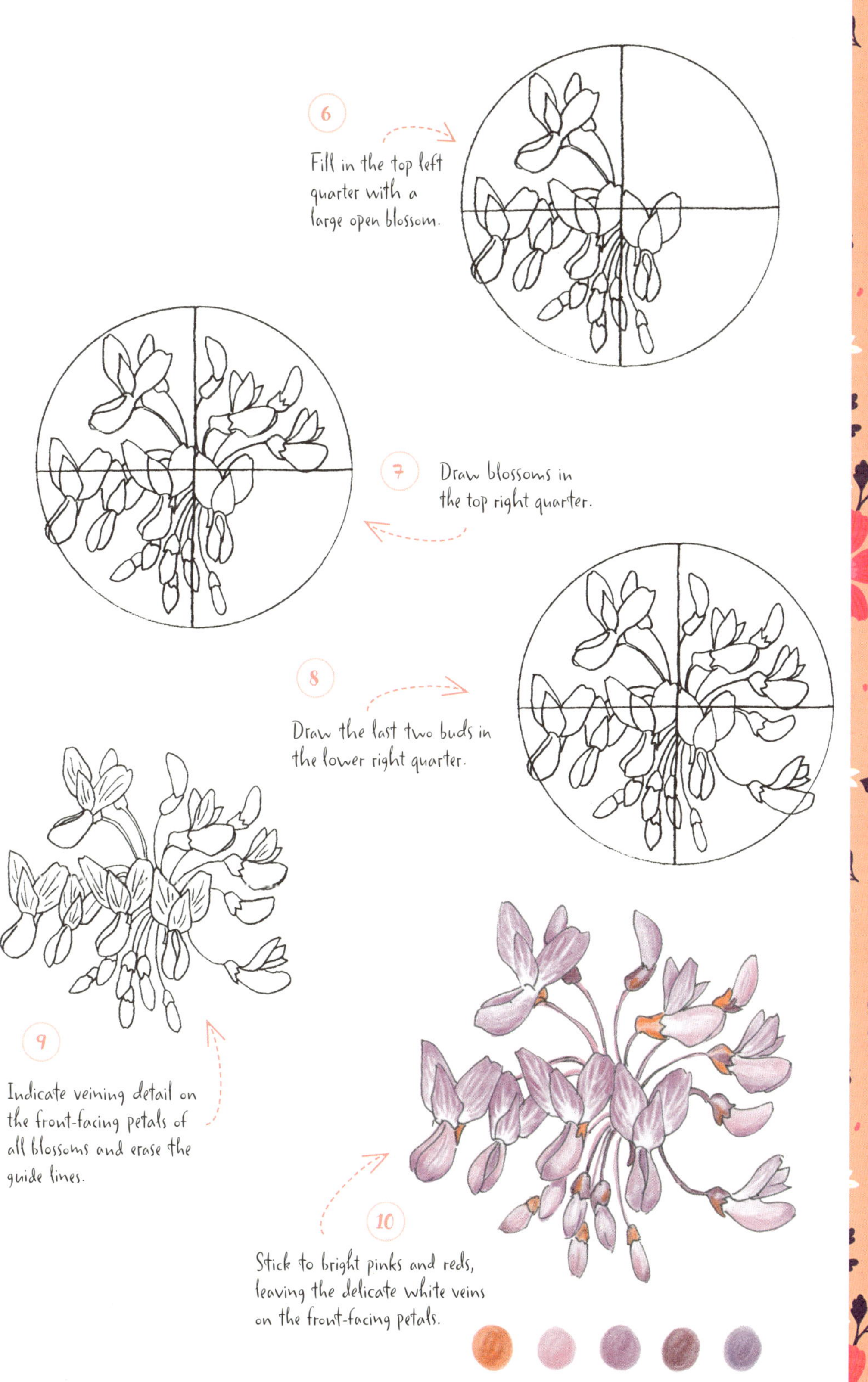

6 Fill in the top left quarter with a large open blossom.

7 Draw blossoms in the top right quarter.

8 Draw the last two buds in the lower right quarter.

9 Indicate veining detail on the front-facing petals of all blossoms and erase the guide lines.

10 Stick to bright pinks and reds, leaving the delicate white veins on the front-facing petals.

Venus Dogwood

The dogwood is not necessarily the most popular flowering tree, but its simple and fresh looking white flowers are worthy of inclusion.

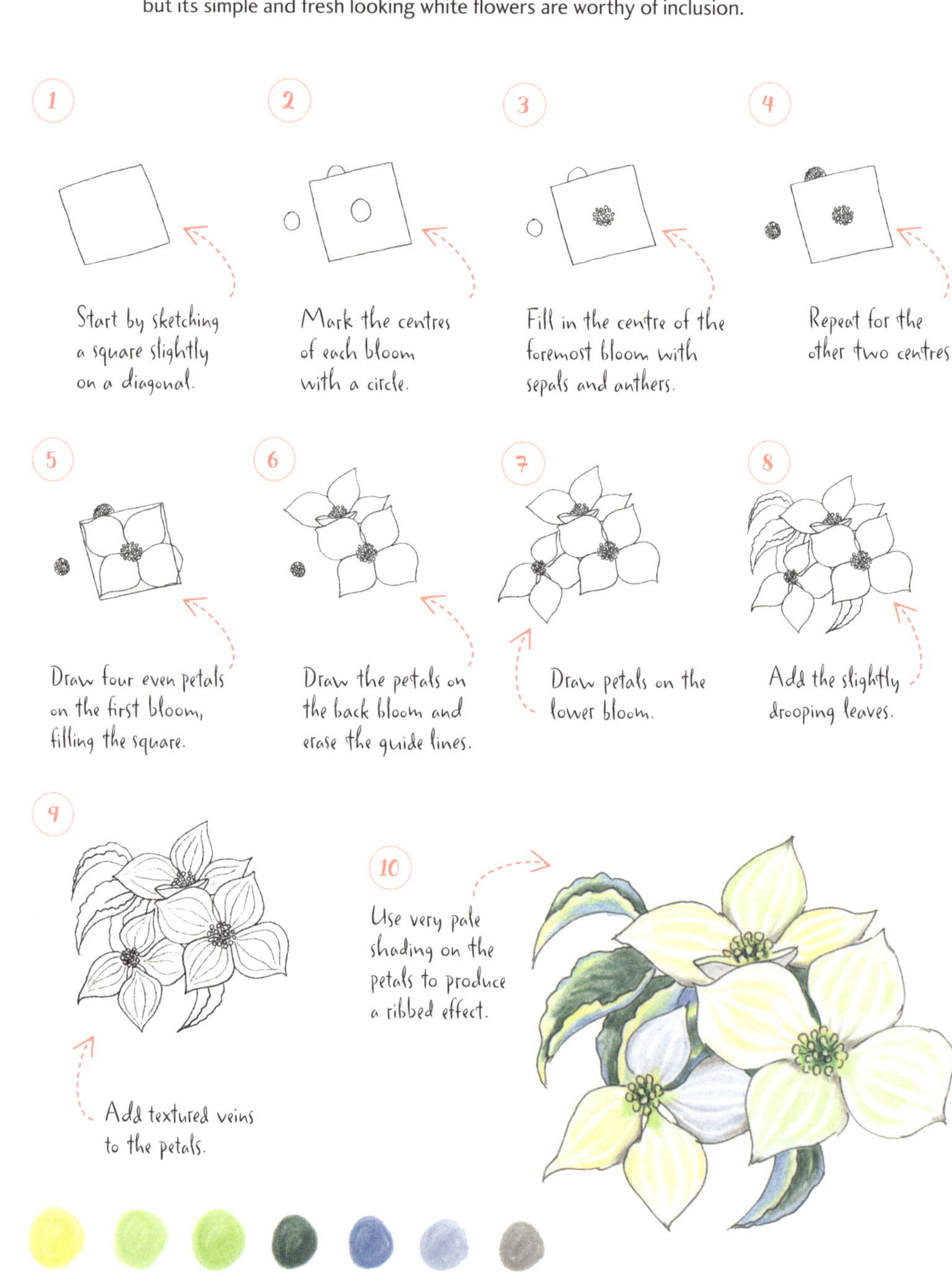

Cherry Blossom

This pretty pink blossoming tree is most associated with Japan and provides the most exquisite striking pink flowers.

1

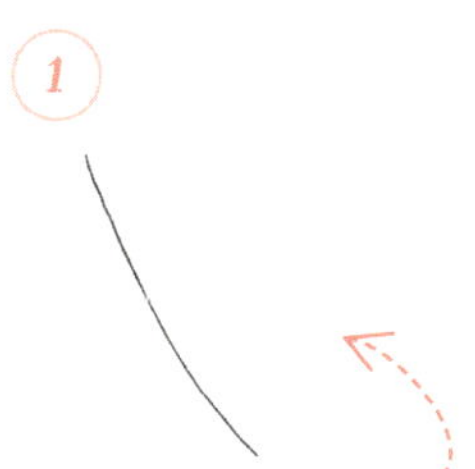

Draw a diagonal line for the direction of the stem.

2

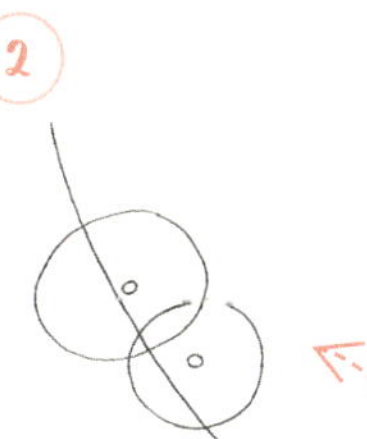

Sketch two circles with centres for the two main blossoms.

3

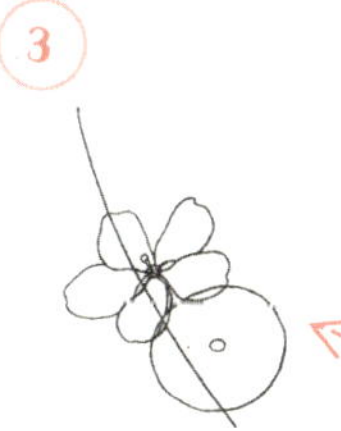

Draw the five petals and the centre of the first blossom.

4

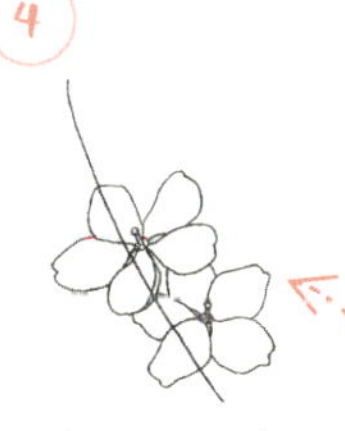

Repeat for the second blossom and erase the circular guides.

5

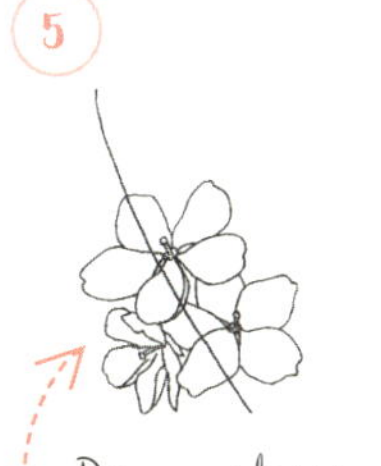

Draw a side-view blossom.

6

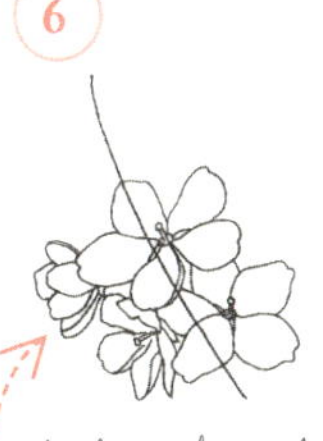

Add another side-view blossom.

7

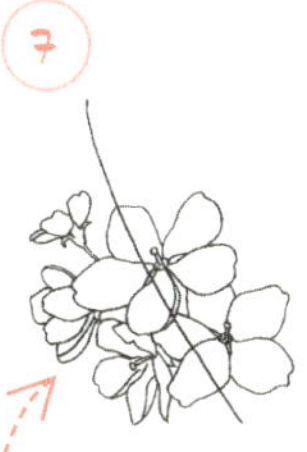

And another smaller side-view blossom.

8

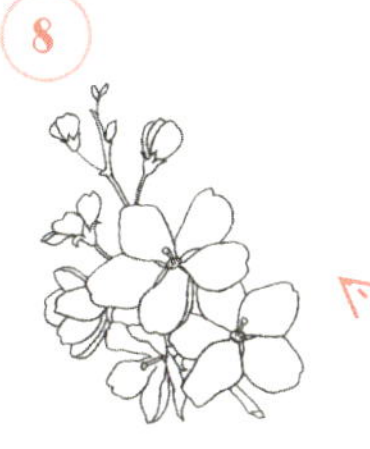

Fill in the twig at the top and add some buds and erase the guide line.

9

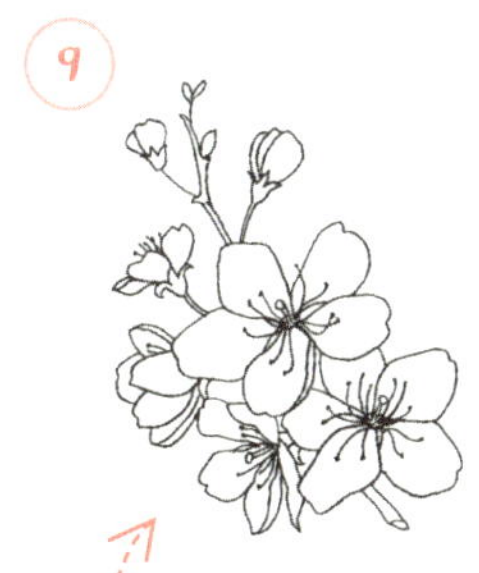

Add anthers to the centre of the blossoms.

10

Keep the petals very pale but create texture by layering pencil strokes along their length. Use a dark maroon for the very centre to hold the flowers together.

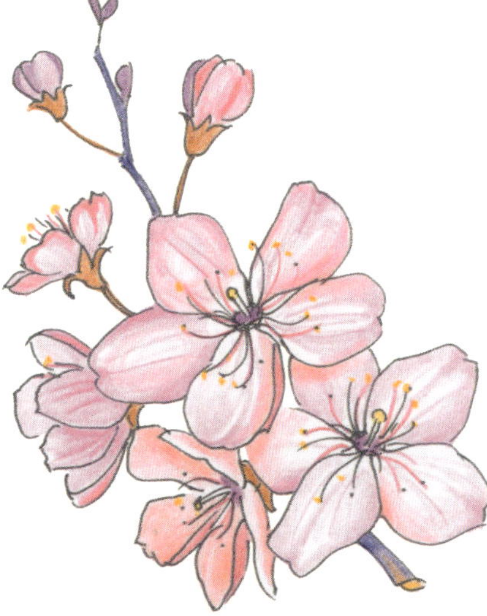

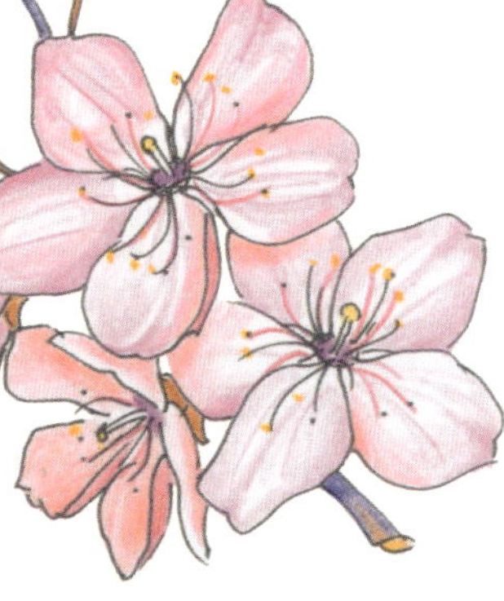

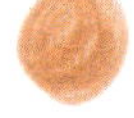   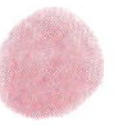  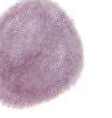 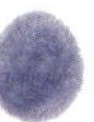

Crab Apple

The long-lasting, scented flowers of the crab apple tree come in a variety of pretty white, pink and purple blossoms.

1

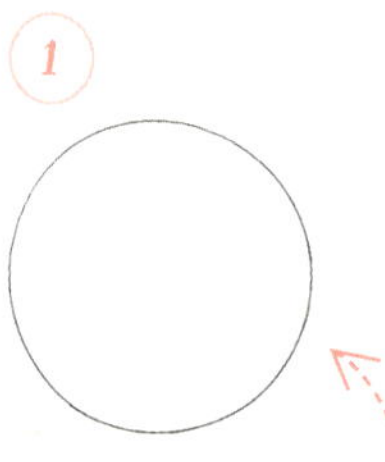

Draw a circle as a guide outline.

2

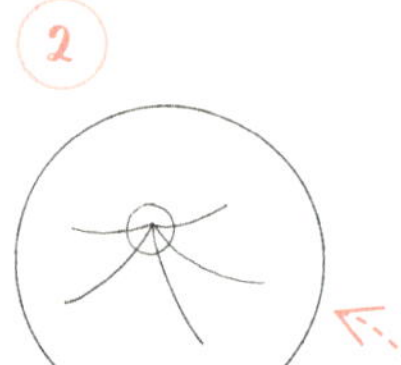

Mark the centre of the main blossom and draw lines radiating out from it.

3

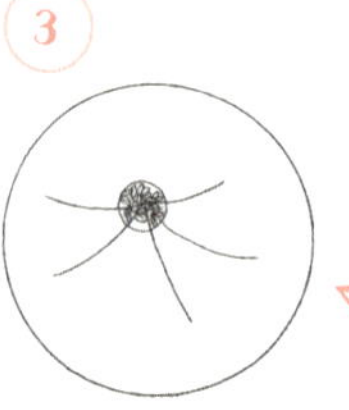

Draw the anthers in the centre of the main blossom.

4

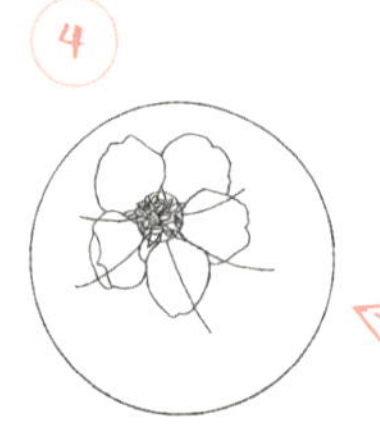

Draw the main five-petalled open blossom.

5

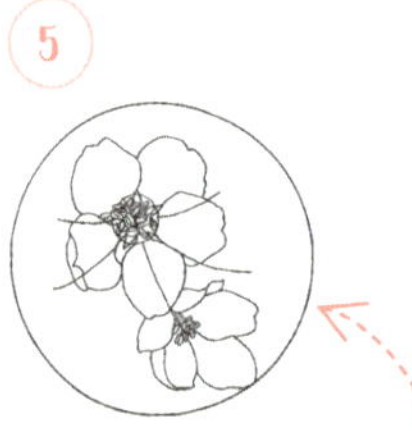

Draw a second open blossom just below.

6

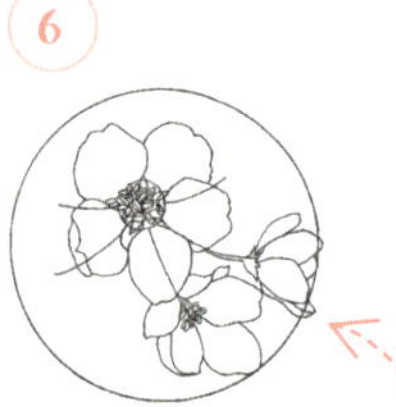

Add a side-view blossom.

7

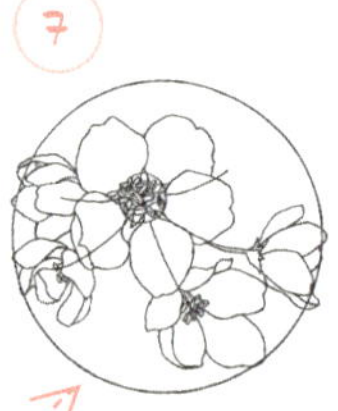

Add two opening buds on the left-hand side.

8

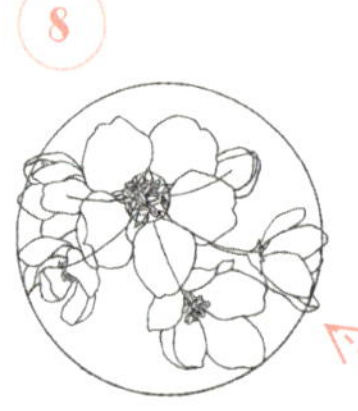

Add a closed bud on the right-hand side.

9

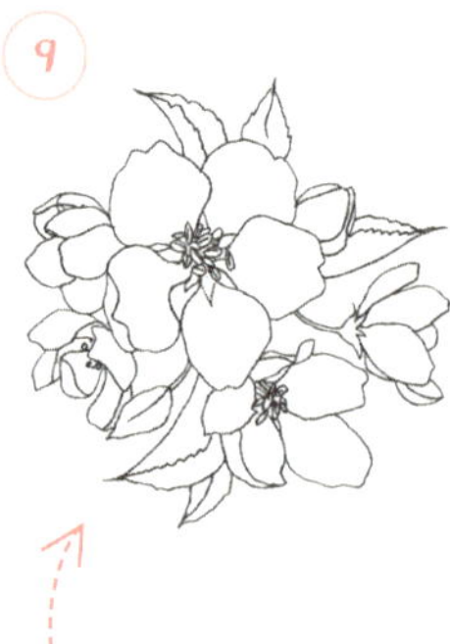

Add leaves and erase the guide circle.

Colour with deep rich pinks while retaining some lighter highlights and white veins originating from the centre of the petals.

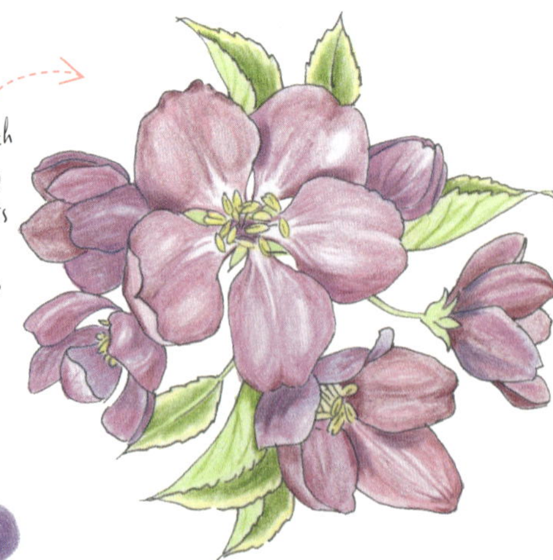

  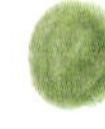 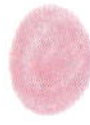 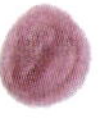 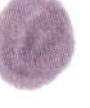 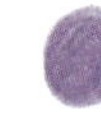

Red Robin

This is also known as a Photinia and, owing to its tight white flowers on red shoots, it is a distinctive evergreen shrub.

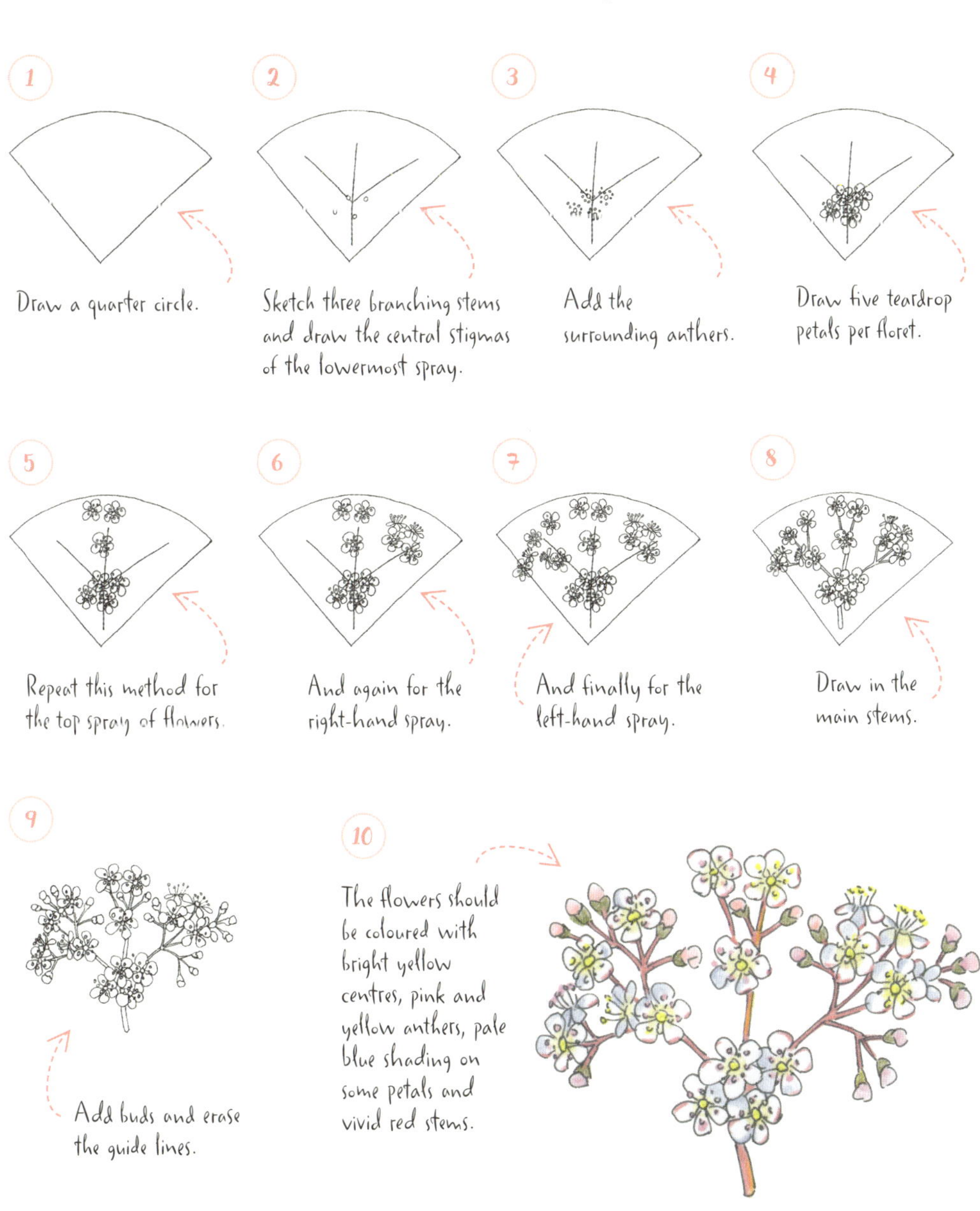

Paul's Scarlet

Crataegus Laevigata Paul's Scarlet is the full name for this plant, also commonly known as hawthorn. It displays these pretty blousy flowers, which make way for its distinctive red berries.

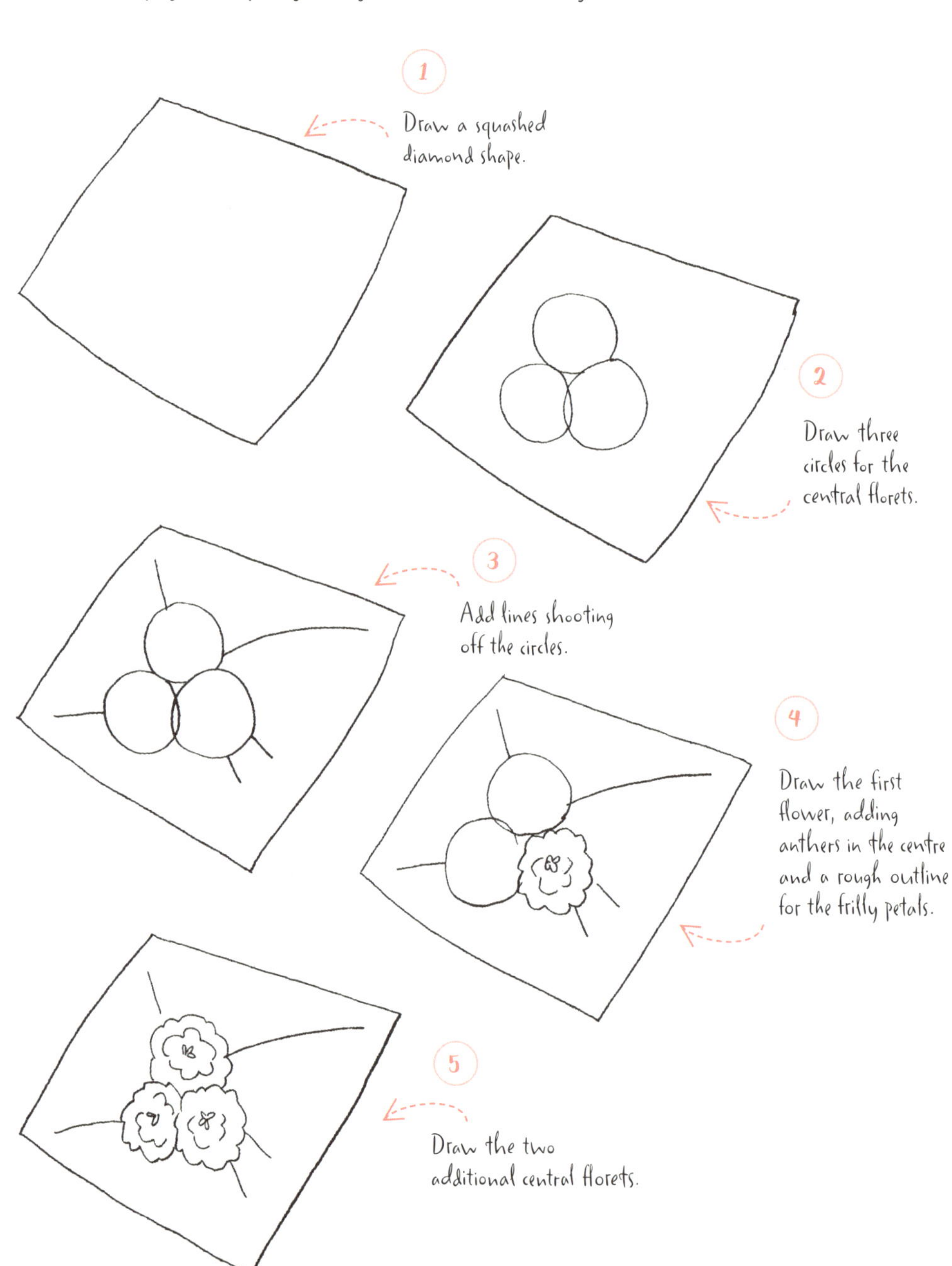

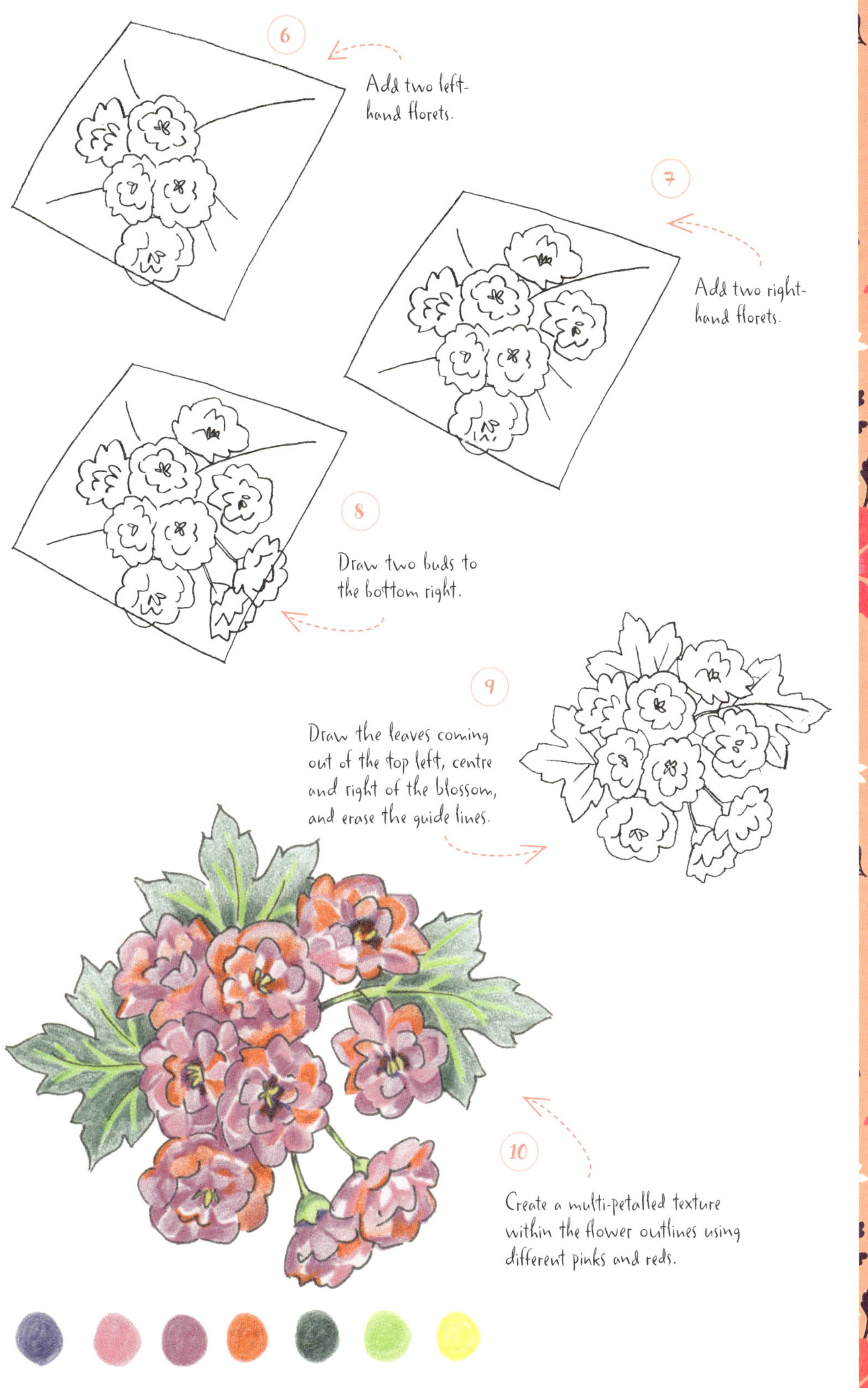
6
Add two left-hand florets.
7
Add two right-hand florets.
8
Draw two buds to the bottom right.
9
Draw the leaves coming out of the top left, centre and right of the blossom, and erase the guide lines.
10
Create a multi-petalled texture within the flower outlines using different pinks and reds.

Prunus Kanzan

This flowering cherry tree produces tight pink blossoms. Master the individual blooms before experimenting with a larger section of the tree.

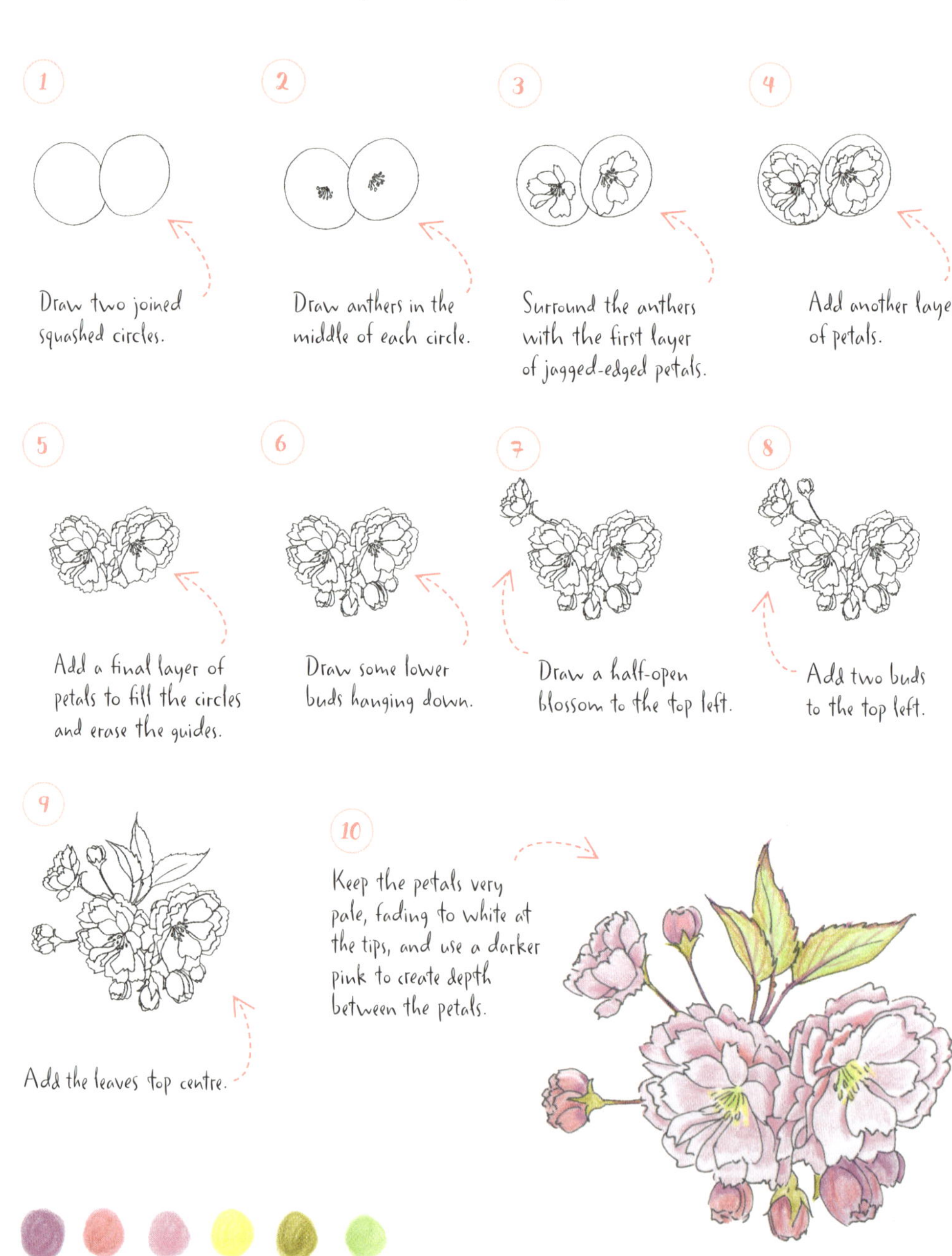

American Fringe

The American fringe tree is native to the eastern United States. It has simple leaves in pairs and loose, long white flowers.

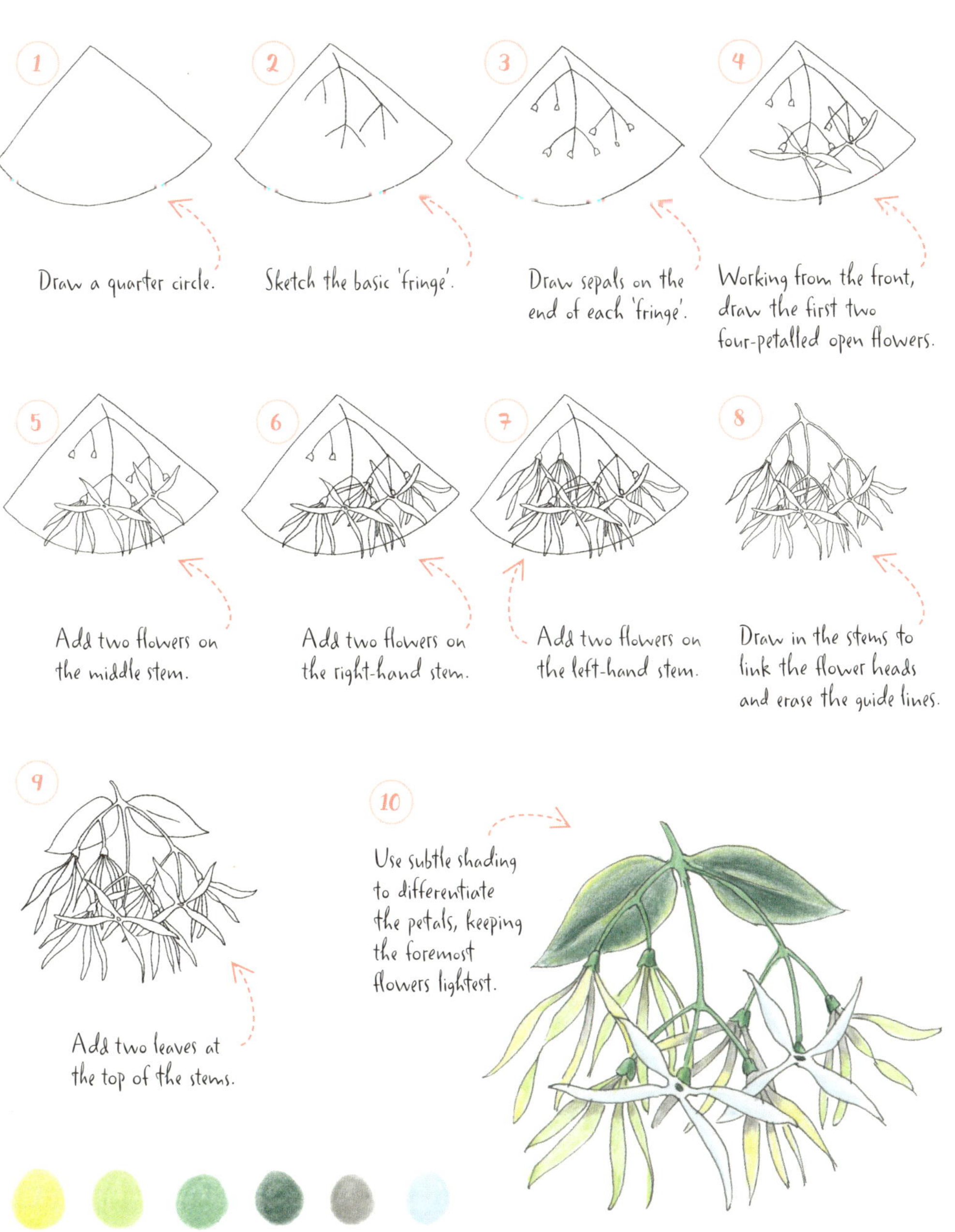

'Star Wars' Magnolia

This multi-stem magnolia has big thick leaves and a dramatic display of large rich pink flowers that appear in the springtime.

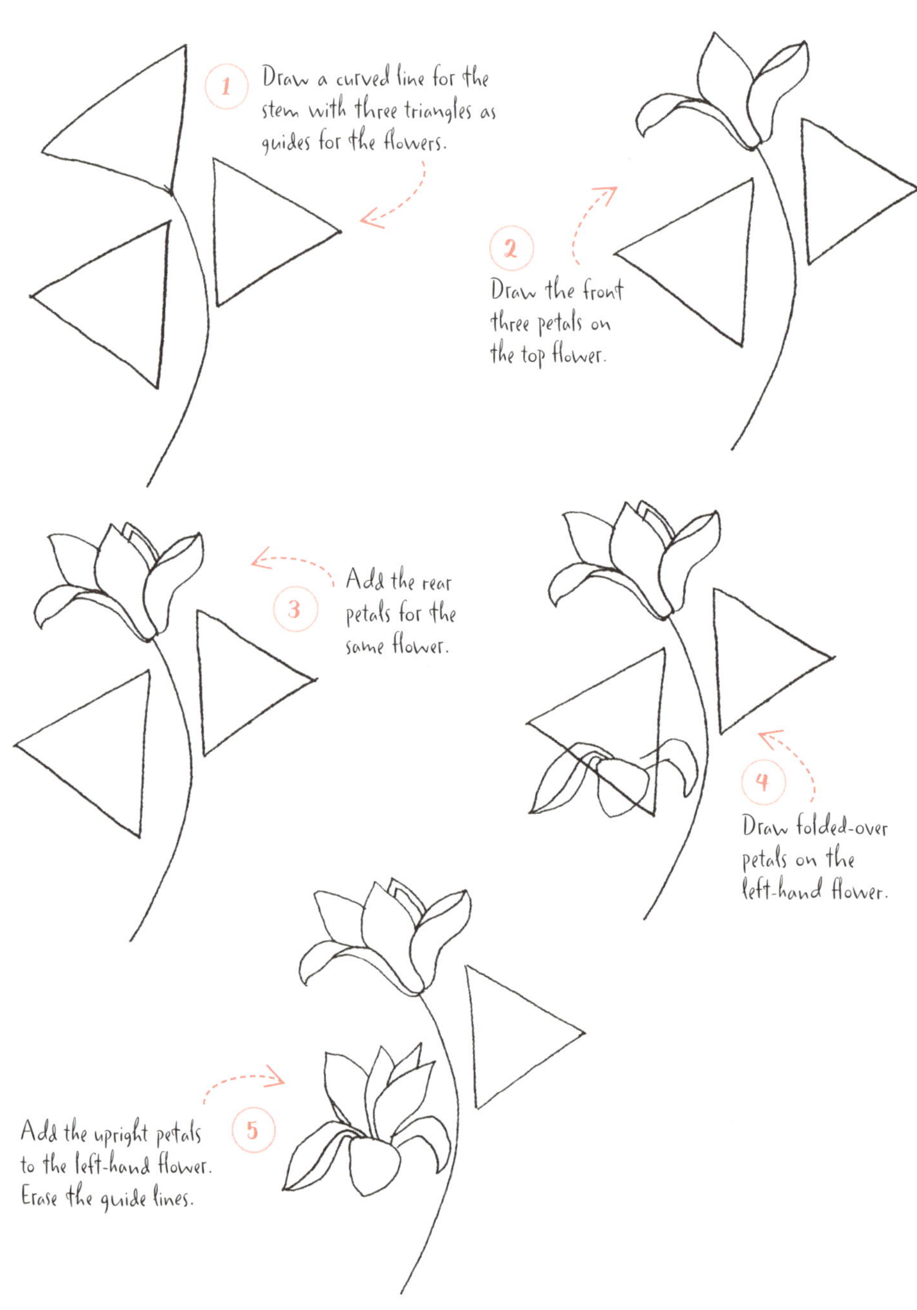

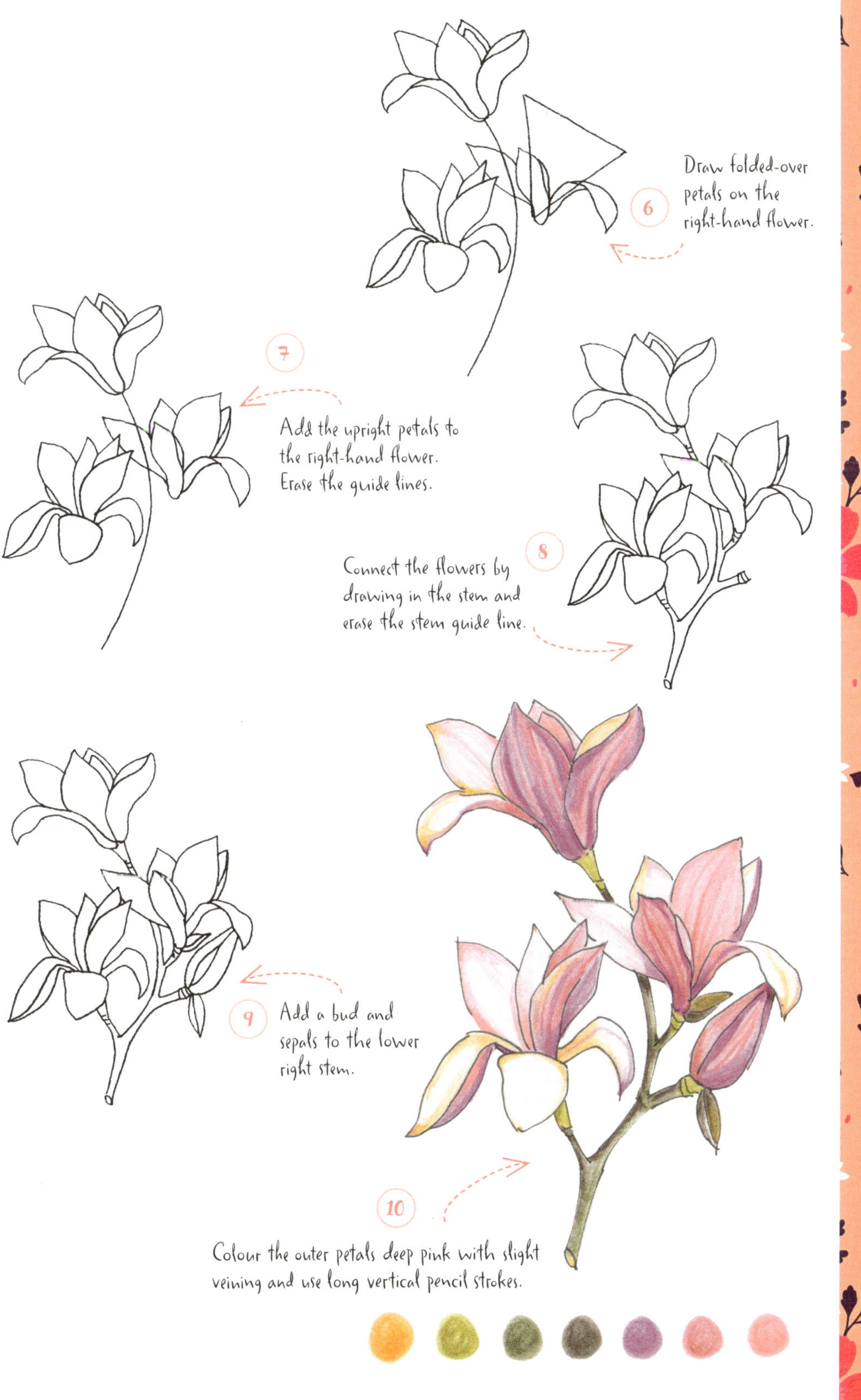
6
Draw folded-over petals on the right-hand flower.
7
Add the upright petals to the right-hand flower. Erase the guide lines.
8
Connect the flowers by drawing in the stem and erase the stem guide line.
9
Add a bud and sepals to the lower right stem.
10
Colour the outer petals deep pink with slight veining and use long vertical pencil strokes.

Double Flowering Plum

The frothy pink blossom on this popular garden shrub will create a full and interesting drawing.

1

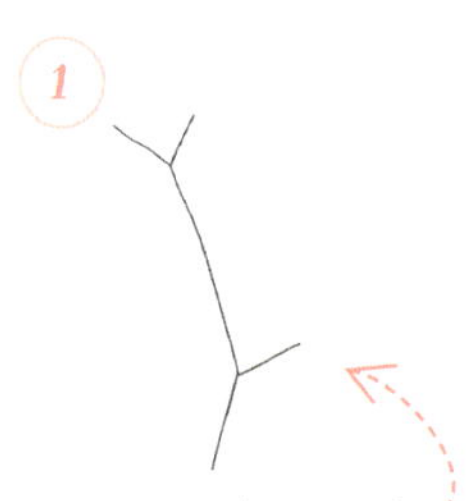

Draw the branch.

2

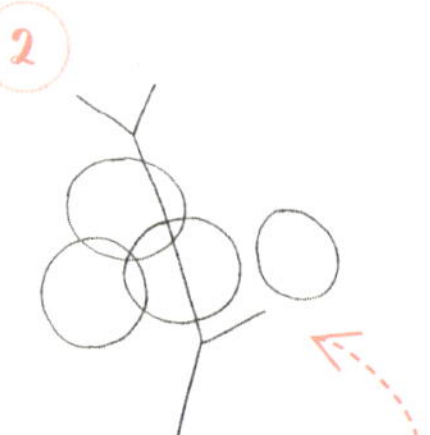

Add circles as guides for the flowers.

3

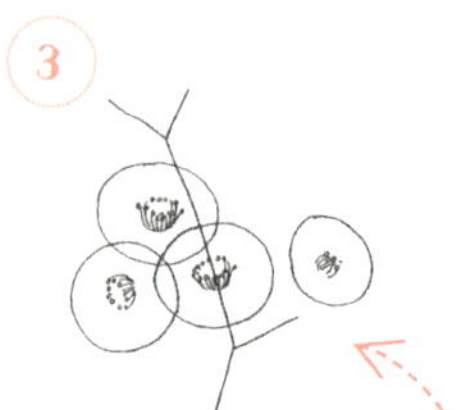

Draw stamens in the centre of each blossom.

4

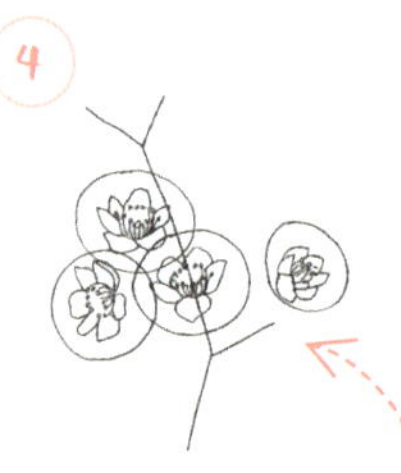

Surround each centre with the first layer of petals.

5

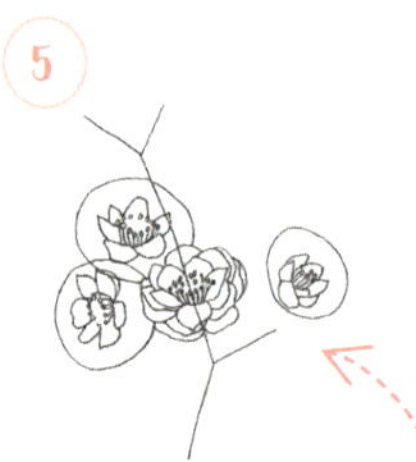

Draw remaining petals on the centre foremost flower, filling the circle.

6

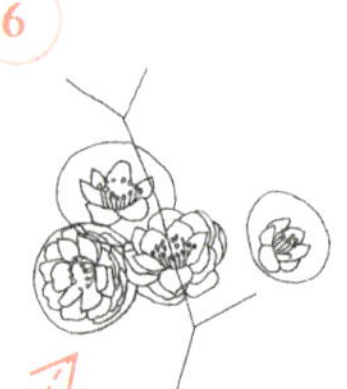

Add the remaining petals to the left-hand flower.

7

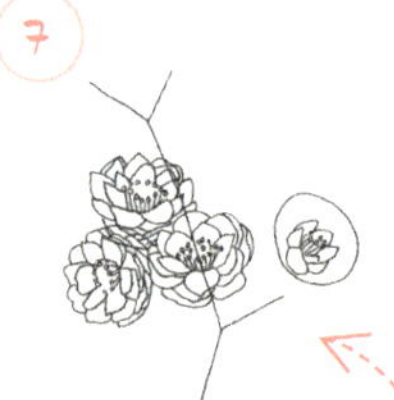

Add the remaining petals to the top flower.

8

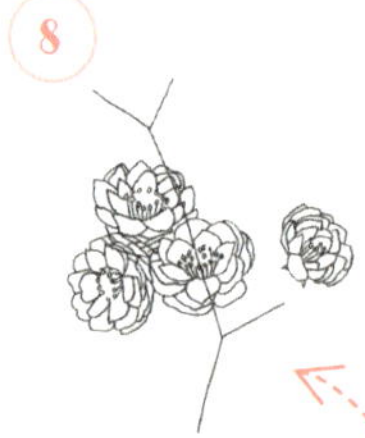

Add remaining petals to the half-open flower on the right.

9

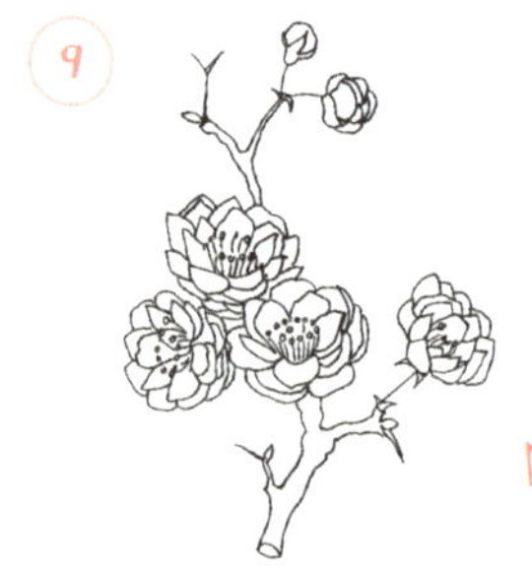

Draw in the branch and a few buds and erase the guide lines.

10

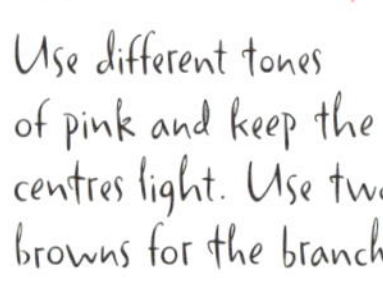

Use different tones of pink and keep the centres light. Use two browns for the branch.

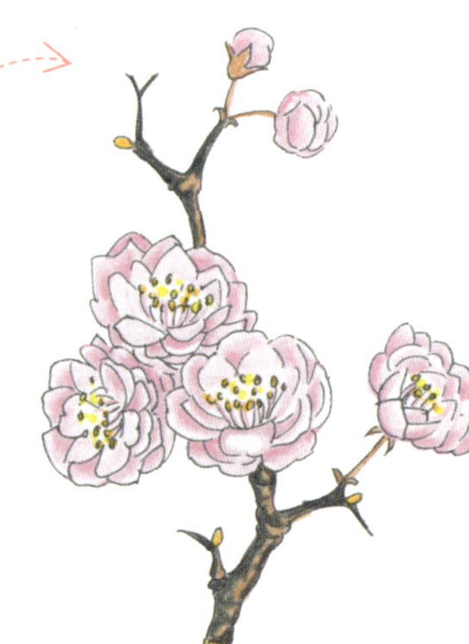

  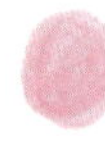 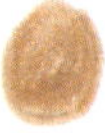 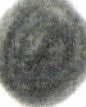

Orange Blossom

This pretty white flower is the blossom of the fragrant Sinensis tree and is often used in perfumes and aromatics. It makes it the perfect choice for a scented bouquet (see page 126).

1. Draw a star shape with lines.

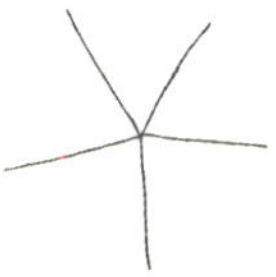

2. Working from the centre of the flower outwards, draw the central pistil.

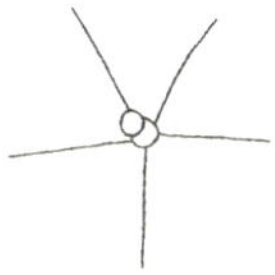

3. Add a ring of stamens around the pistil.

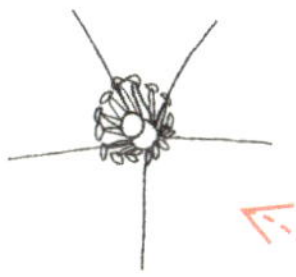

4. Add five pointed, evenly shaped petals.

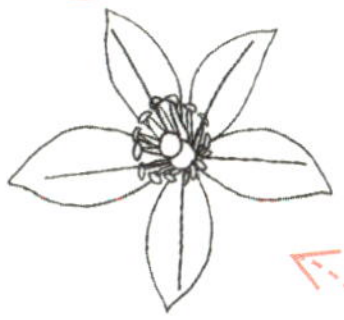

5. Draw the pistil and stamen of the second flower and erase the guide lines

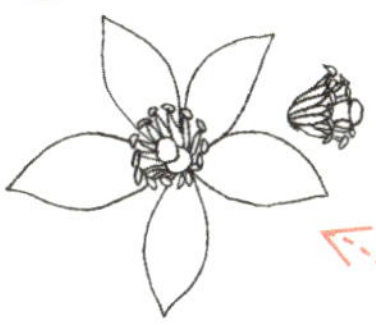

6. Draw the petals of the second flower.

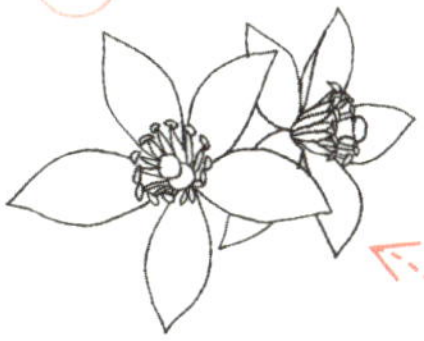

7. Add circular, tightly closed buds.

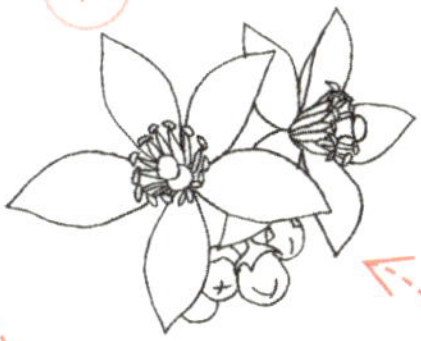

8. Add elongated buds hanging down.

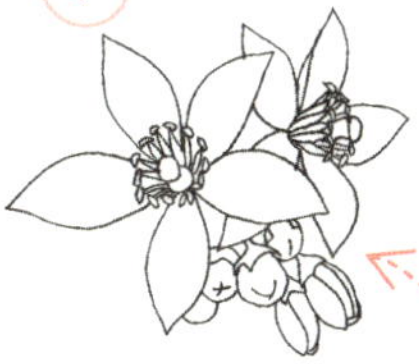

9. 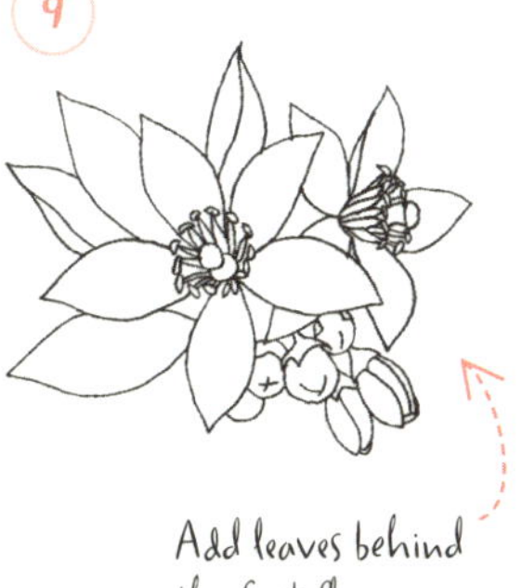

   Add leaves behind the first flower.

10. Add veins and shading to the leaves to make them look glossy and keep the flowers very pale in colour.

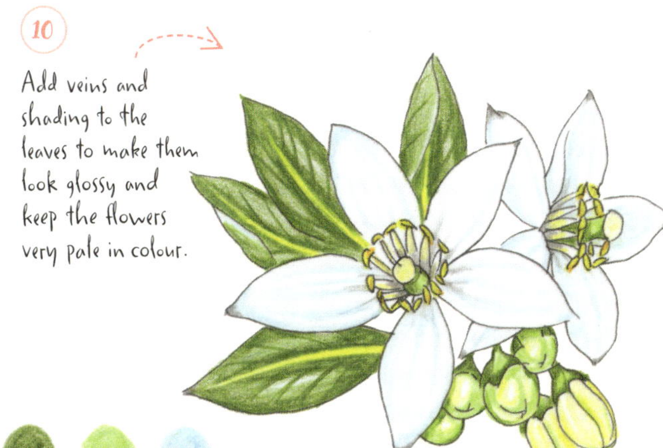

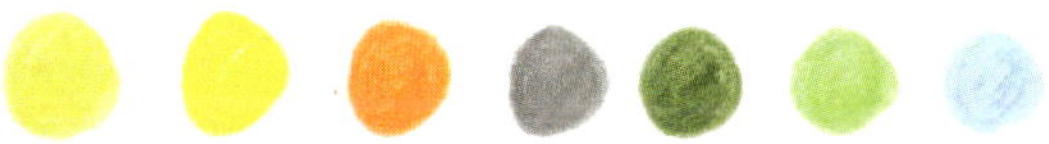

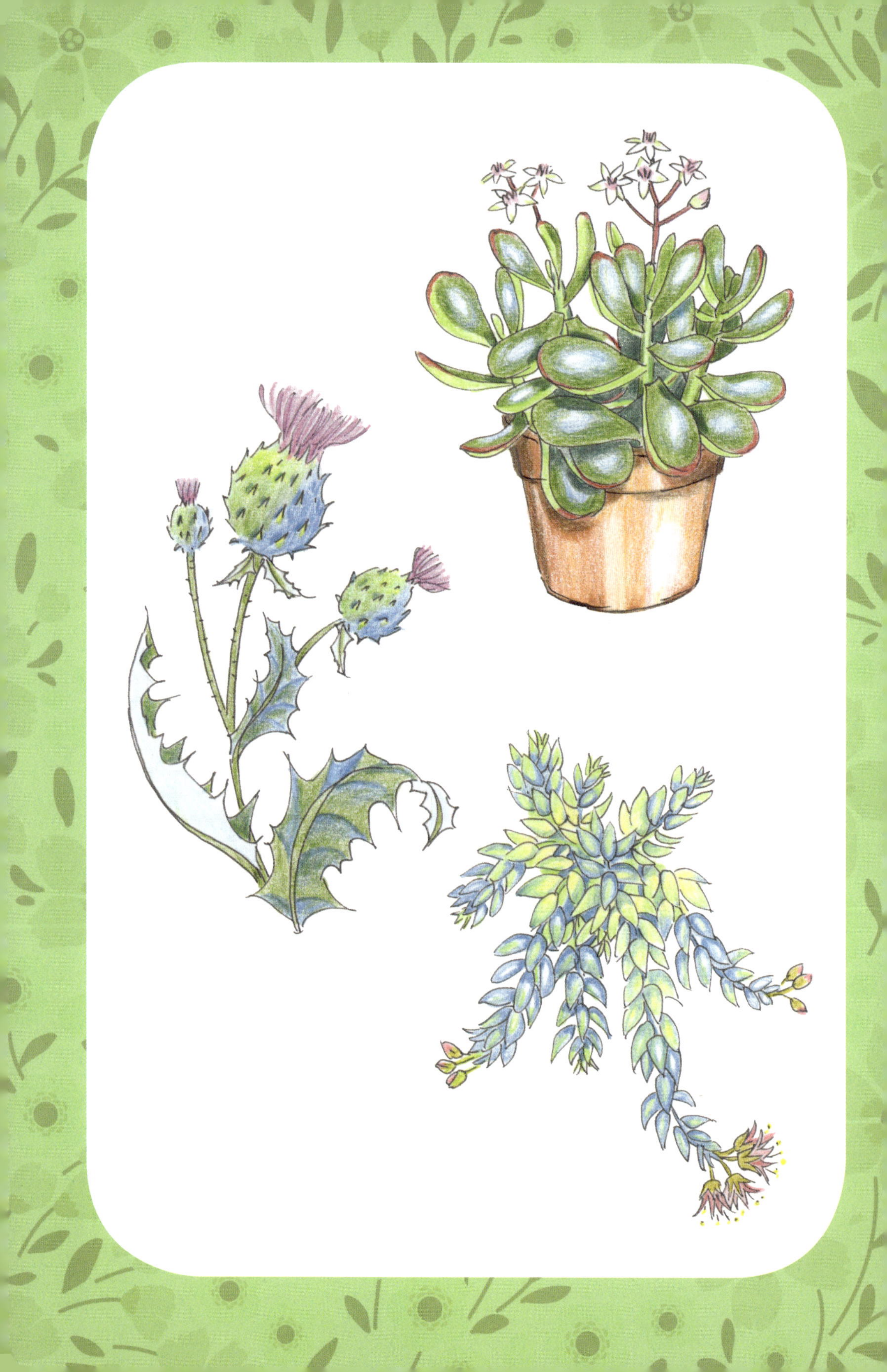

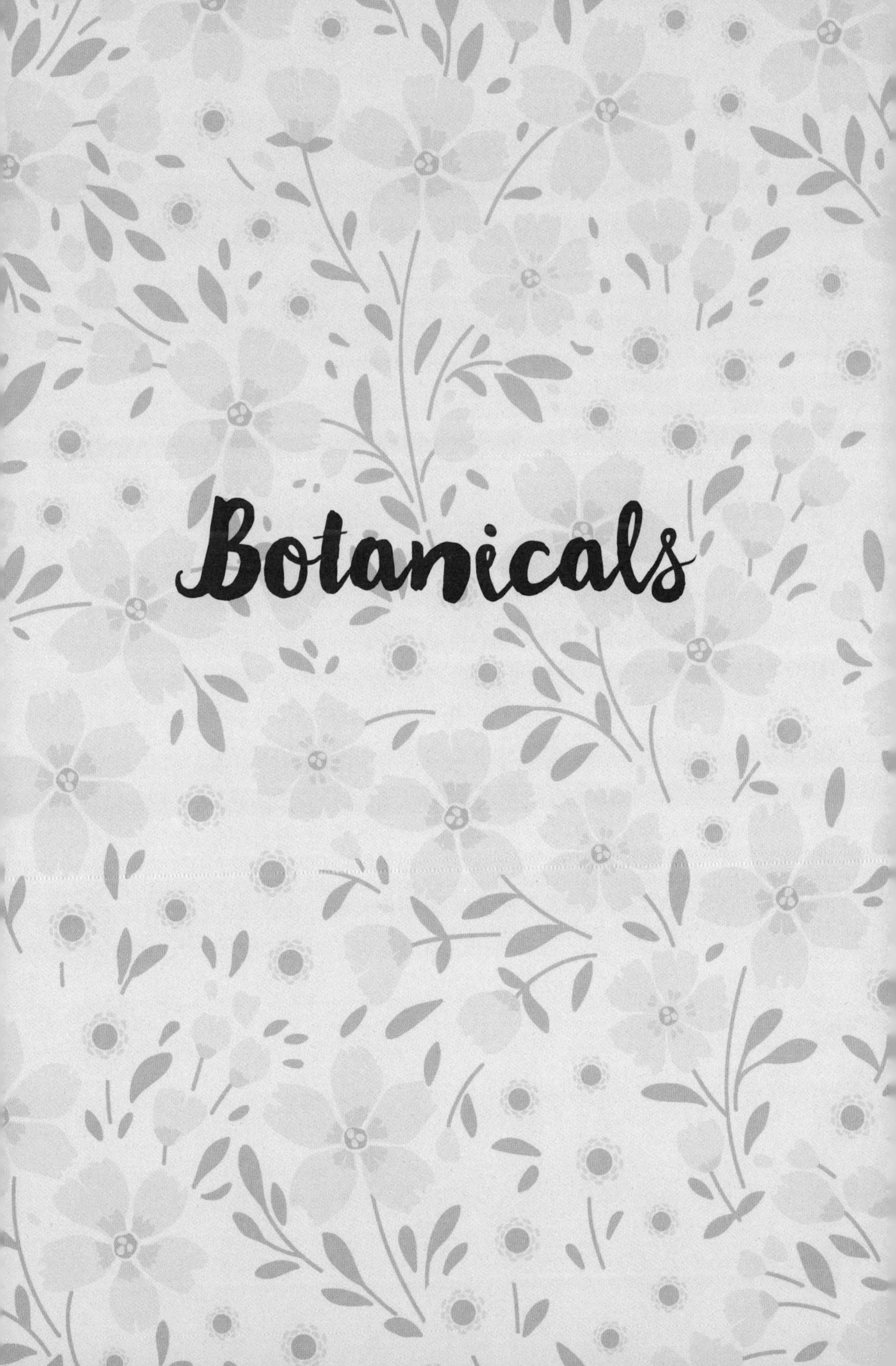

Botanicals

Blue Thistle

The intricate detail on this thistle head and strong blue and purple tones make for a beautifully dramatic drawing.

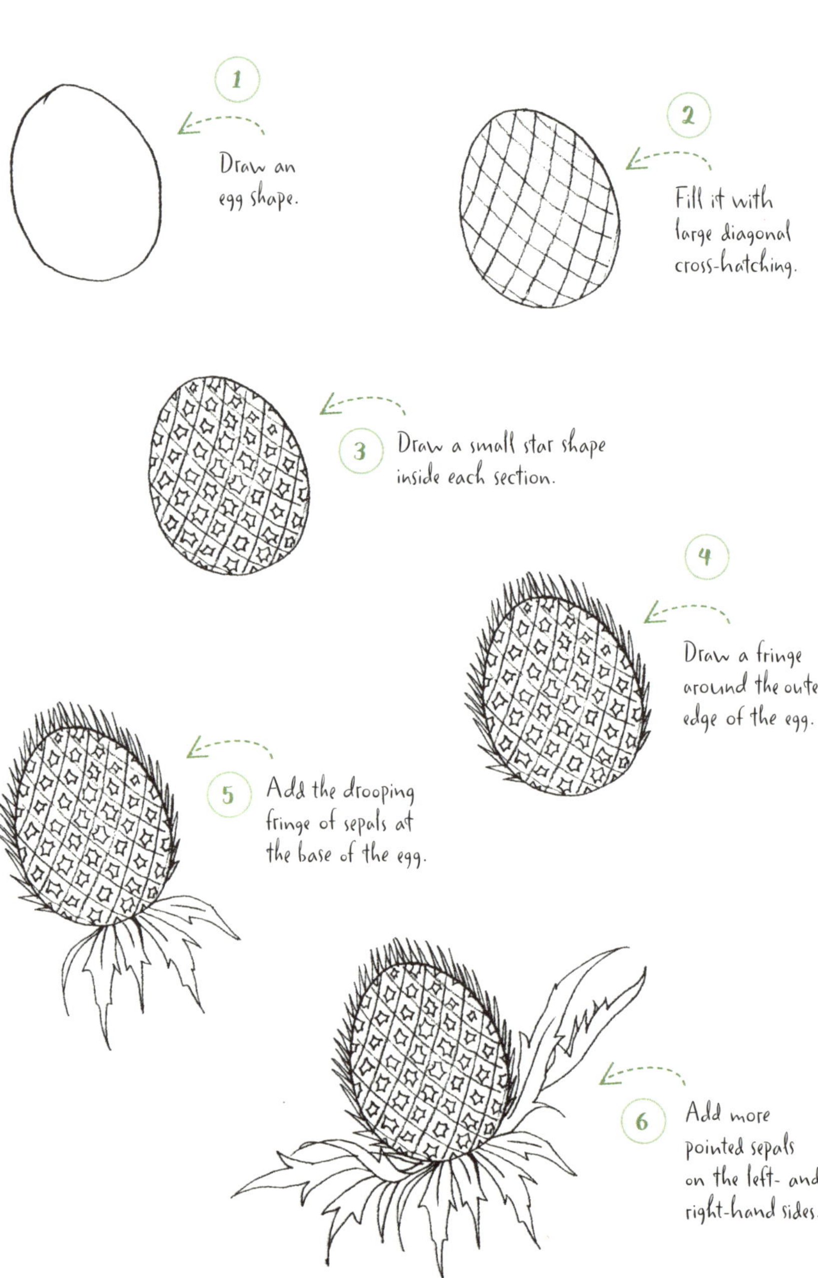

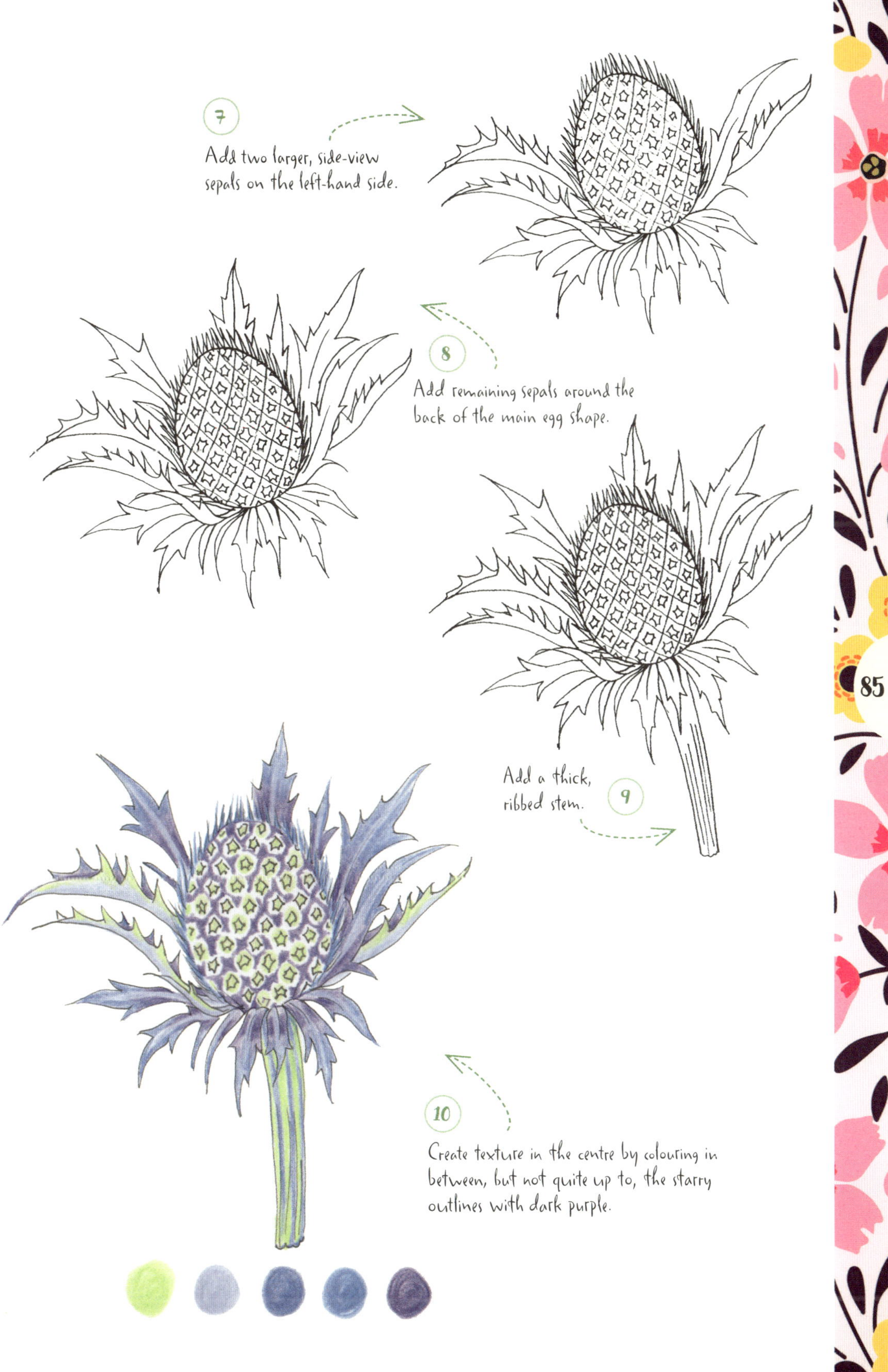
7
Add two larger, side-view sepals on the left-hand side.
8
Add remaining sepals around the back of the main egg shape.
9
Add a thick, ribbed stem.
10
Create texture in the centre by colouring in between, but not quite up to, the starry outlines with dark purple.

Desert Rose

The desert rose is a striking plant with a thick, succulent stem and pretty pink flowers.

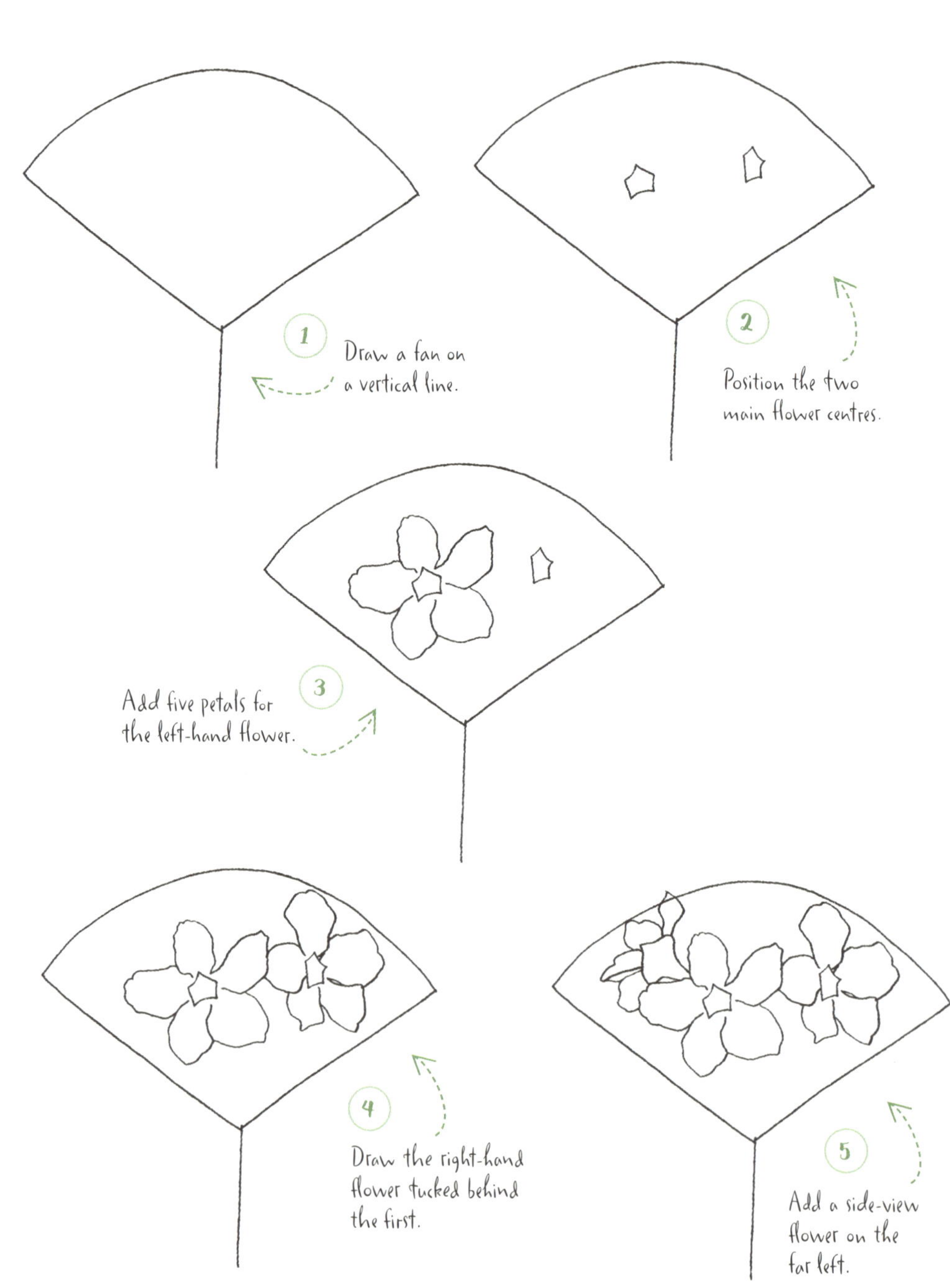

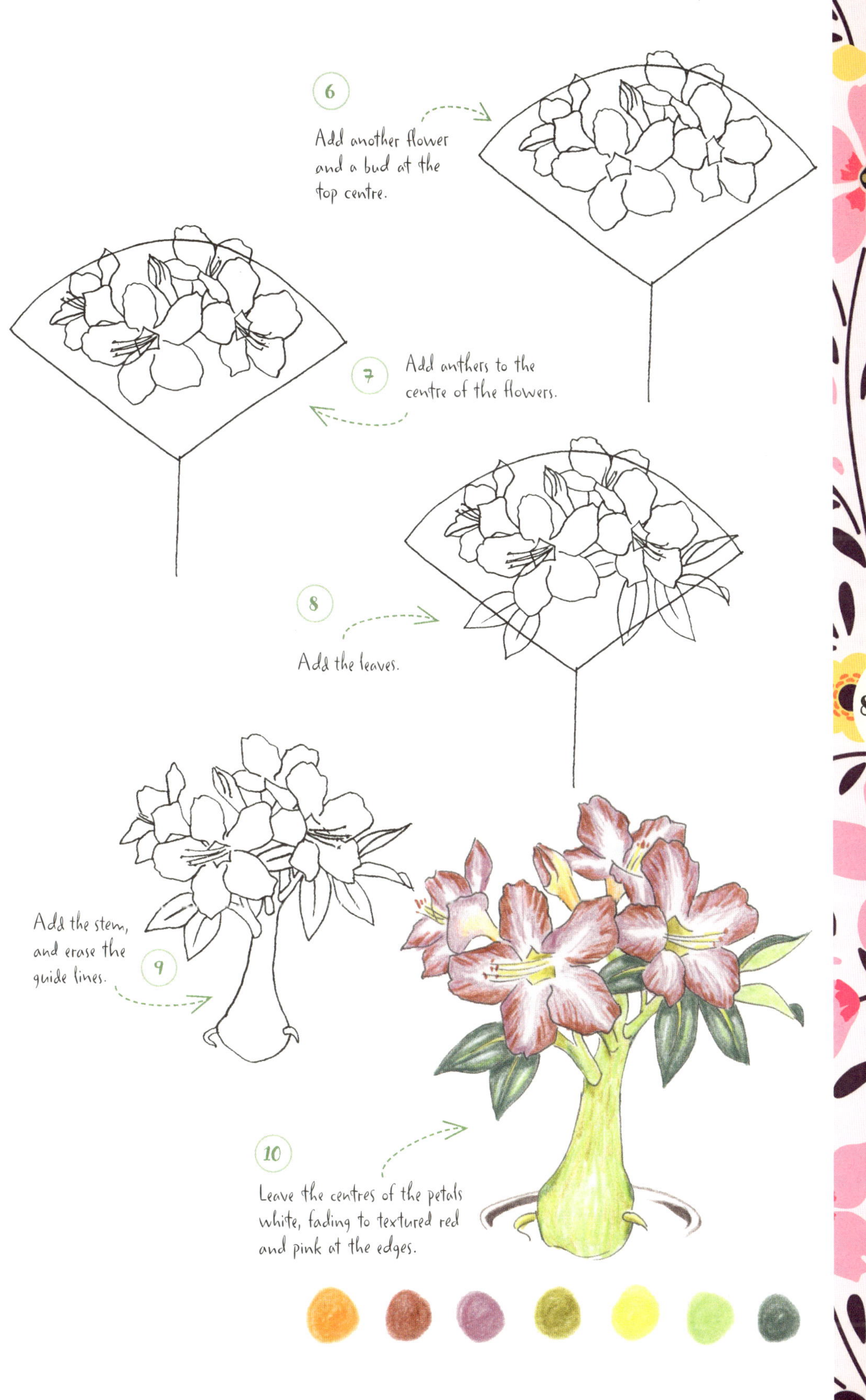
6
Add another flower and a bud at the top centre.
7
Add anthers to the centre of the flowers.
8
Add the leaves.
Add the stem, and erase the guide lines.
9
10
Leave the centres of the petals white, fading to textured red and pink at the edges.

Jade

Commonly known as a friendship or money tree, this succulent is considered good luck to have in the home.

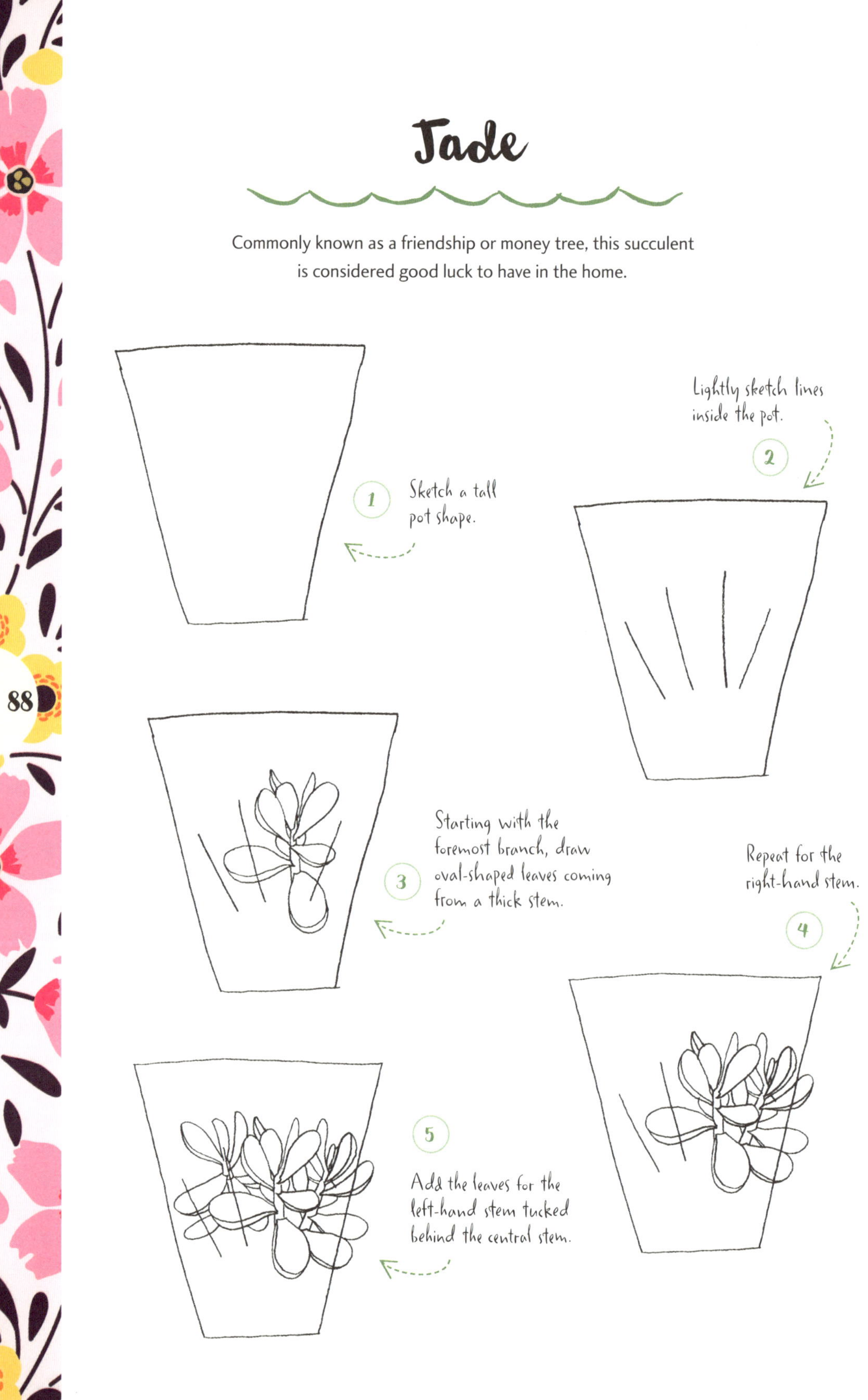

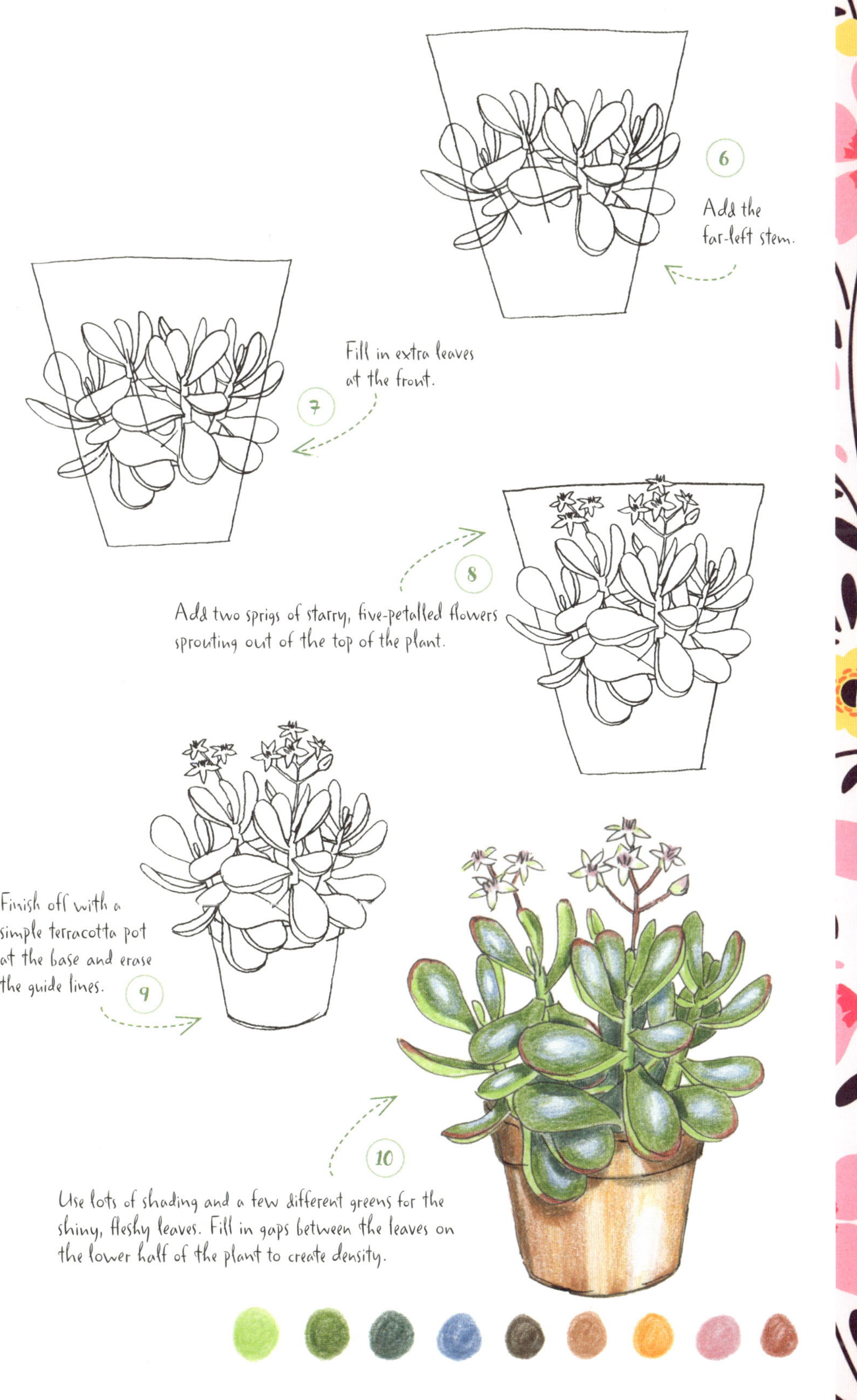
6
Add the far-left stem.
Fill in extra leaves at the front.
7
8
Add two sprigs of starry, five-petalled flowers sprouting out of the top of the plant.
Finish off with a simple terracotta pot at the base and erase the guide lines.
9
10
Use lots of shading and a few different greens for the shiny, fleshy leaves. Fill in gaps between the leaves on the lower half of the plant to create density.

Aloe Vera

This succulent has so many health benefits, and its natural, spiky shape makes it an interesting plant to draw.

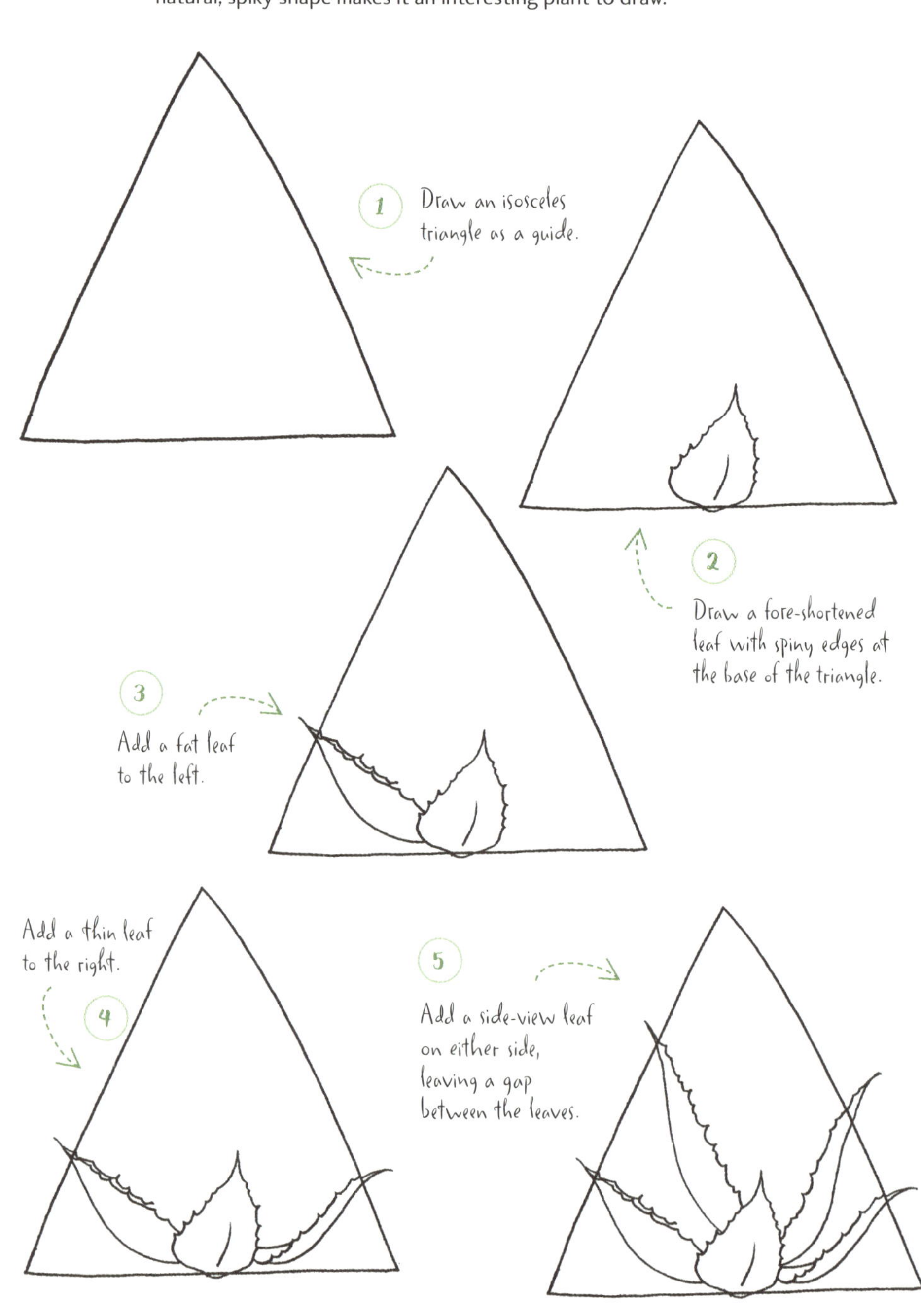

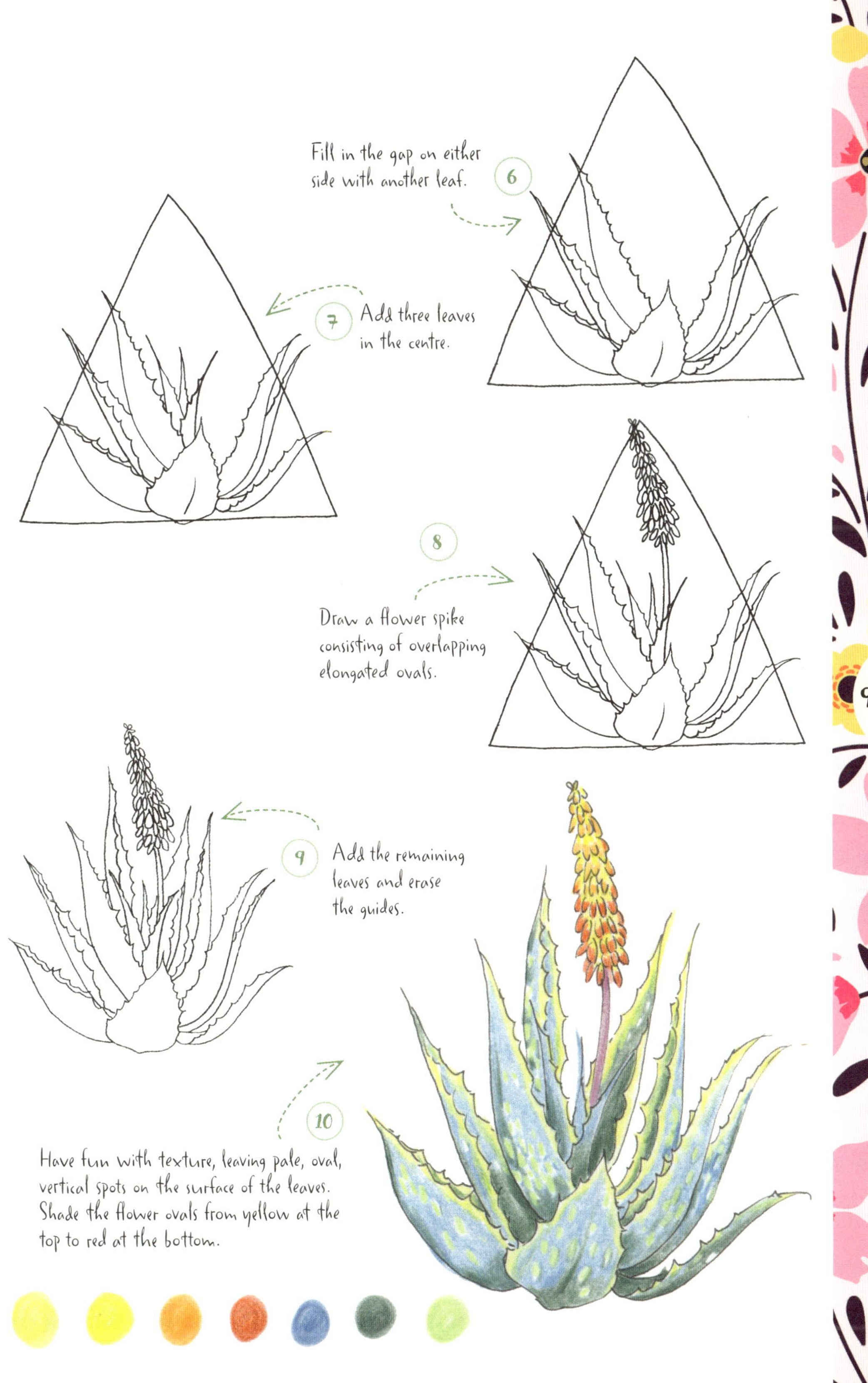

6
Fill in the gap on either side with another leaf.
7
Add three leaves in the centre.
8
Draw a flower spike consisting of overlapping elongated ovals.
9
Add the remaining leaves and erase the guides.
10
Have fun with texture, leaving pale, oval, vertical spots on the surface of the leaves. Shade the flower ovals from yellow at the top to red at the bottom.

Baby Rubber

Forget the usual greens of a boring leafy houseplant – the leaves on this baby rubber plant have interesting shapes and blends of colours.

1

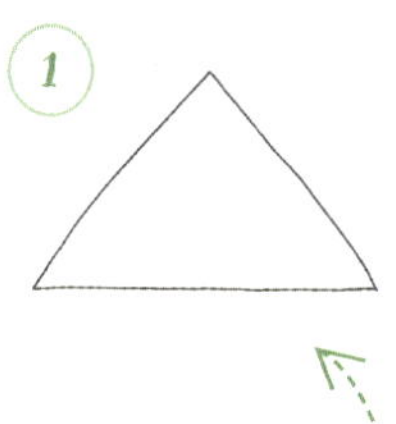

Draw a wide-bottomed triangle.

2

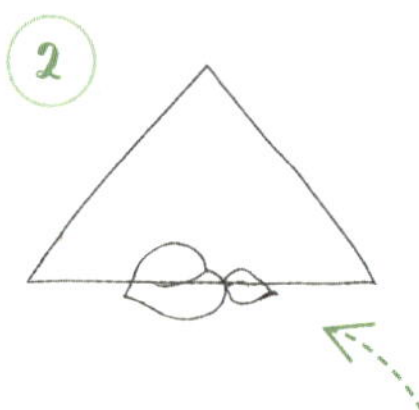

Draw two heart-shaped leaves in the centre of the bottom line.

3

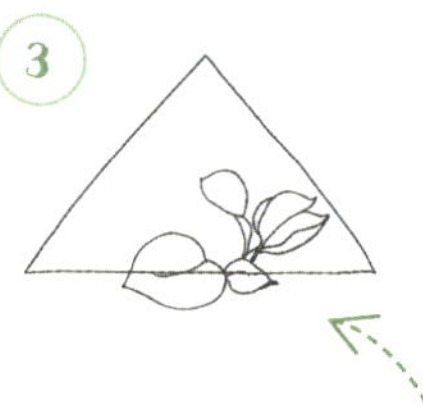

Add three twisted leaves on the right-hand side.

4

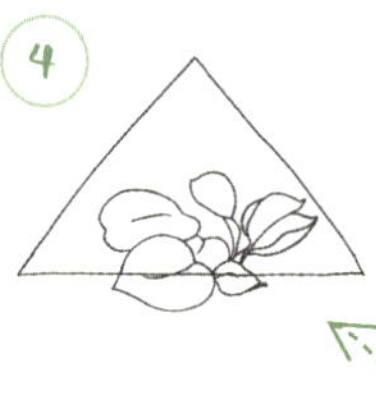

Add two leaves to the left-hand side.

5

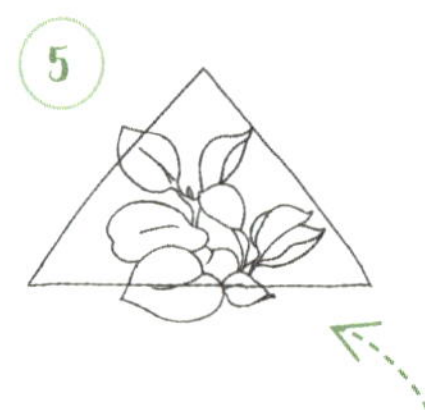

Draw the top two leaves and the stem.

6

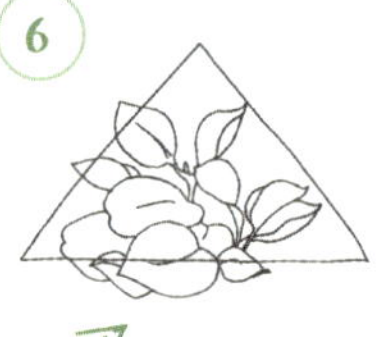

Add two more leaves on the left-hand side.

7

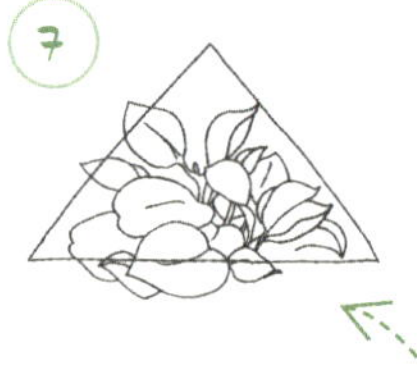

Add leaves on the right-hand side.

8

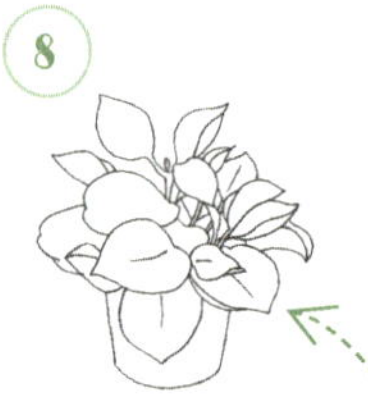

Draw the pot and lower leaves and erase the guides.

9

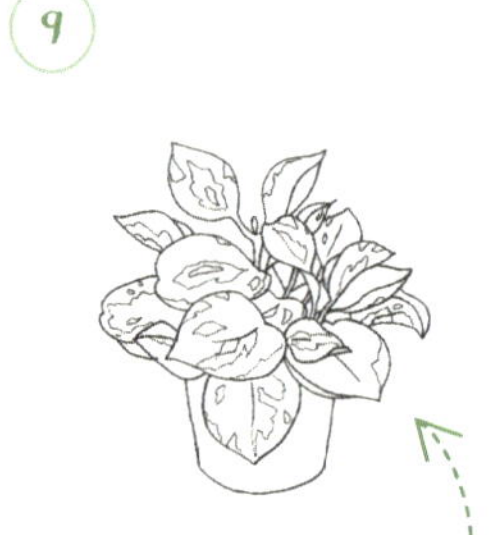

Sketch some detail for the variegated texture on the leaves.

10

Start with the dark green and blue splotches, then shade from mid to light.

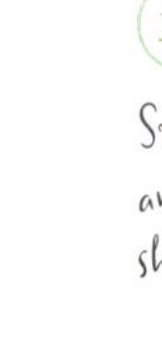

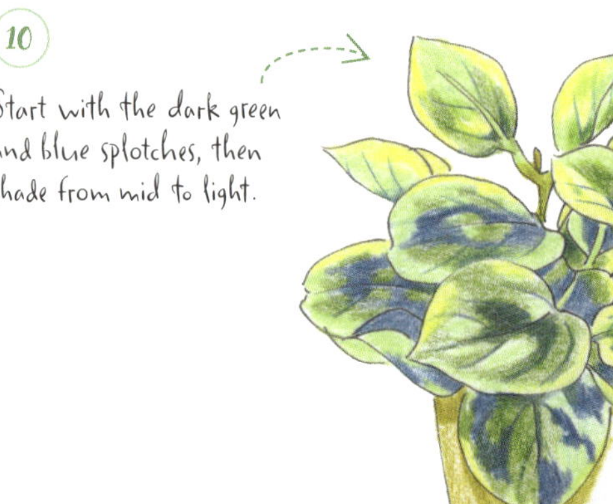

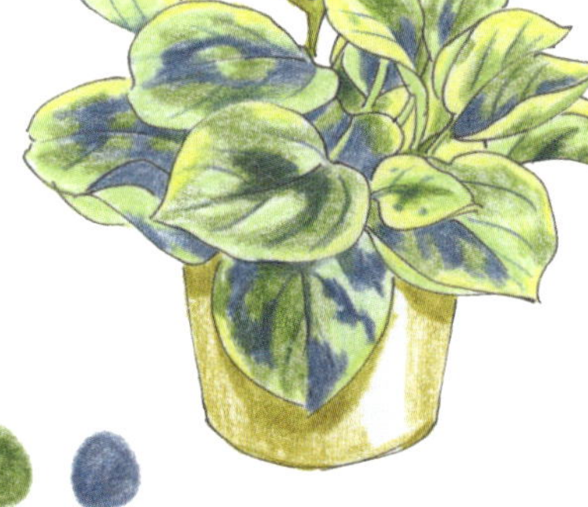

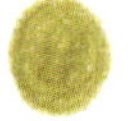

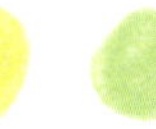

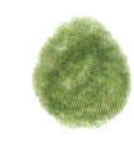

Pitcher

The pitcher plant is a type of carnivorous plant with a prey-trapping mechanism, known as a pitfall trap, within its leaves.

1 Draw two slightly curved vertical lines.

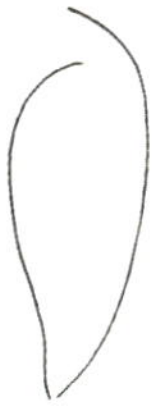

2 Add two ovals towards the top of the lines.

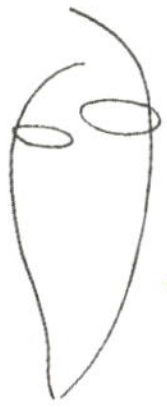

3 Draw the frilly edged mouth rims.

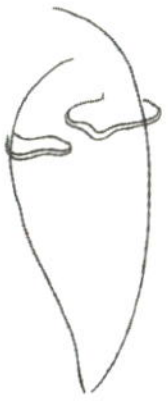

4 Draw the front of the lid on the stem.

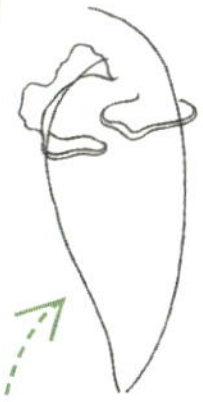

5 Complete the far side of the lid.

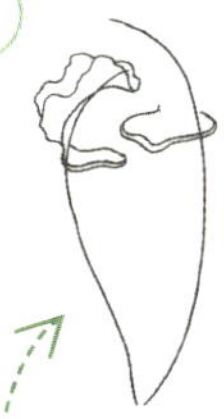

6 Draw the lid on the second stem.

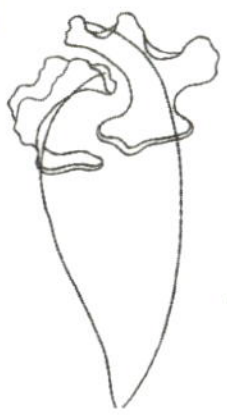

7 Add the left-hand tube.

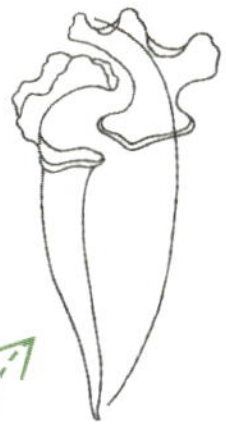

8 Add the right-hand tube and erase the guides.

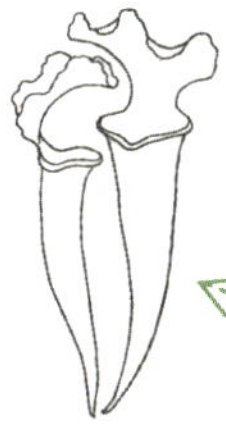

9

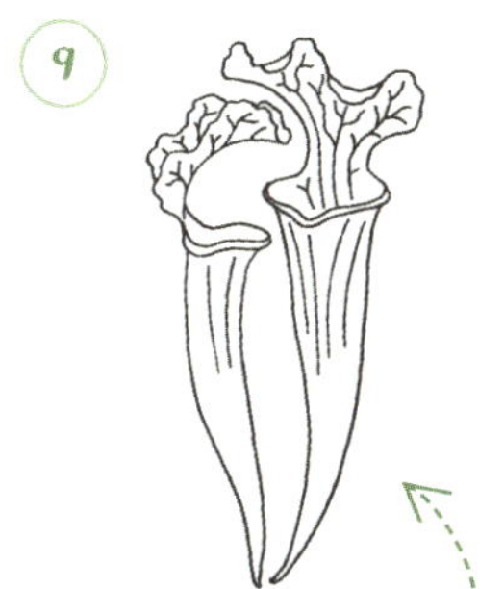

Indicate the vein patterns on the pitchers.

10 Keep the colours very simple so as not to detract from the subtle patterns created by the veins.

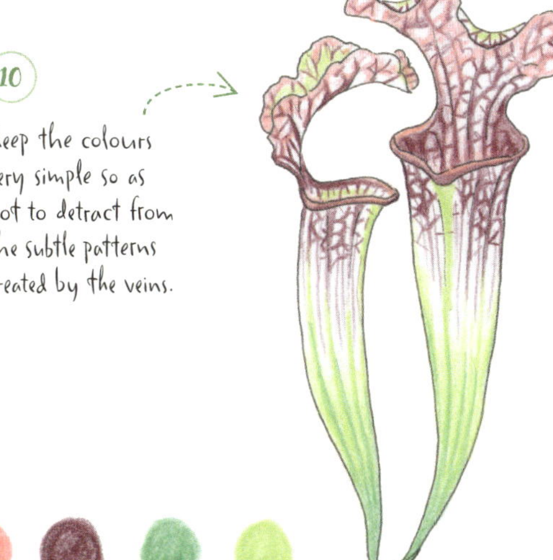

Persian Shield

The luminous purple leaves of this houseplant create quite a striking figure and provide a great example of how to blend a series of colours together.

1

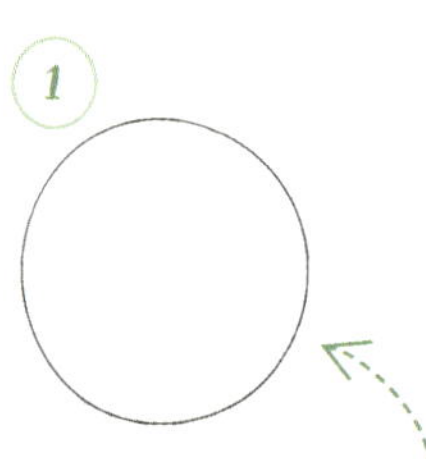

Sketch a guide circle.

2

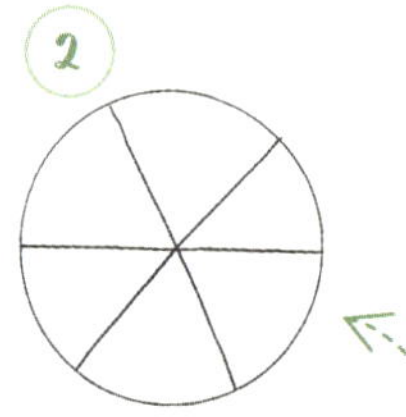

Divide the circle into sixths.

3

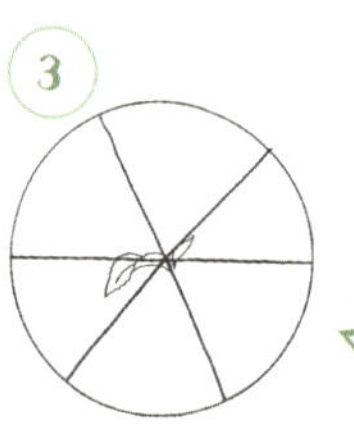

Draw two small leaves in the centre of the circle.

4

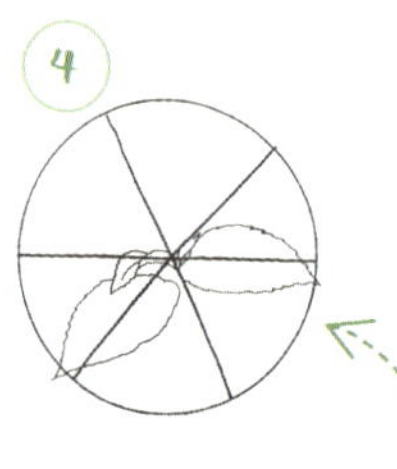

Add larger pointed leaves.

5

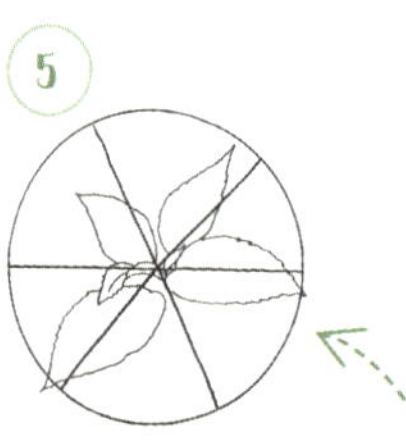

Add slightly smaller pointed leaves.

6

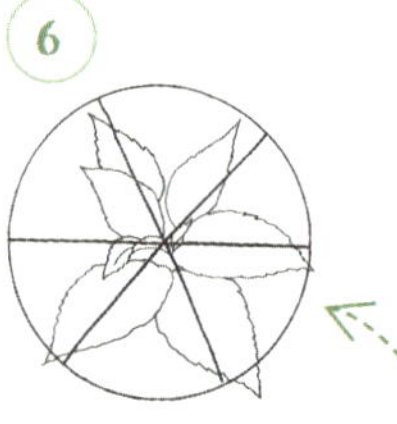

Add two more leaves.

7

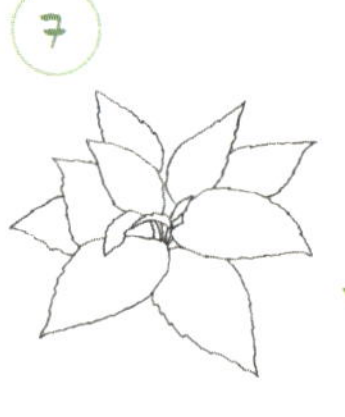

Add in the remaining leaves to fill the circle and erase the guide lines.

8

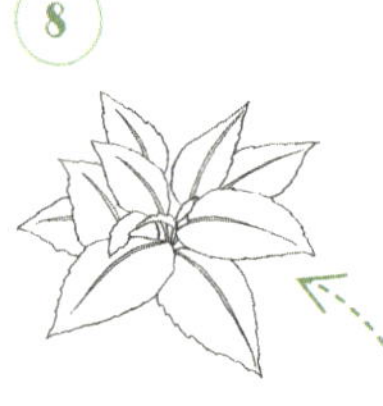

Draw the mid rib on each leaf.

9

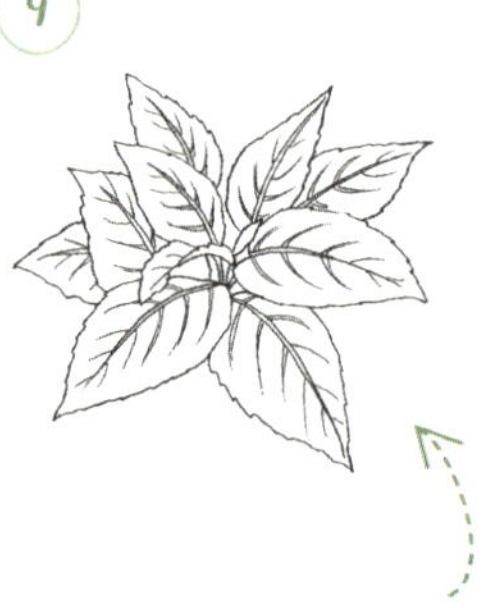

Add the veins to the leaves.

Keep all the veins and ribs a uniform pale green but vary the shading on the leaves. Give some purple centres fading to green, and others a white centre fading to pink, then green.

10

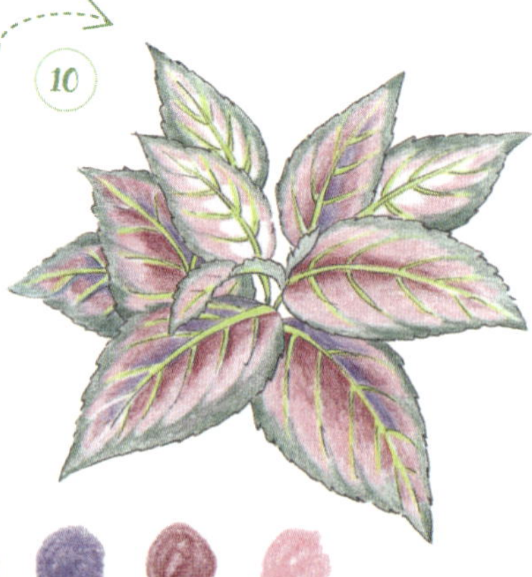

Spear Thistle

This robust thistle grows wild in the Scottish Highlands and is topped with a vibrant purple flower.

1

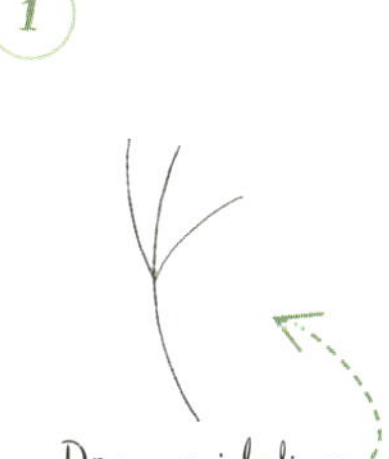

Draw guide lines.

2

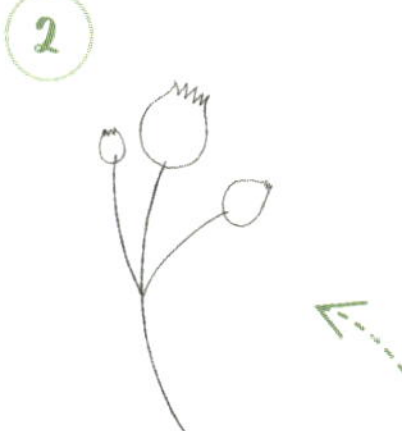

Draw the base of three flowers at the ends of the lines.

3

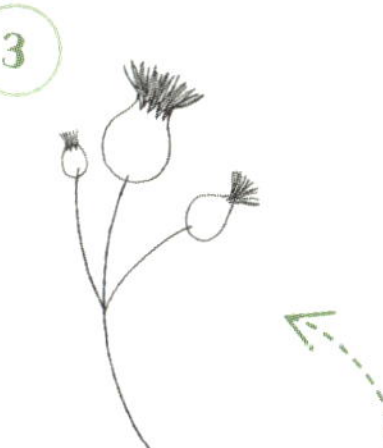

Add petals to the top of the flowers.

4

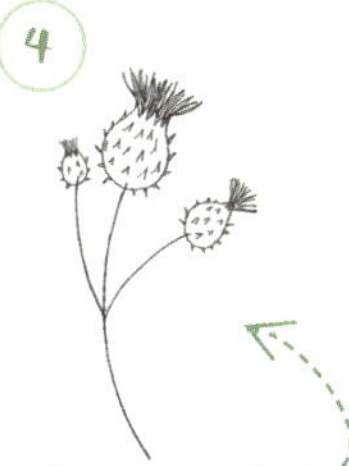

Add spiny details to the base of the flowers.

5

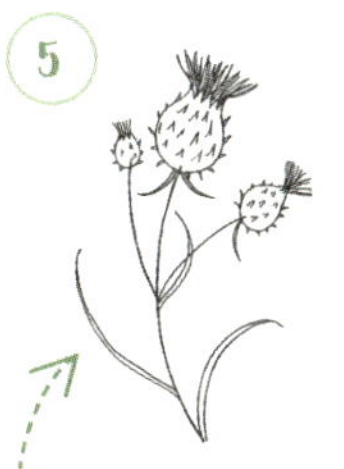

Add the leaf ribs lower down the stem.

6

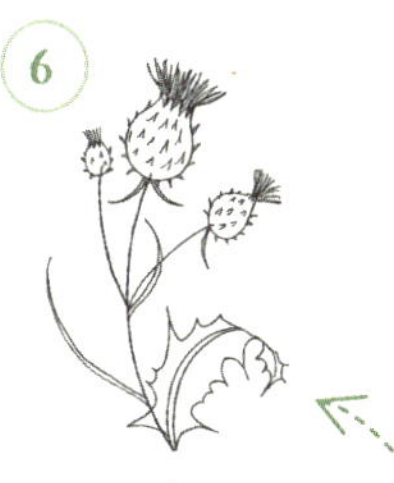

Draw the lower right-hand leaf with jagged edges.

7

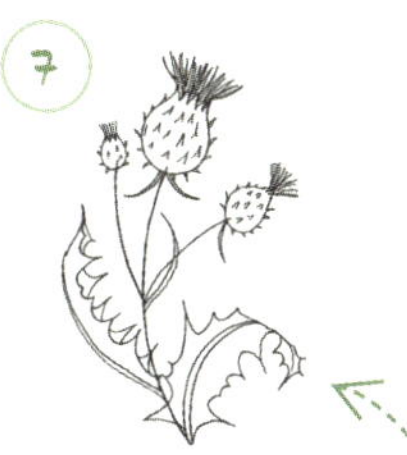

Draw the left-hand, side-view leaf.

8

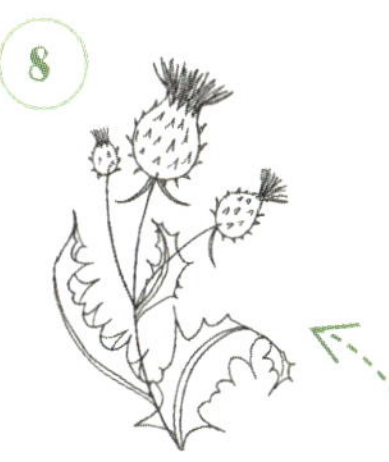

Add a small leaf in the middle.

9

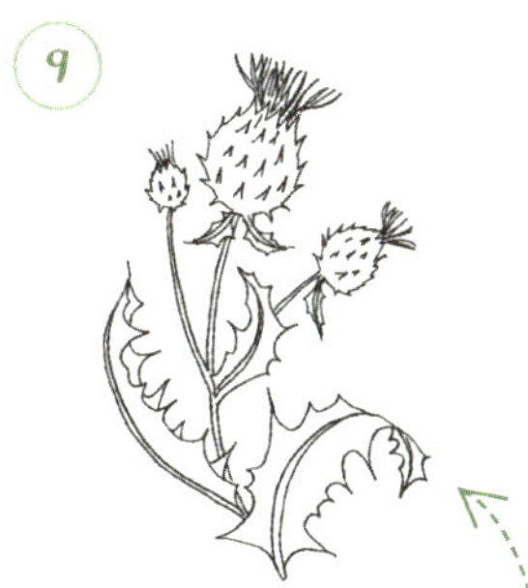

Add the stem and tiny leaflets under the flower heads.

10

Use contrasting greens to give texture to the leaves and flower heads.

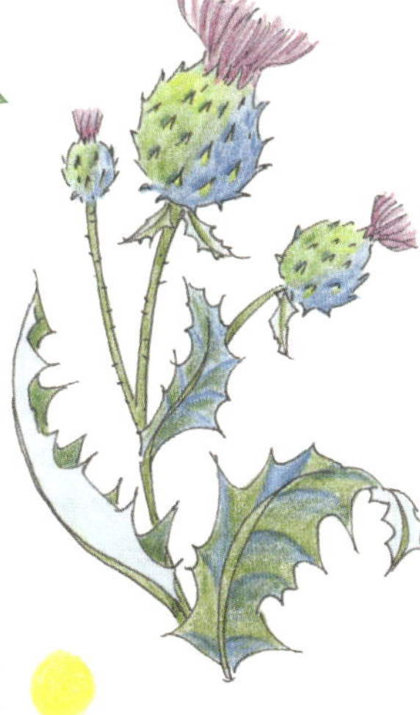

Bromeliad Guzmania

This exotic looking plant with long drooping leaves and spiky flowers makes a change from drawing more rounded shapes.

1

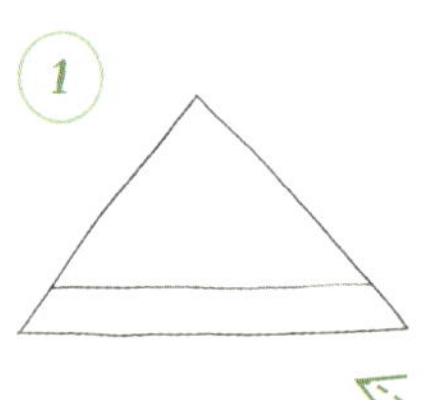

Draw a wide-bottomed triangle with two parallel horizontals.

2

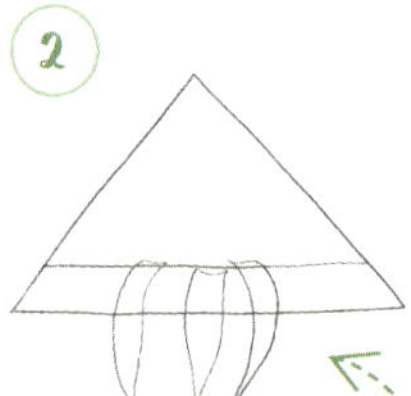

Draw three central forward-folded leaves from the top line.

3

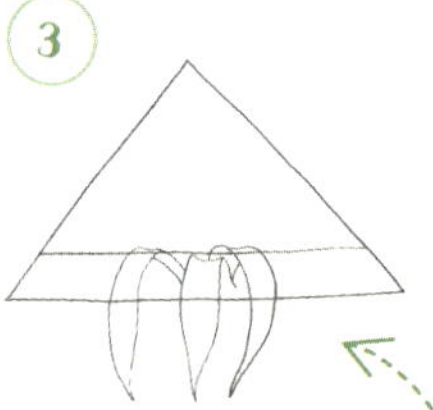

Add the undersides of the leaves.

4

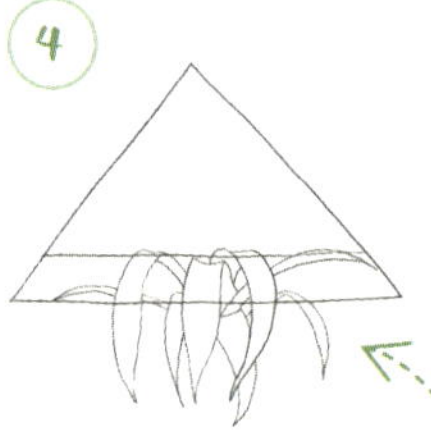

Draw leaves stemming from the lower line.

5

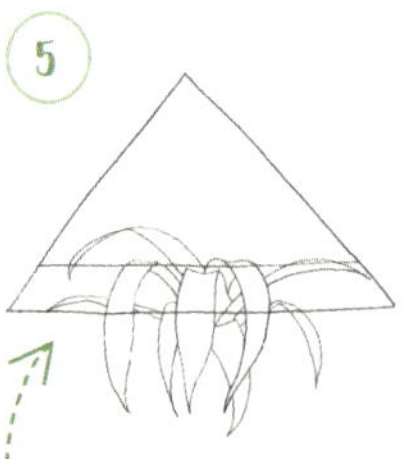

Add an arching left-hand leaf at the top.

6

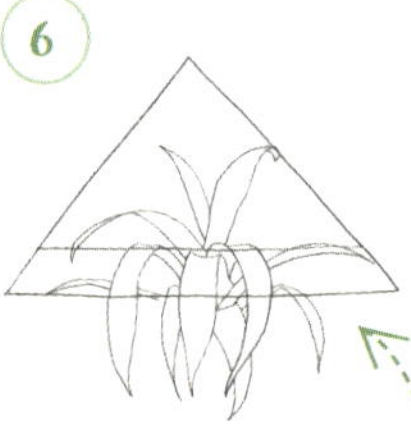

Add a pair of upright leaves.

7

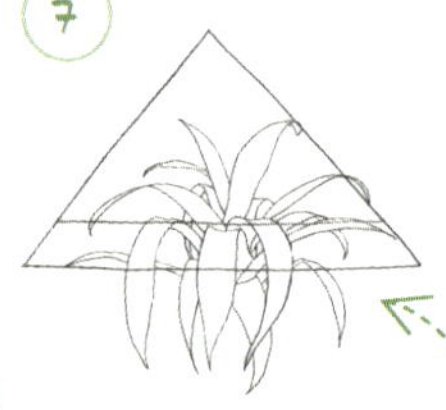

Add the right-hand side leaves in the background.

8

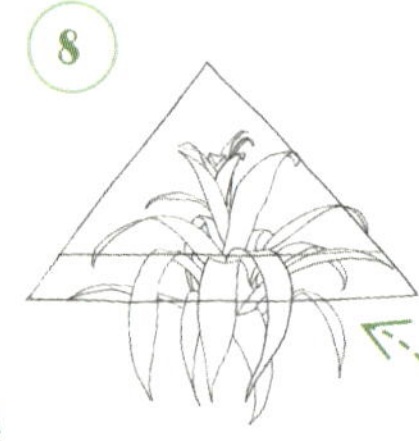

Draw the lower half of the flower sprouting from the centre of the leaves.

9

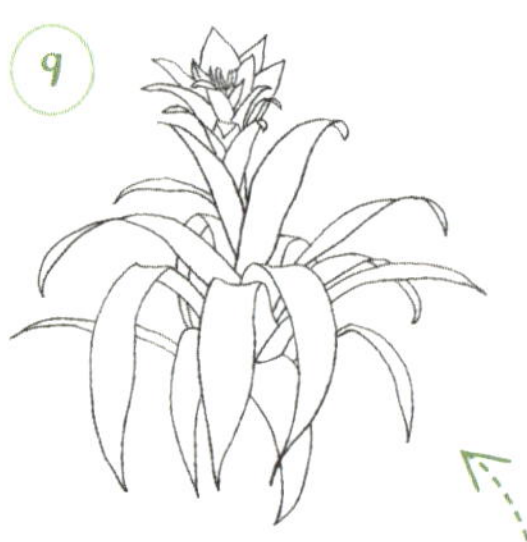

Add the rest of the flower by adding overlapping spiky petals.

Use long vertical pencil strokes to create striations on the leaves and leave a white highlight on the curve of each leaf.

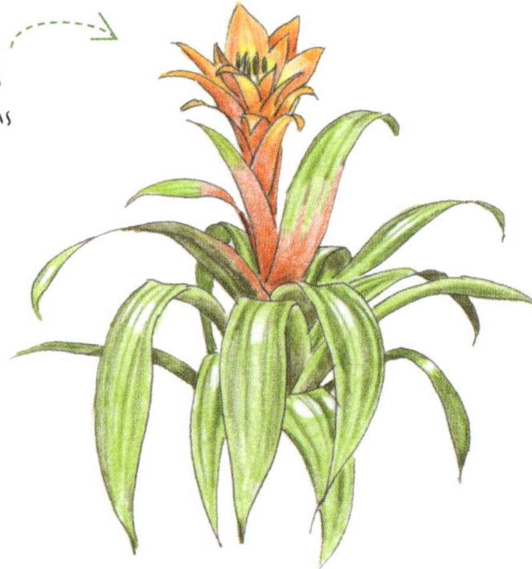

  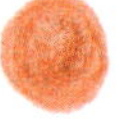 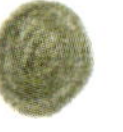 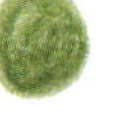 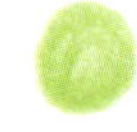

Anthurium

The large waxy flowers of this popular houseplant have a very unusual texture, which makes for an interesting plant to draw.

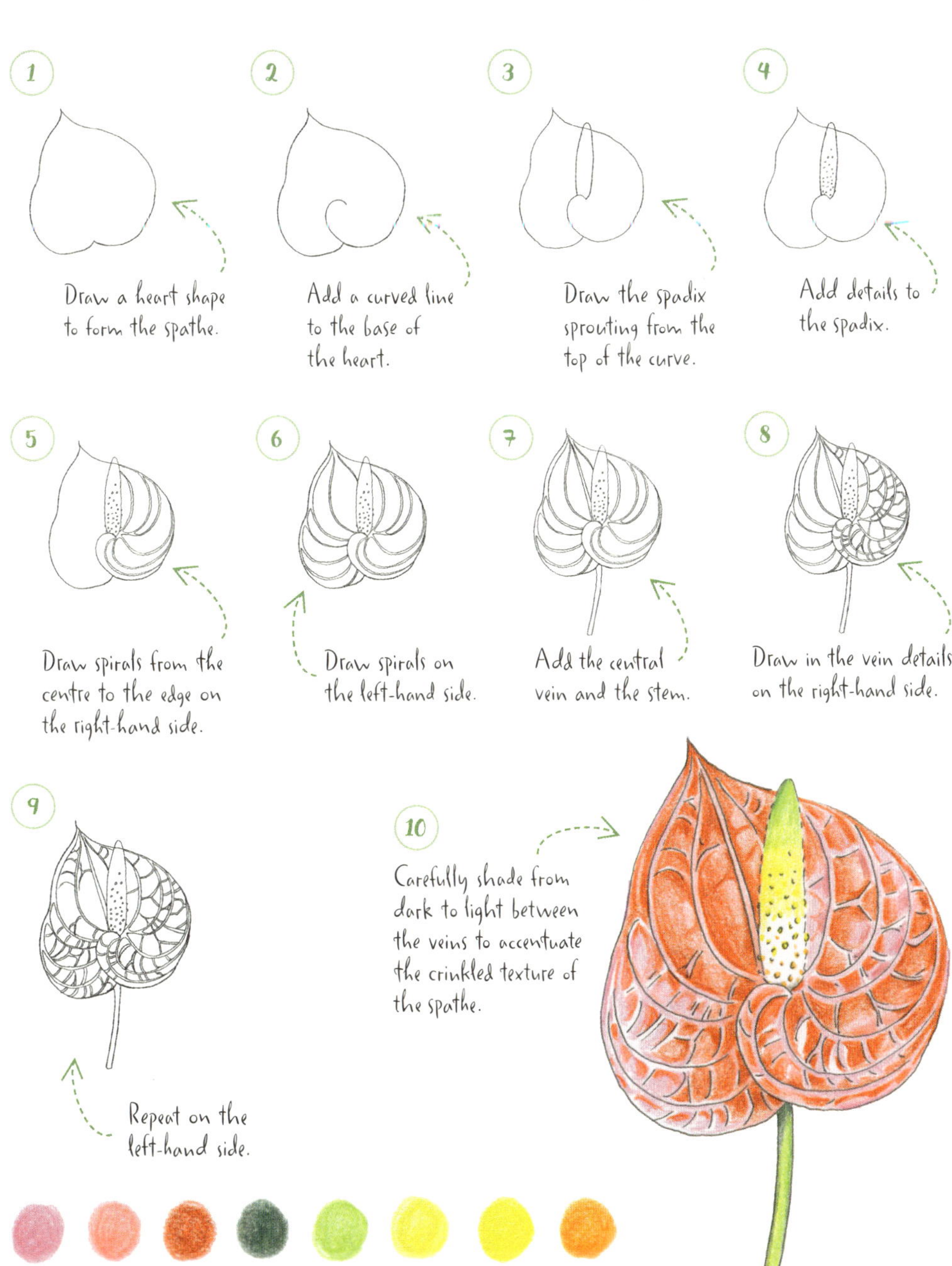

Blackberry

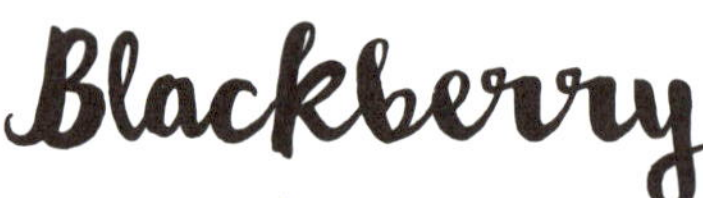

This juicy berry is packed with detail, as it is made up of multiple tiny berries in a rich blueish purple.

1

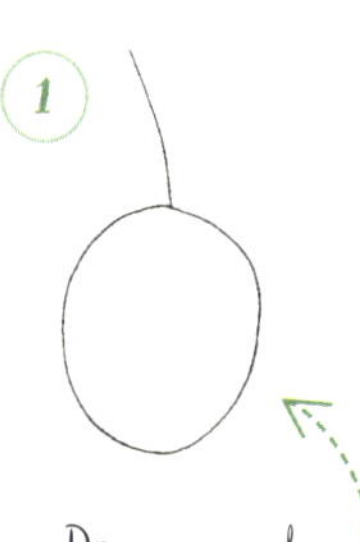

Draw an oval guide hanging off a vertical stick.

2

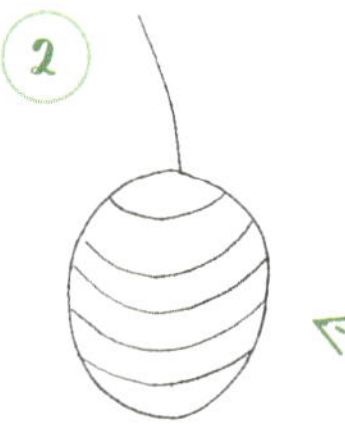

Divide the oval with horizontal bands.

3

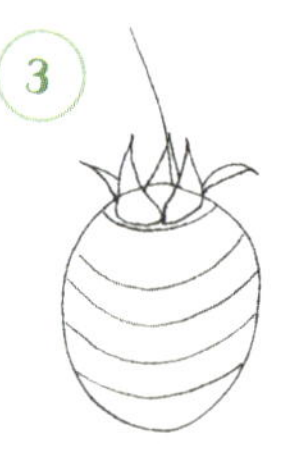

Draw five sepals around the top of the oval.

4

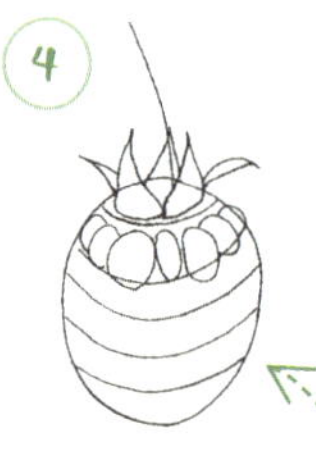

Fill in the top band with droplets of uneven sizes.

5

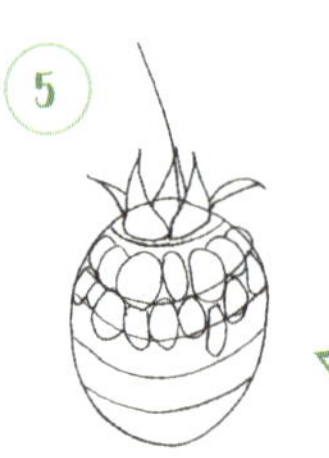

Fill in the next band.

6

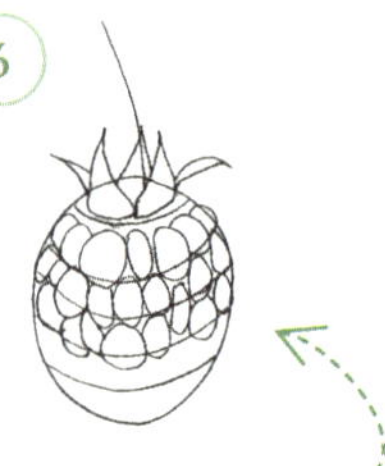

Repeat for the third band.

7

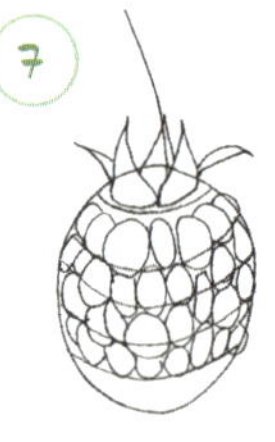

And for the fourth band.

8

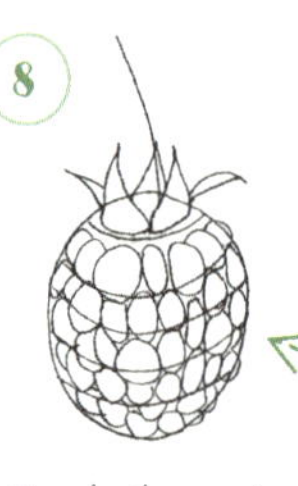

Finish the droplets in the final band.

9

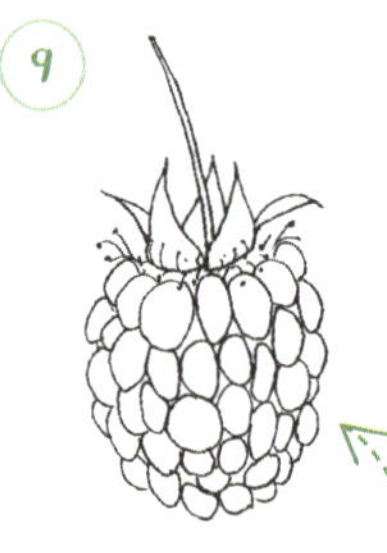

Add the stalk and erase the guide shape.

10

Leave a white highlight on each droplet and shade one side of the blackberry darker than the other to give it volume.

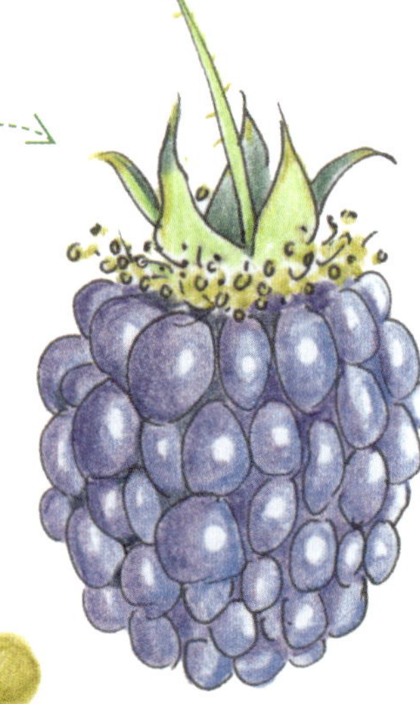

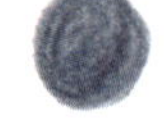 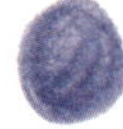 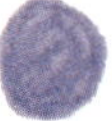   

Christmas Cactus

This festive cactus has a particularly striking appearance and is good for practising a more dramatic style of drawing.

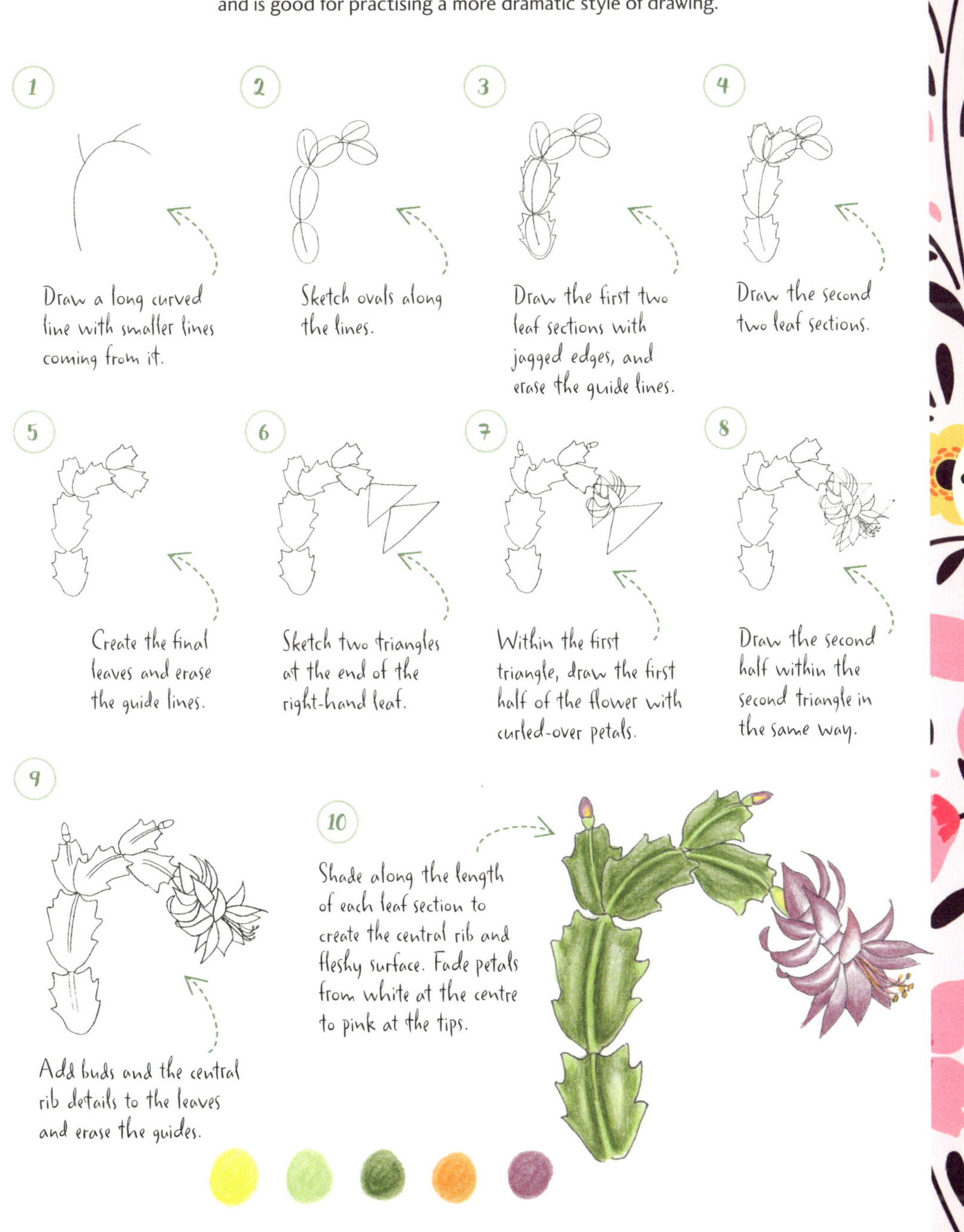

1. Draw a long curved line with smaller lines coming from it.
2. Sketch ovals along the lines.
3. Draw the first two leaf sections with jagged edges, and erase the guide lines.
4. Draw the second two leaf sections.
5. Create the final leaves and erase the guide lines.
6. Sketch two triangles at the end of the right-hand leaf.
7. Within the first triangle, draw the first half of the flower with curled-over petals.
8. Draw the second half within the second triangle in the same way.
9. Add buds and the central rib details to the leaves and erase the guides.
10. Shade along the length of each leaf section to create the central rib and fleshy surface. Fade petals from white at the centre to pink at the tips.

Globe Thistle

This thriving but prickly plant has rough, spiny leaves and the thistle heads are a distinctive blue.

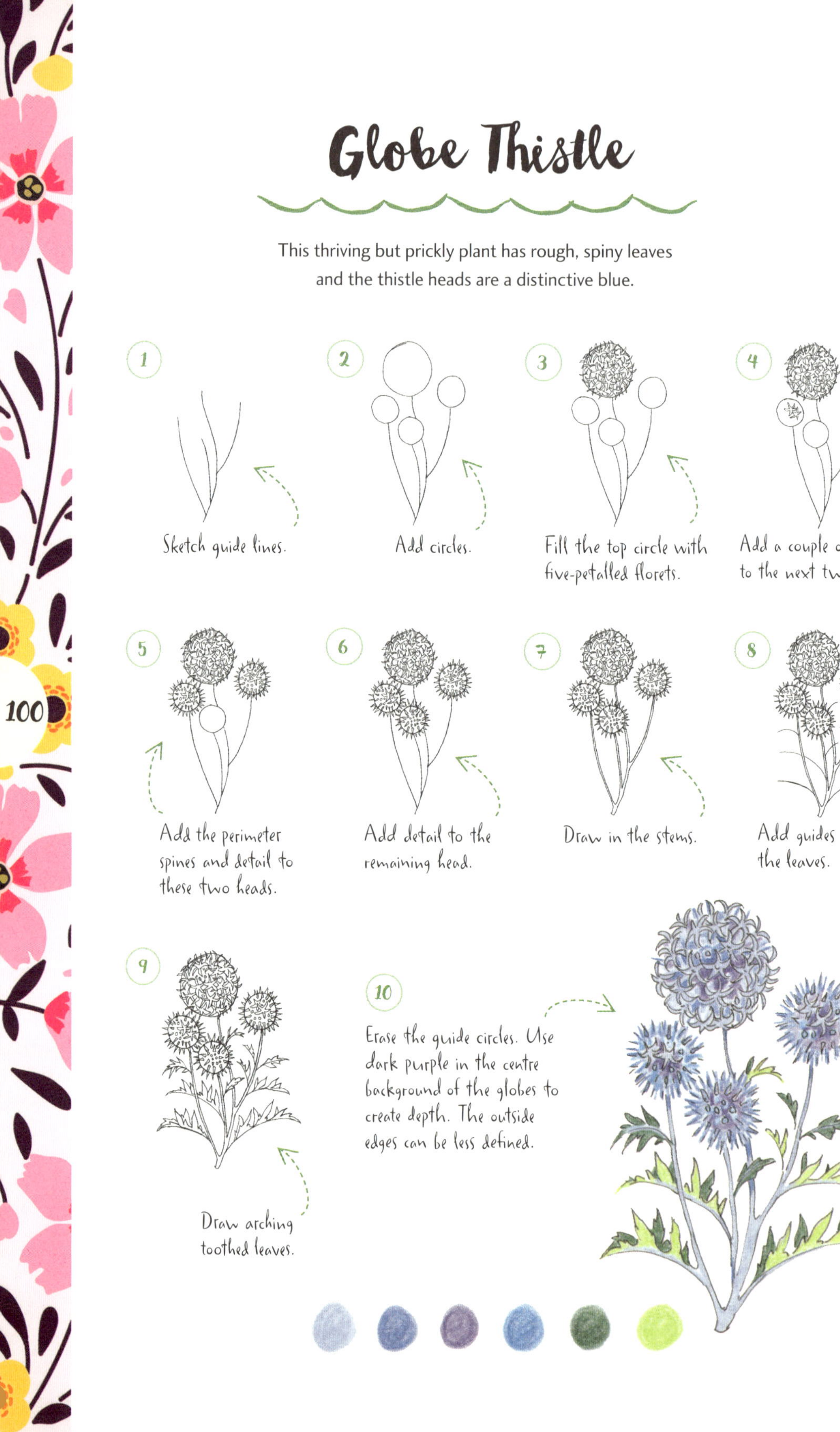

Sloe Berries

Sloes, or blackthorn, are popular berries to be foraged and made into sloe gin. The dark purple berries are indicative of the approaching winter months.

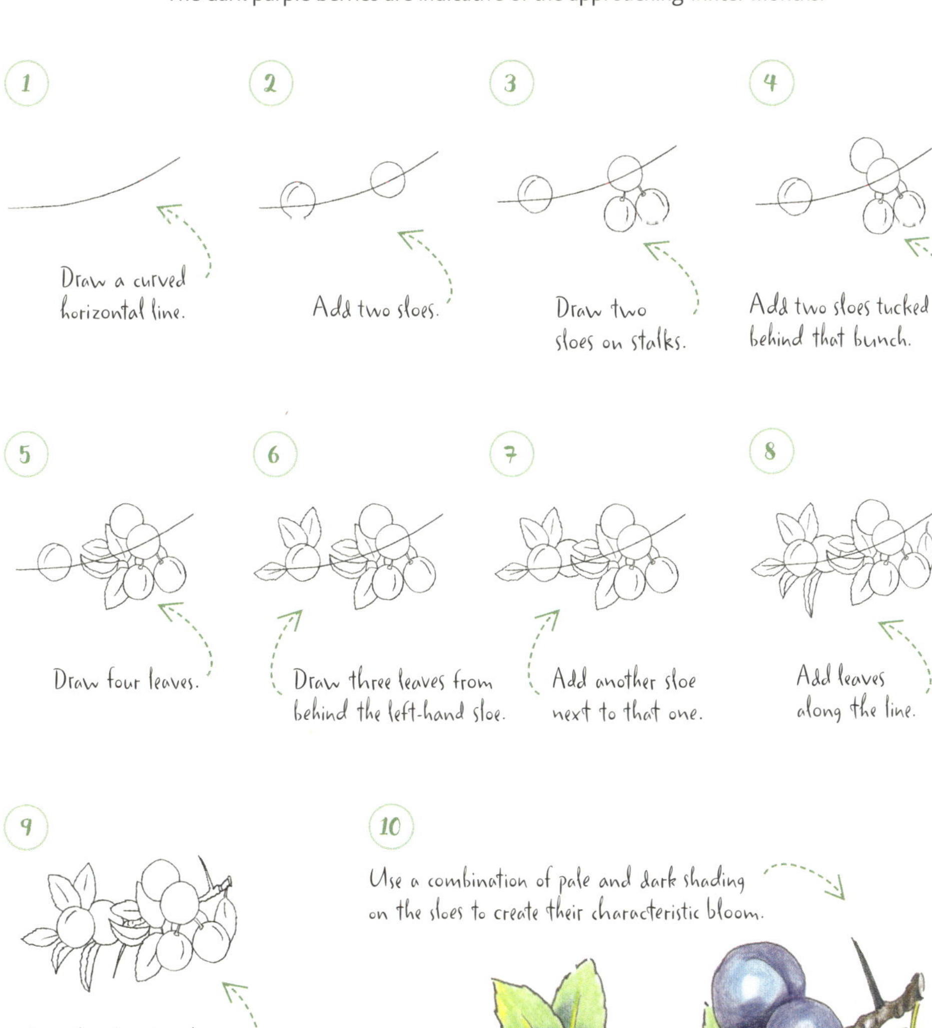

10

Use a combination of pale and dark shading on the sloes to create their characteristic bloom.

Redcurrant

The juicy berries on this plant should be shaded with a white highlight so as to indicate the high shine on the berries.

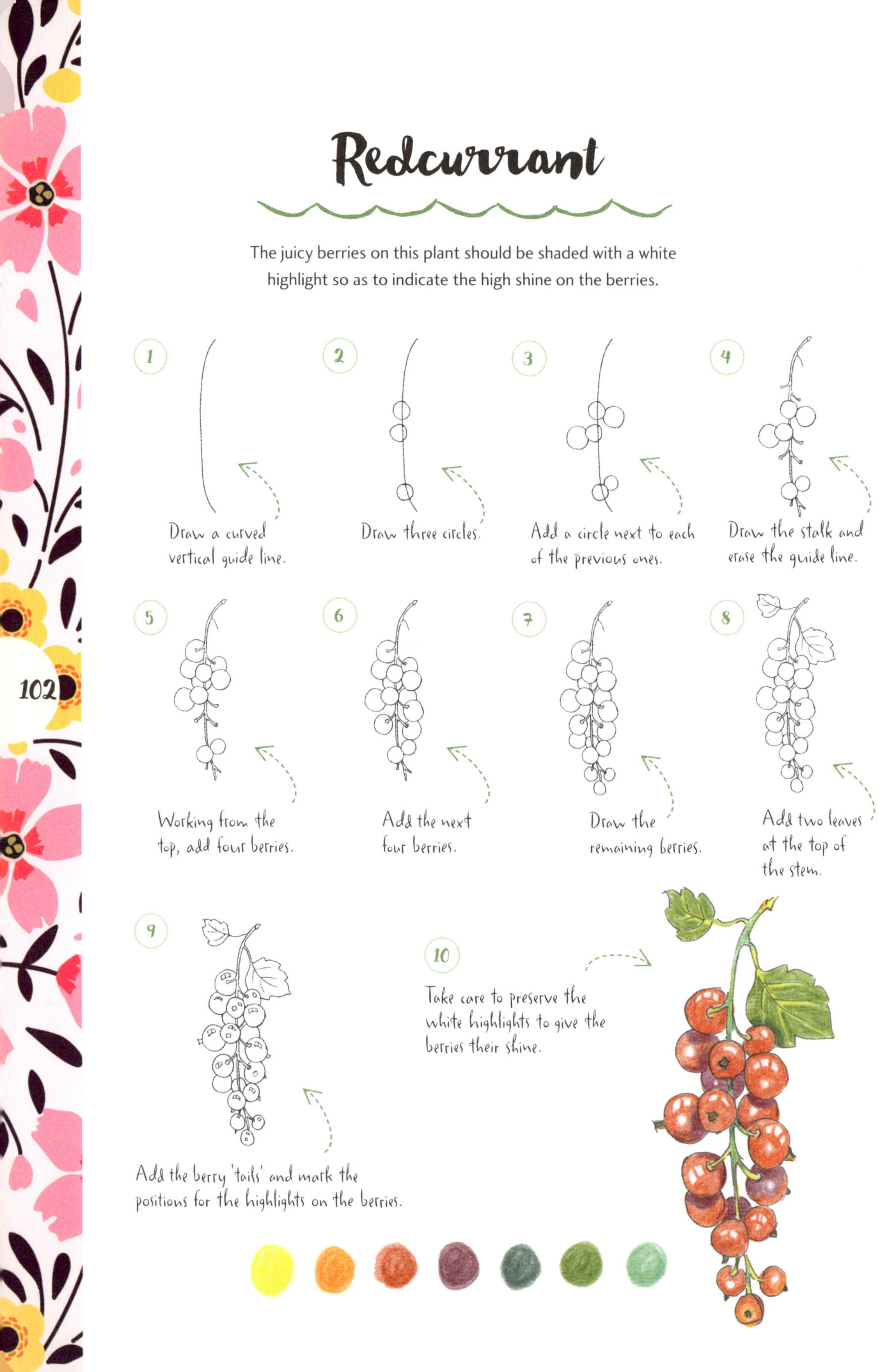

Burro's Tail

This succulent is very compact but has wonderful detail in its small, spiky leaves.

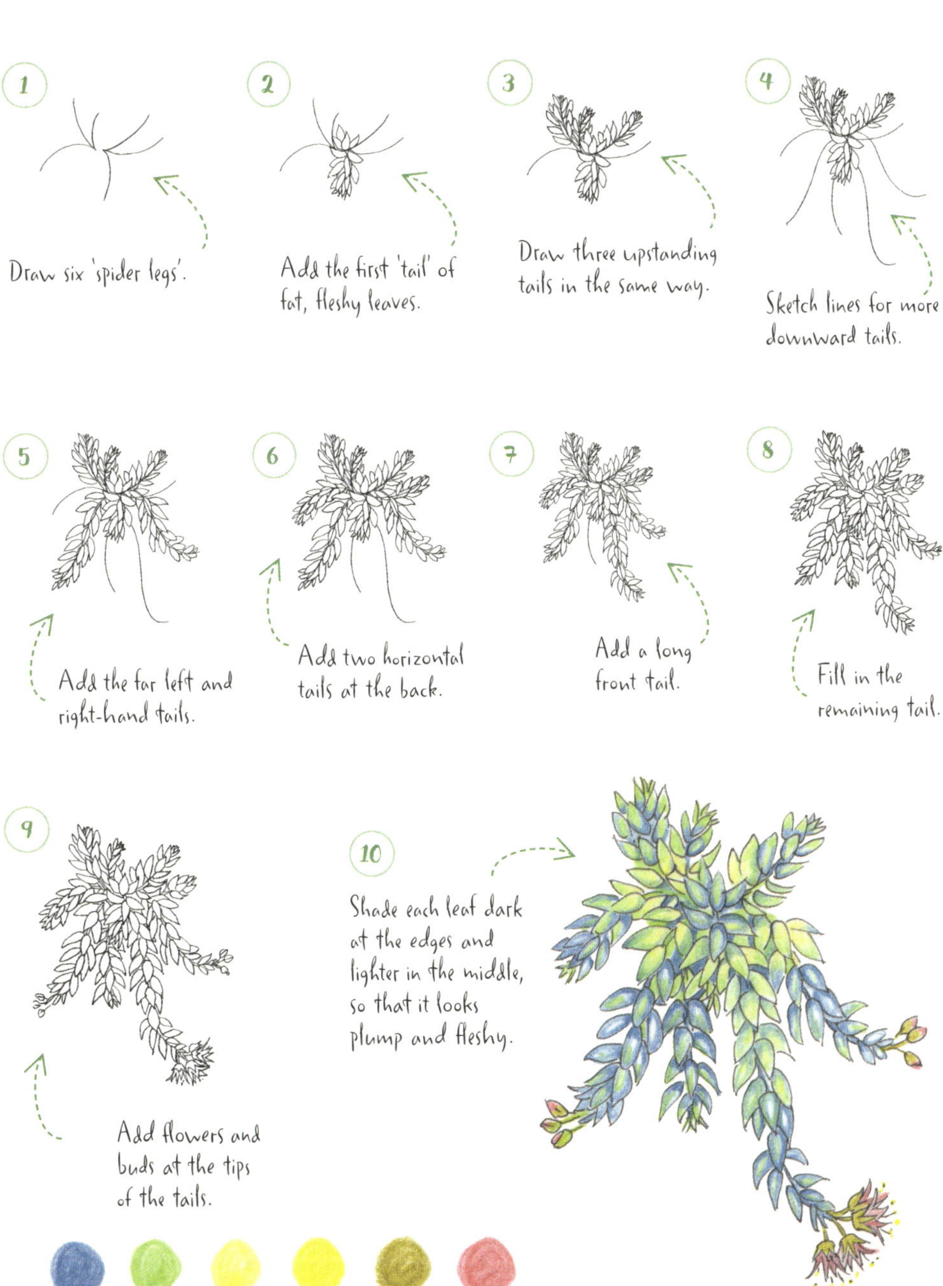

Hen & Chicks

The lovely greens and reds on the succulent leaves make this a striking plant.

1

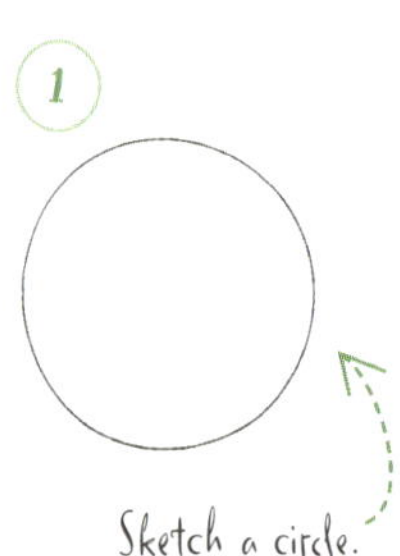

Sketch a circle.

2

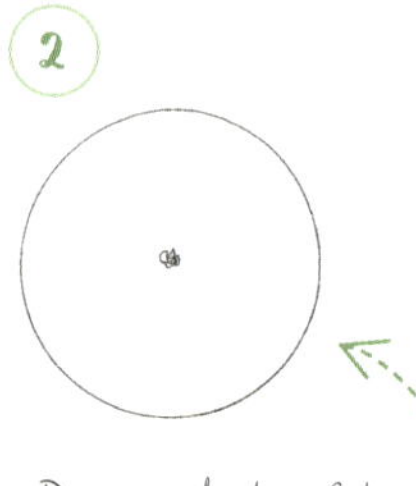

Draw a cluster of tiny triangles in the middle.

3

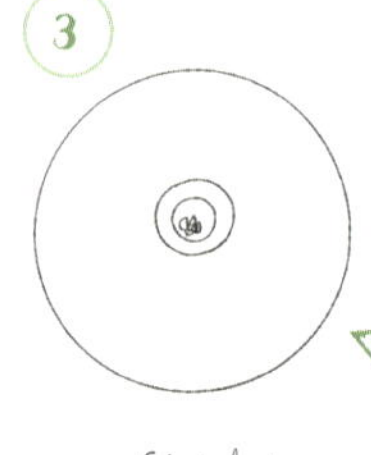

Sketch two pale off-centre circles around the triangles.

4

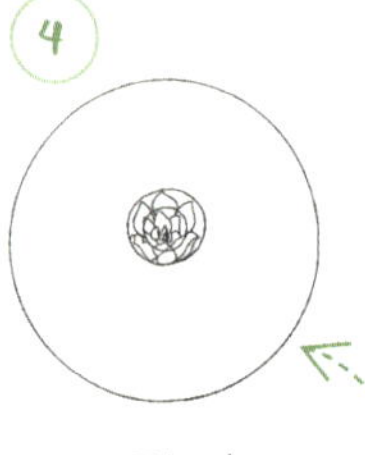

Fill the two circles with pointed leaves.

5

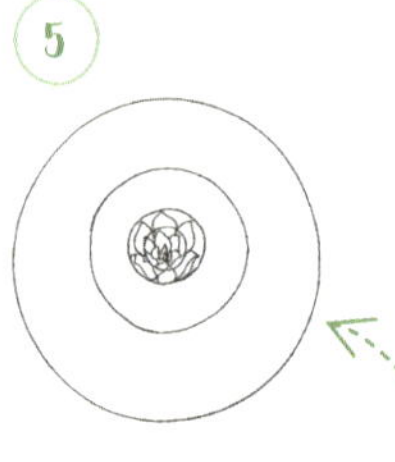

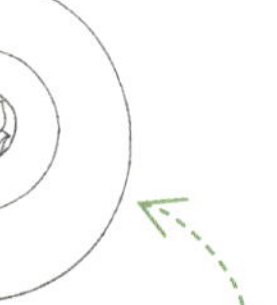

Draw another circle.

6

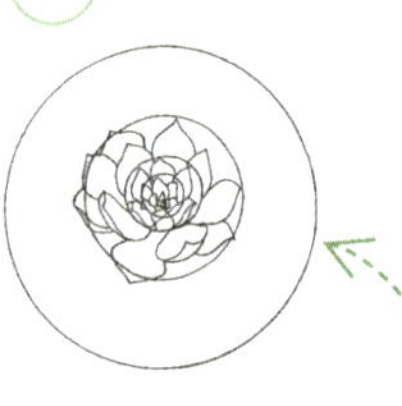

Add more leaves, leaving one or two gaps.

7

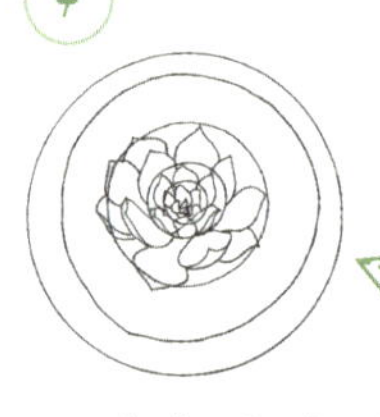

Add a final circle inside the existing two.

8

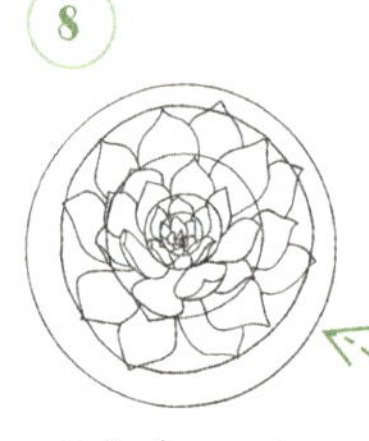

Fill this circle with more pointed leaves.

9

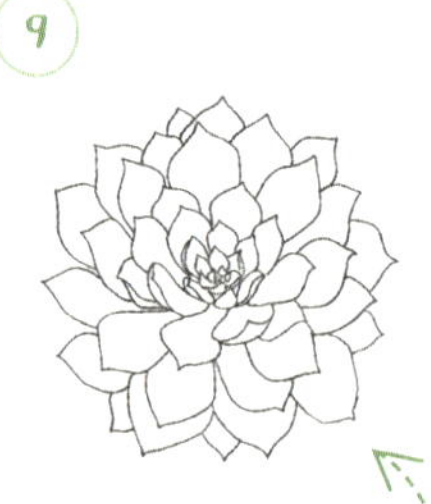

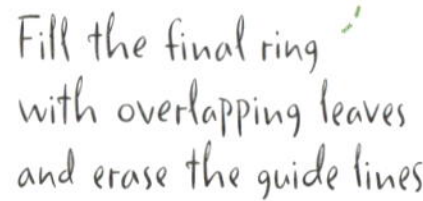

Fill the final ring with overlapping leaves and erase the guide lines.

10

Variegate the leaves with contrasting red and pale green. Keep the colours separate to retain their freshness – if you layer one over the other they will produce a muddy colour.

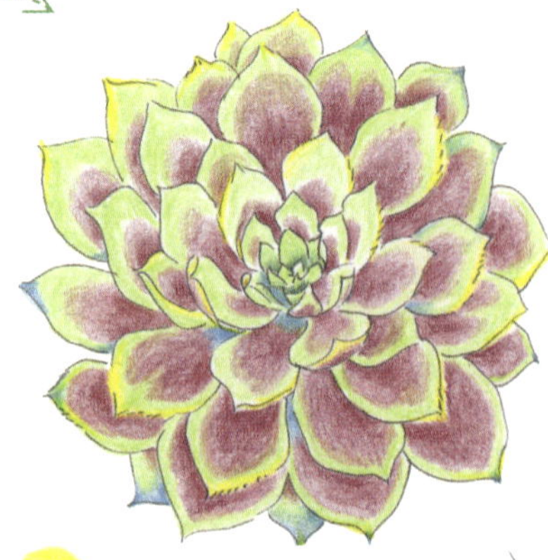

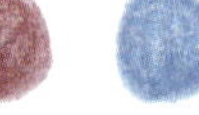

Holly

The prickly leaves and trademark red berries of this festive plant offer wonderful contrast in colours and textures.

1

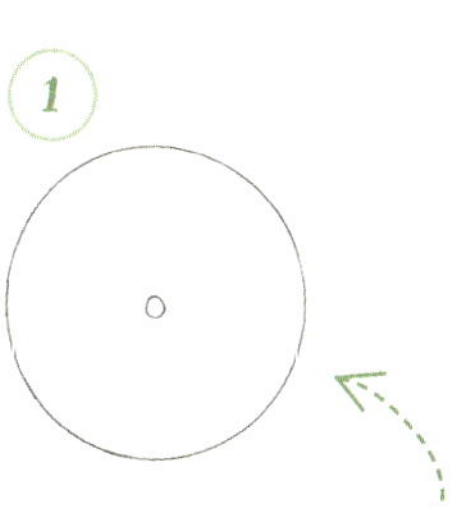

Sketch a circle and draw a single berry in the middle.

2

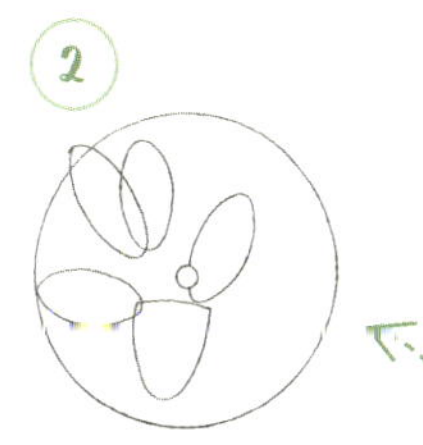

Draw oval outlines at different angles around the central berry.

3

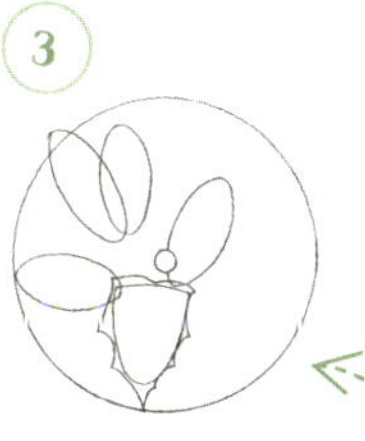

Draw a forward-facing jagged edge around the leaf to make it prickly.

4

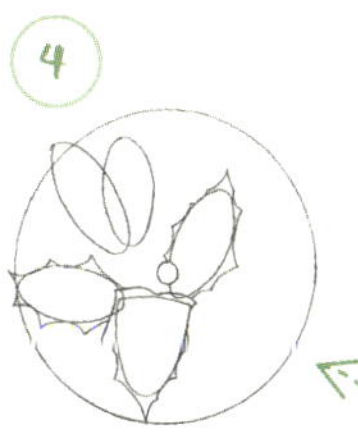

Draw two more prickly leaves adjoining the first.

5

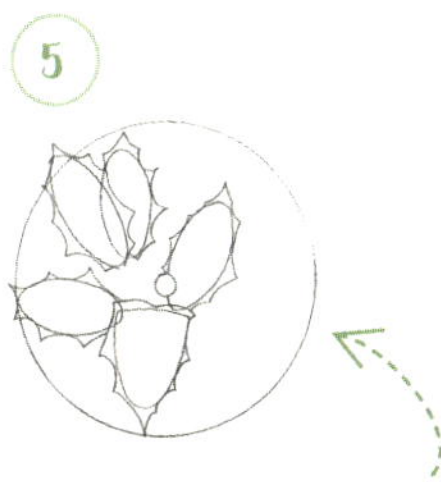

Add two leaves at the back.

6

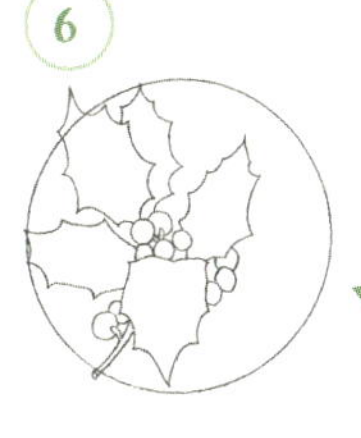

Add more berries and draw in the stem. Erase the leaf outlines.

7

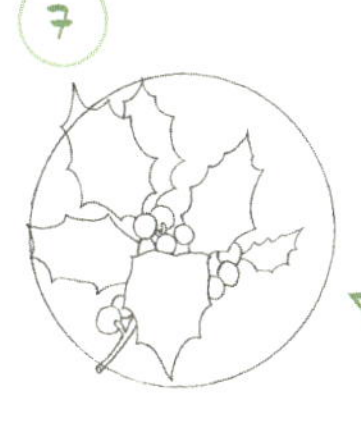

Add a small right-hand leaf.

8

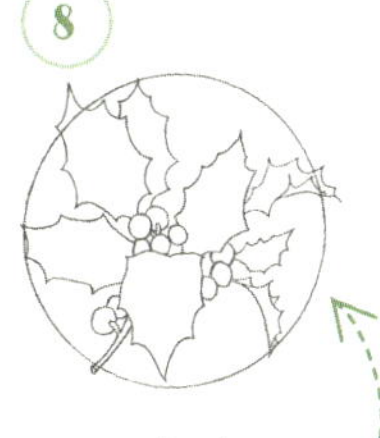

Add some side-facing leaves.

9

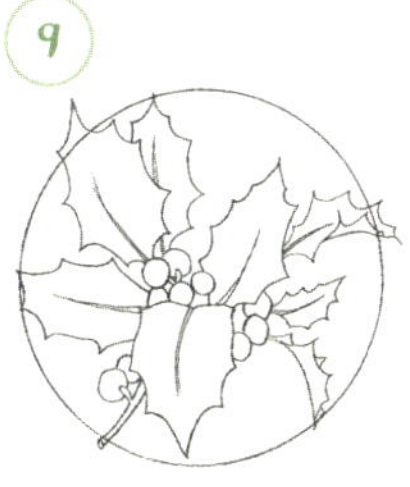

Draw the curved ribs on the leaves.

10

Erase the circle outline. Use blocks of different greens on the leaves to create their typical shine, and leave a white highlight in the same position on each berry.

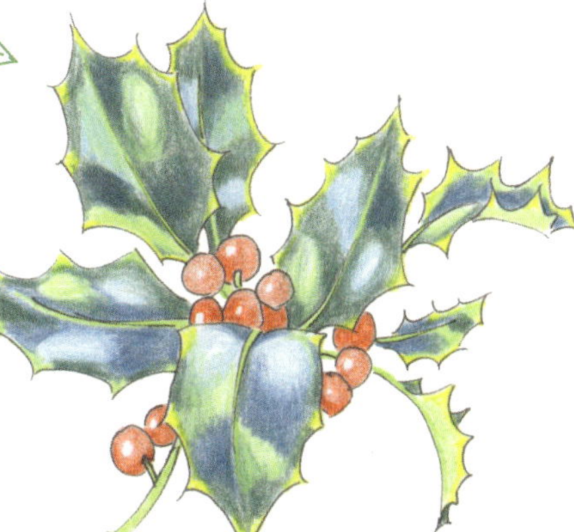

  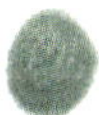 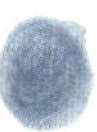  

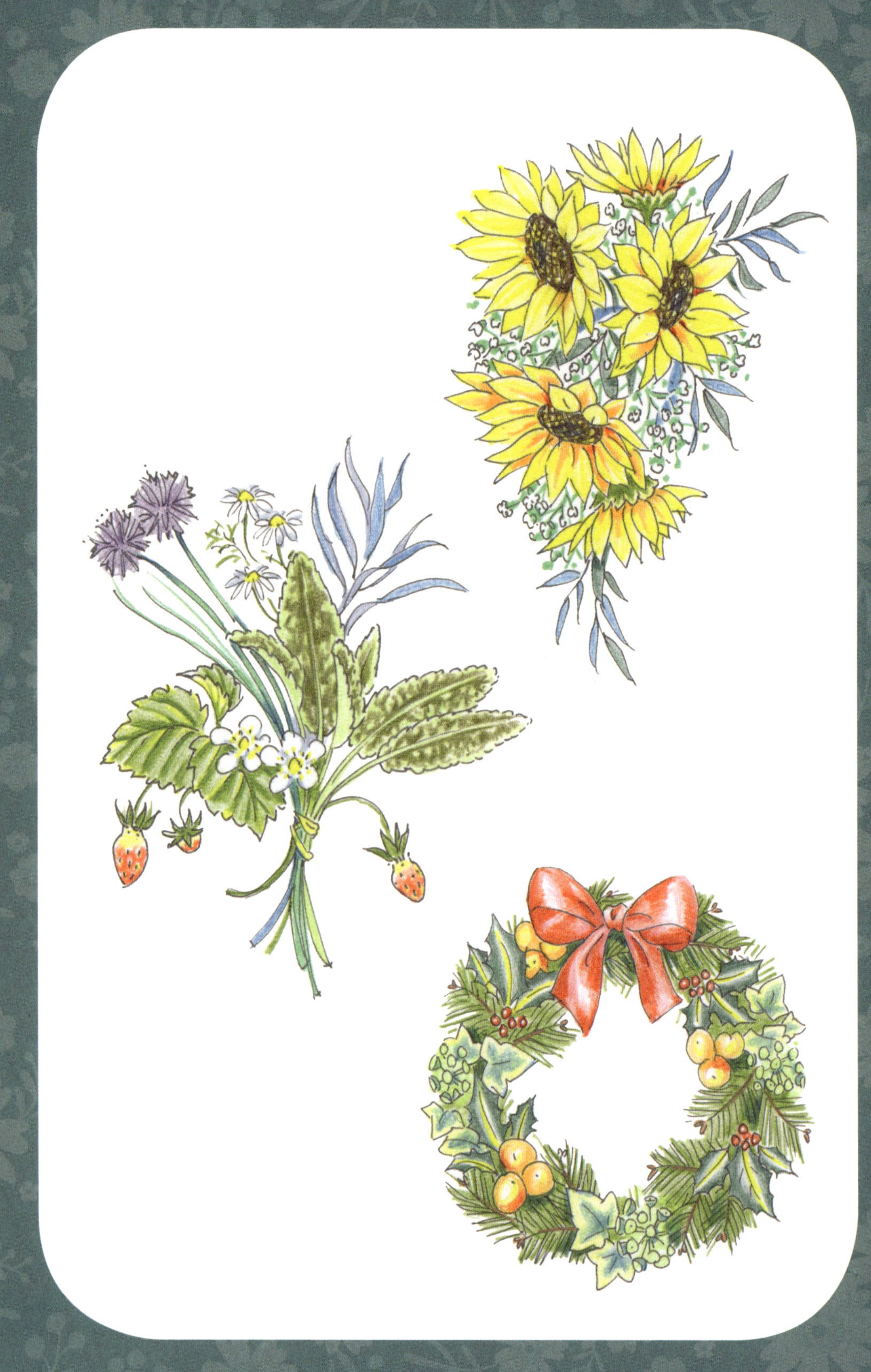

Displays

Festive Wreath

There is nothing better to signify the start of the holidays than placing a wonderfully festive wreath full of holly, fir, ivy and crab apples on your door.

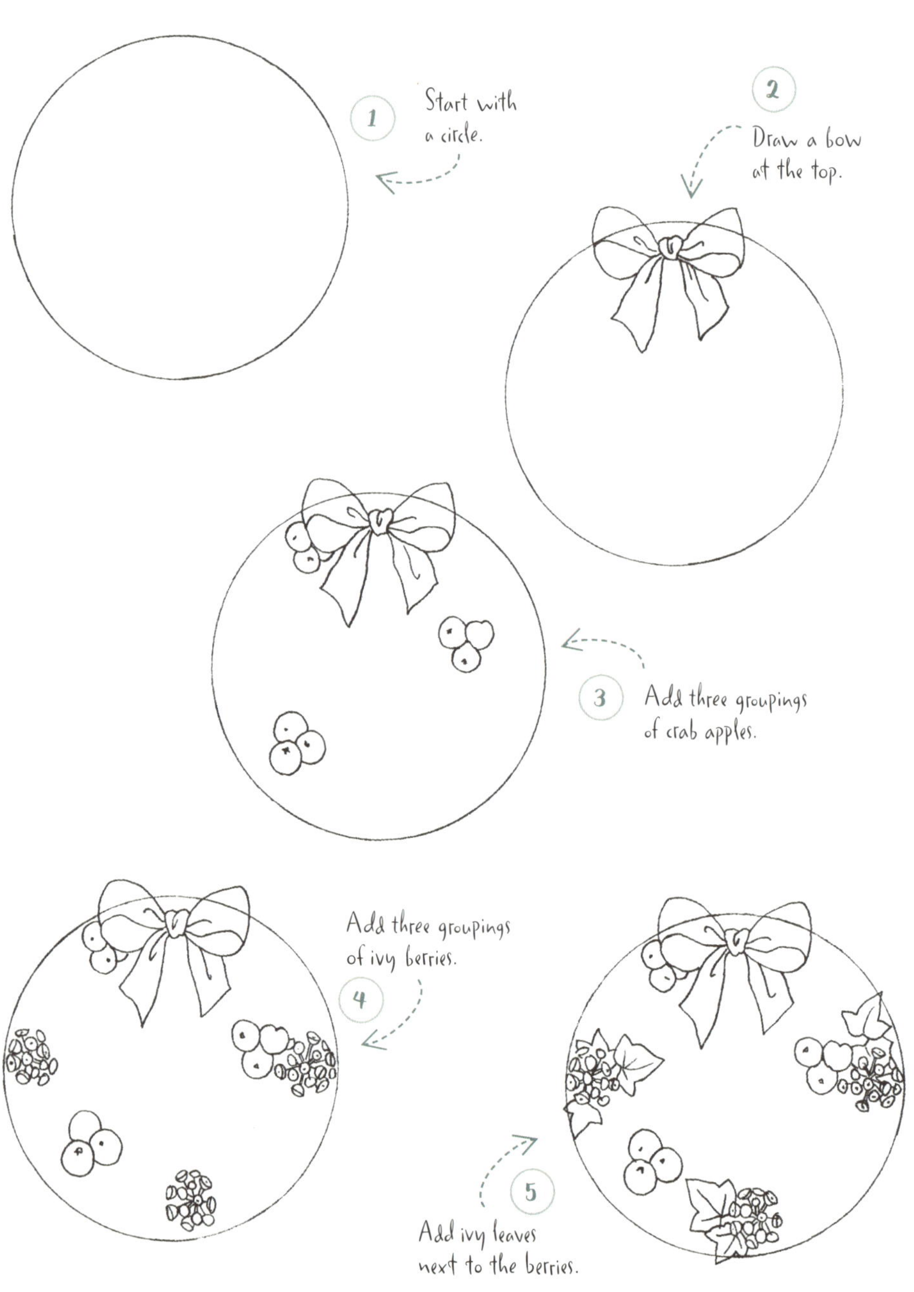

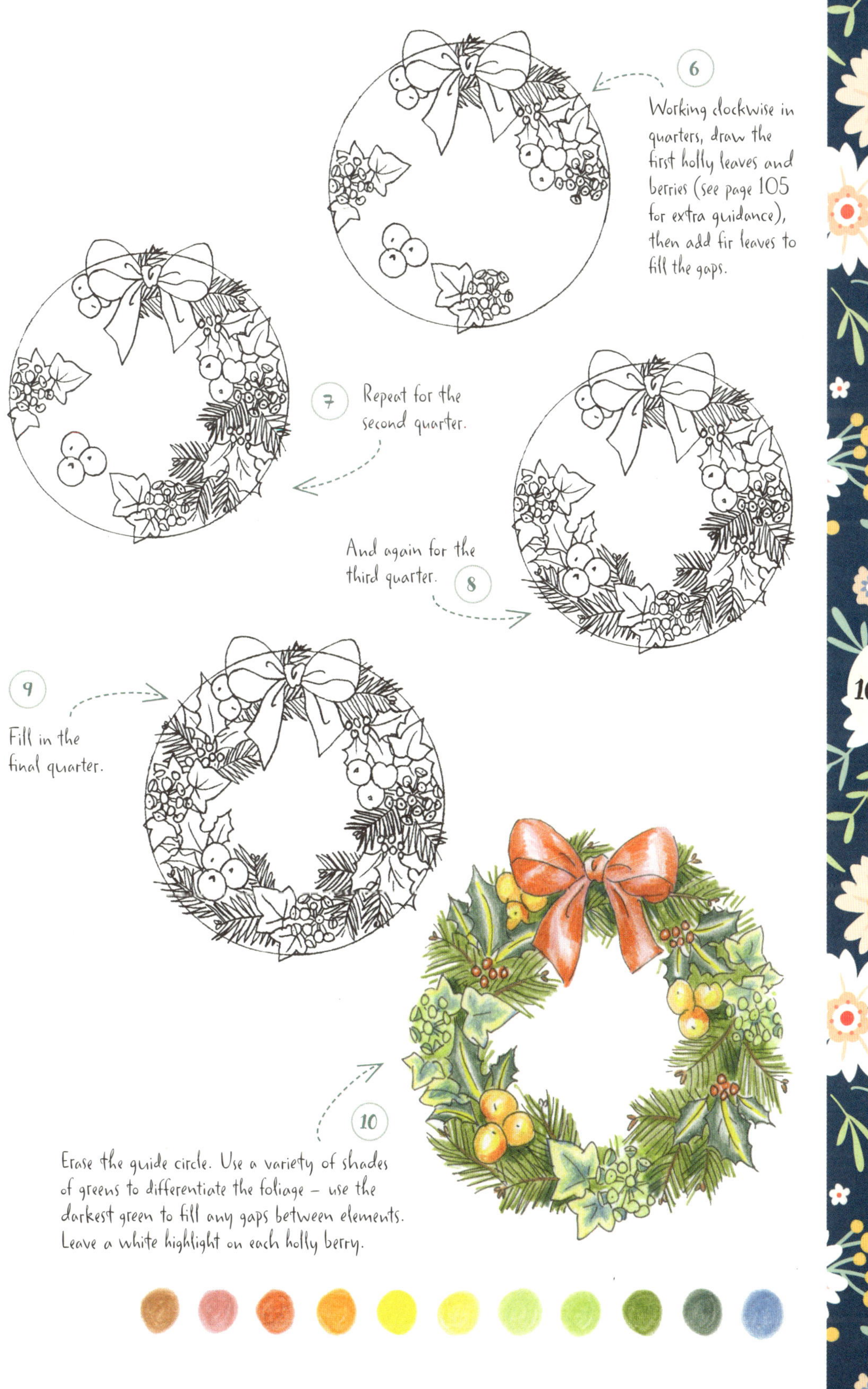
6
Working clockwise in quarters, draw the first holly leaves and berries (see page 105 for extra guidance), then add fir leaves to fill the gaps.
7
Repeat for the second quarter.
And again for the third quarter.
8
9
Fill in the final quarter.
10
Erase the guide circle. Use a variety of shades of greens to differentiate the foliage – use the darkest green to fill any gaps between elements. Leave a white highlight on each holly berry.
109

Herb & Fruit Bouquet

This simple, very natural looking bouquet of wild strawberry, sage, tarragon, chamomile and chives looks like it's been foraged straight out of the garden.

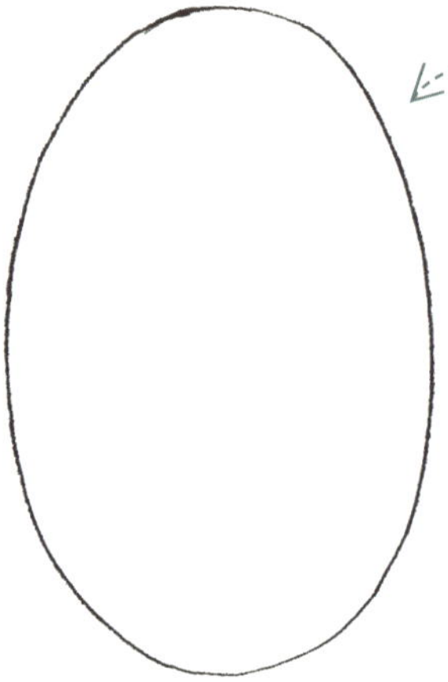

1 Draw an egg-shaped outline.

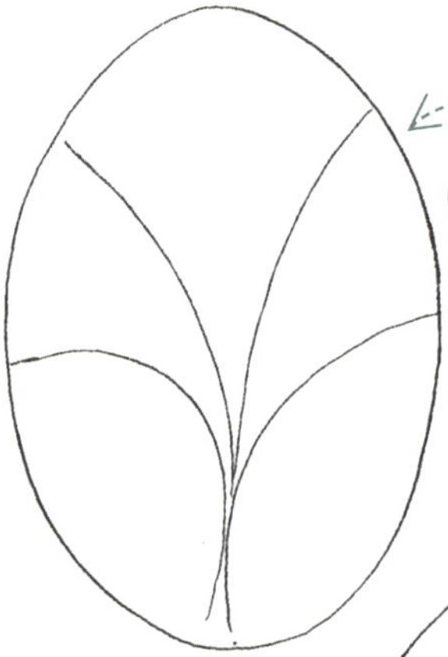

2 Draw four flowing guide lines starting from the base of the egg shape.

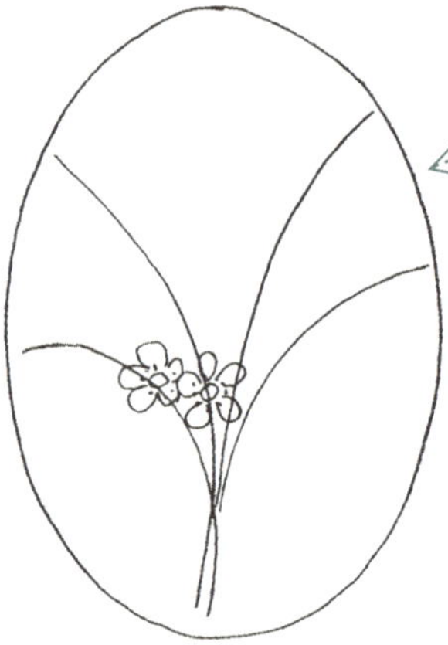

3 Add two strawberry flowers where the lines meet.

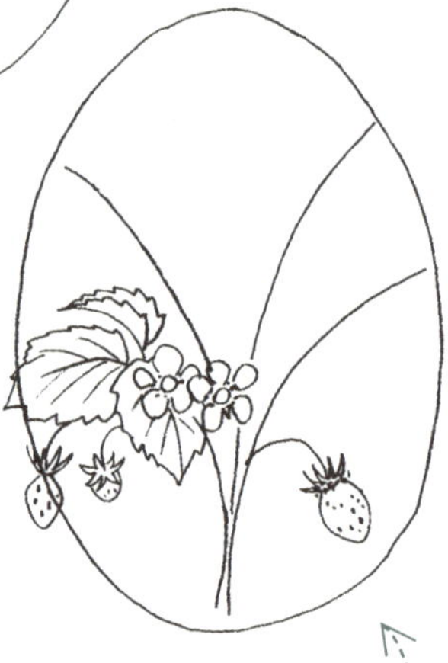

4 Add the strawberries and leaves at the base of the bouquet.

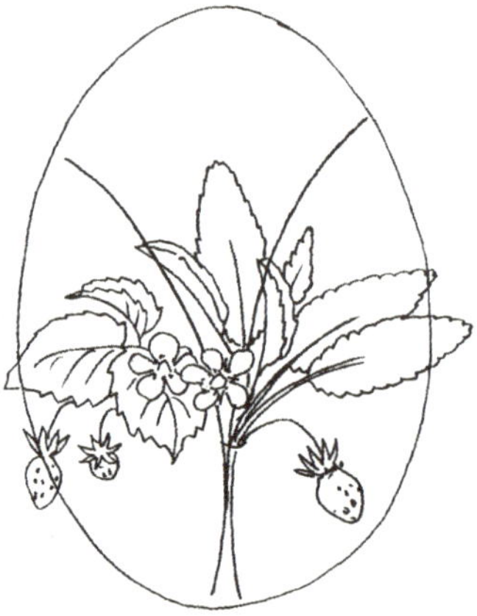

5 Draw some sage leaves above the strawberries and to the right of the bouquet.

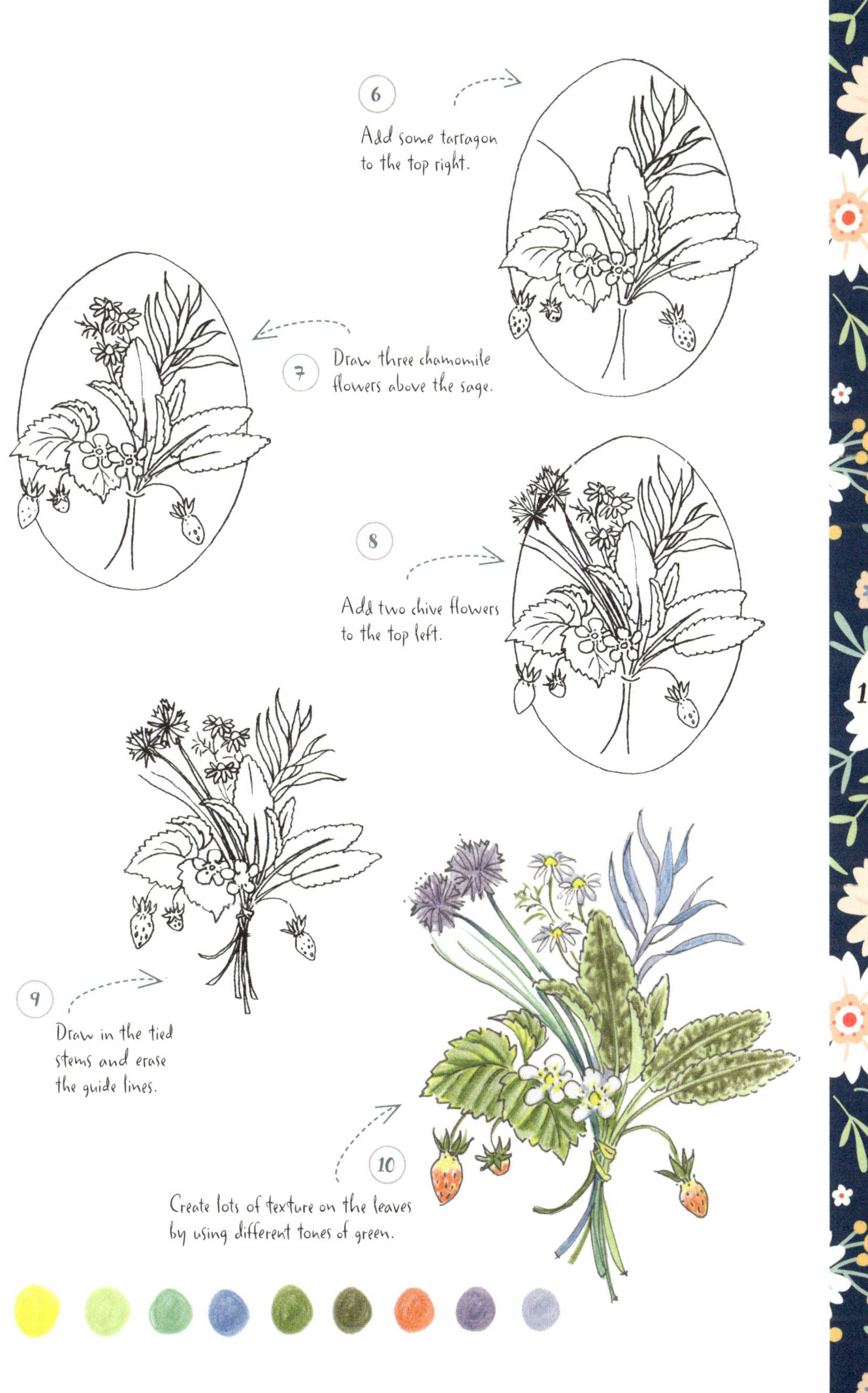
6
Add some tarragon
to the top right.
7
Draw three chamomile
flowers above the sage.
8
Add two chive flowers
to the top left.
9
Draw in the tied
stems and erase
the guide lines.
10
Create lots of texture on the leaves
by using different tones of green.

Sunflower Bouquet

This tall, summery bouquet is full of bright sunflowers and filled out with gypsophila and leafy foliage. Be sure to vary the intensity of yellow on the sunflowers so that they don't look exactly the same.

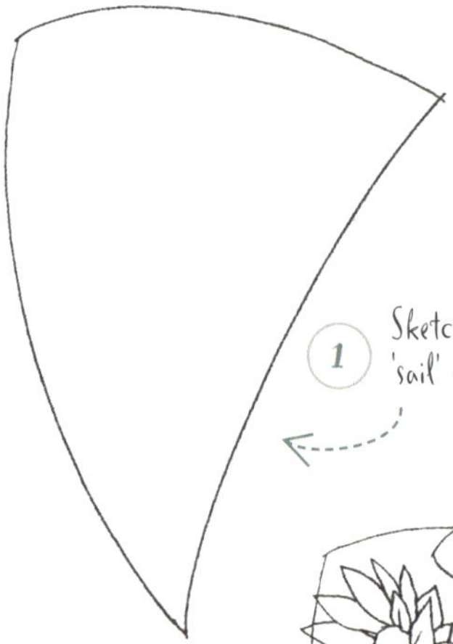

1 Sketch an inverted 'sail' shape as a guide.

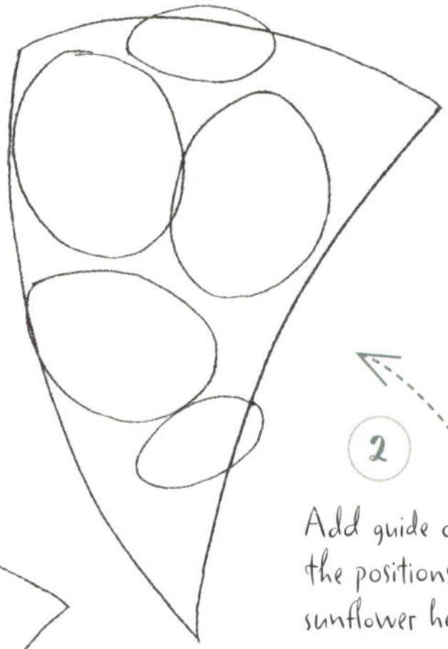

2 Add guide circles for the positions of the sunflower heads.

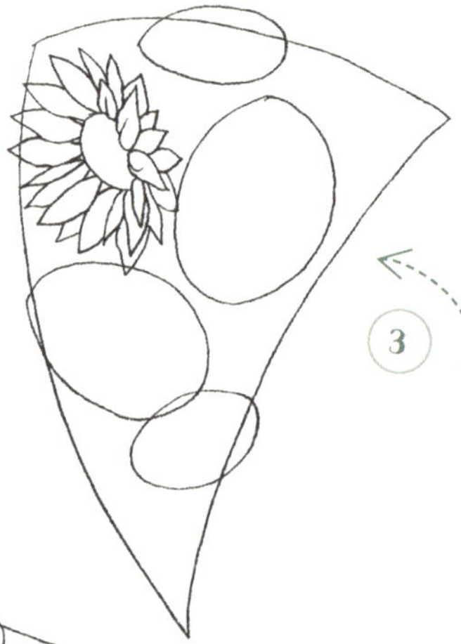

3 Draw the first sunflower (see pages 44–45 for extra guidance).

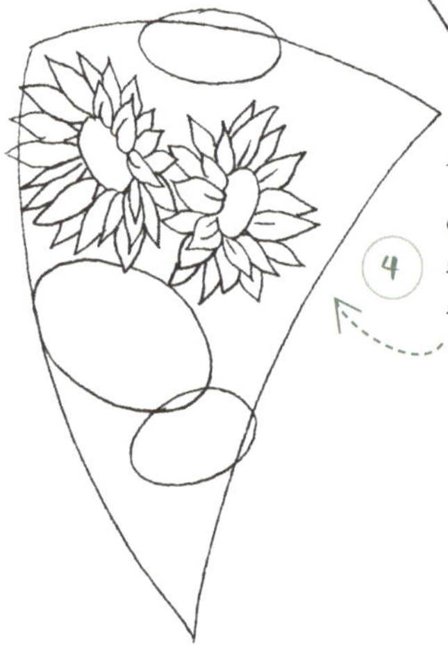

4 Draw the second sunflower, facing away from the first.

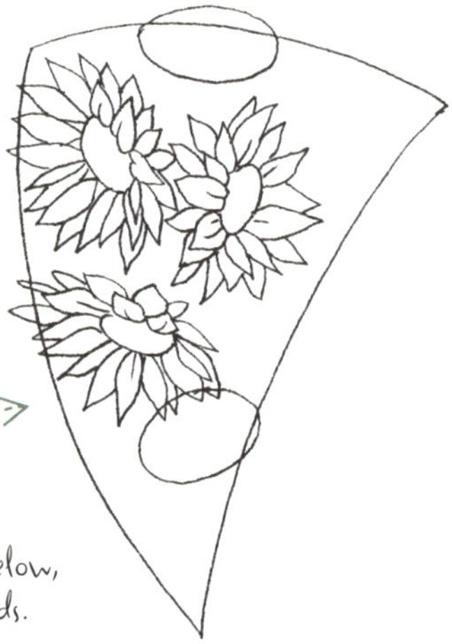

5 Add a third sunflower just below, facing downwards.

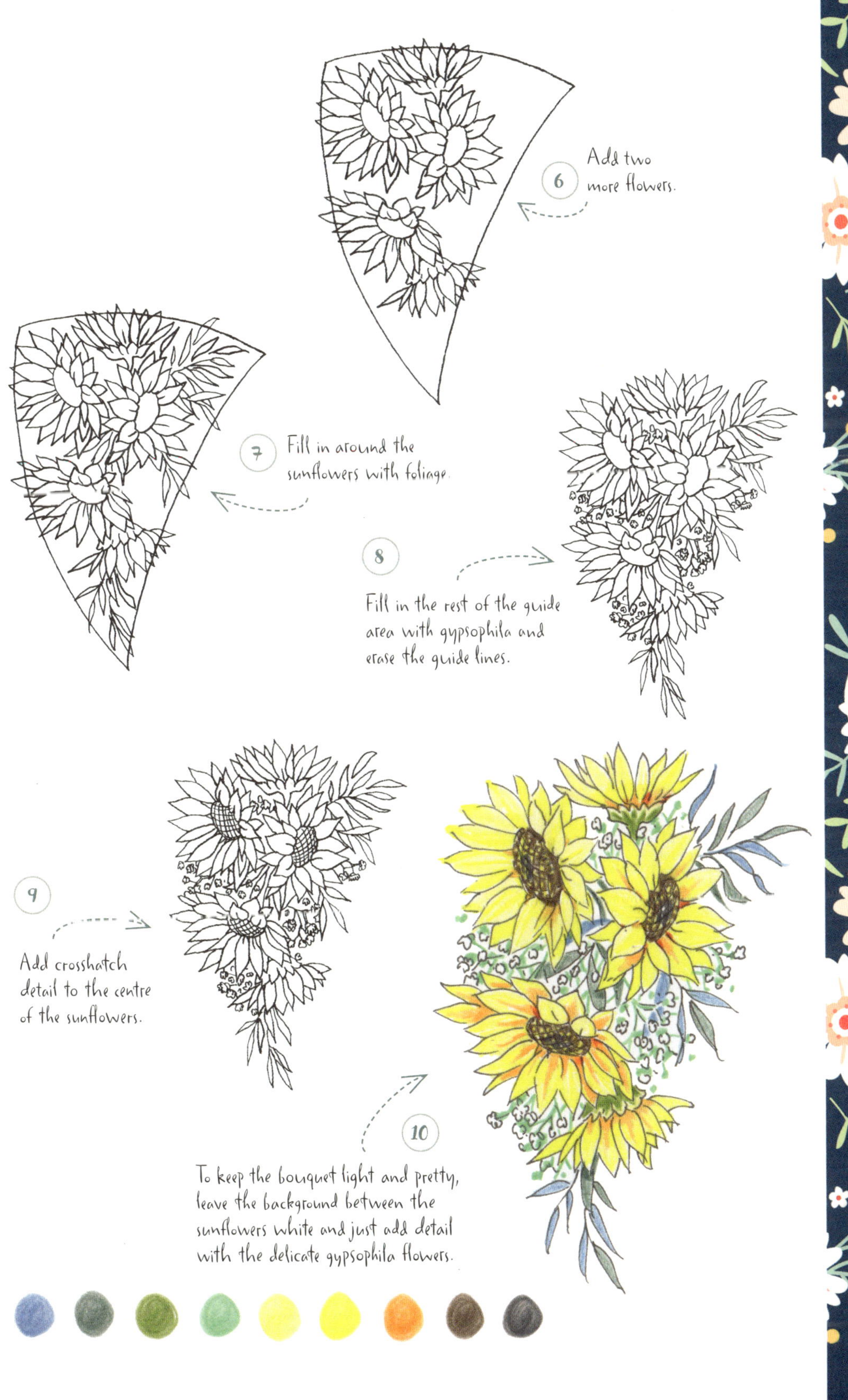
6
Add two
more flowers.
7
Fill in around the
sunflowers with foliage.
8
Fill in the rest of the guide
area with gypsophila and
erase the guide lines.
9
Add crosshatch
detail to the centre
of the sunflowers.
10
To keep the bouquet light and pretty,
leave the background between the
sunflowers white and just add detail
with the delicate gypsophila flowers.

Wild Flower Bouquet

Wild roses, marguerite daisies, cornflower, cow parsley and lady's mantle make up this wild and natural looking bouquet.

1

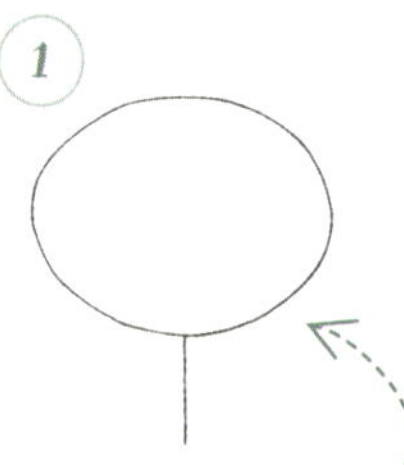

Sketch an oval on a vertical line.

2

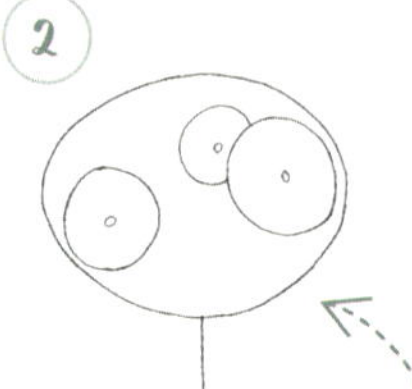

Mark guide circles (with a small central circle) for the roses.

3

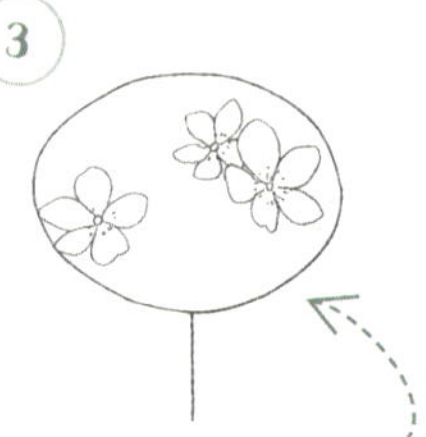

Draw the wild roses with five varying petals and erase the small guide circles.

4

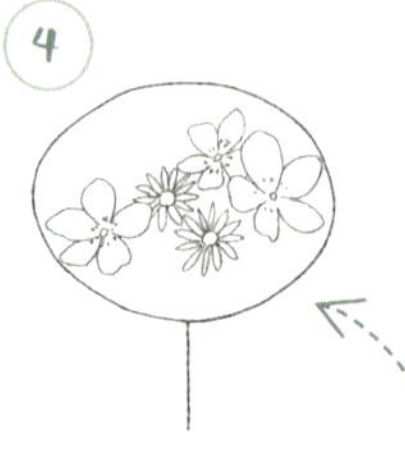

Add two central daisies.

5

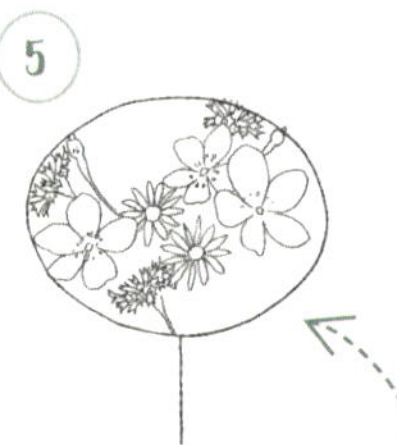

Draw the cornflowers at 6, 10 and 1 o'clock.

6

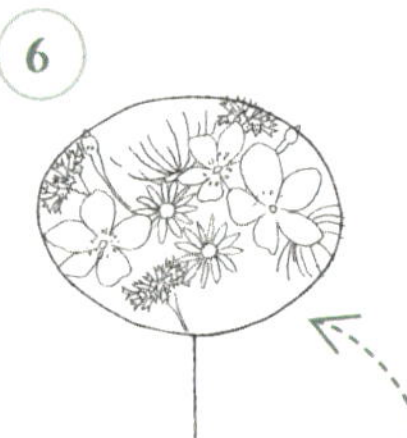

Draw the cow parsley stems.

7

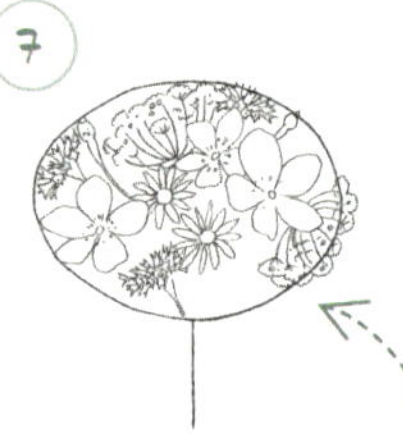

Add the cow parsley florets (there's no need to draw every petal).

8

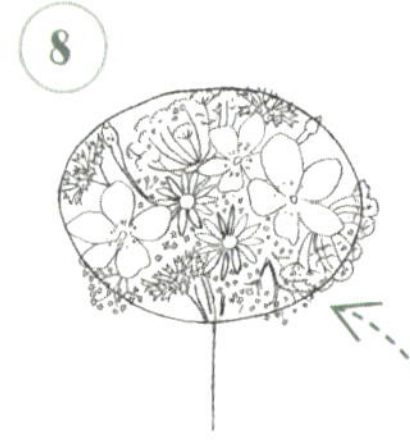

Draw tiny starry blooms for the lady's mantle (no need to draw every one).

9

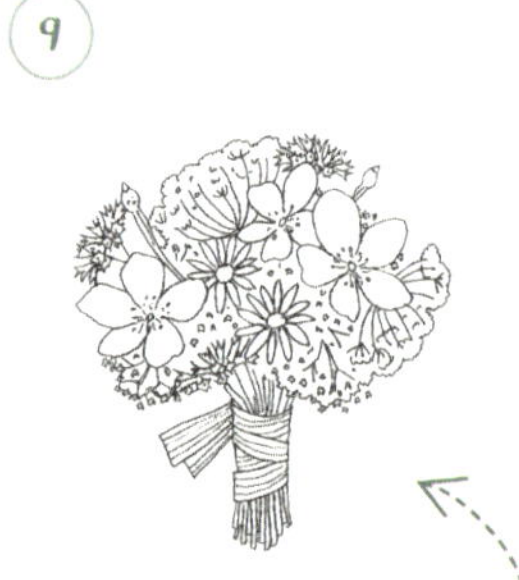

Draw in the stems tied with ribbon and erase the guide circle.

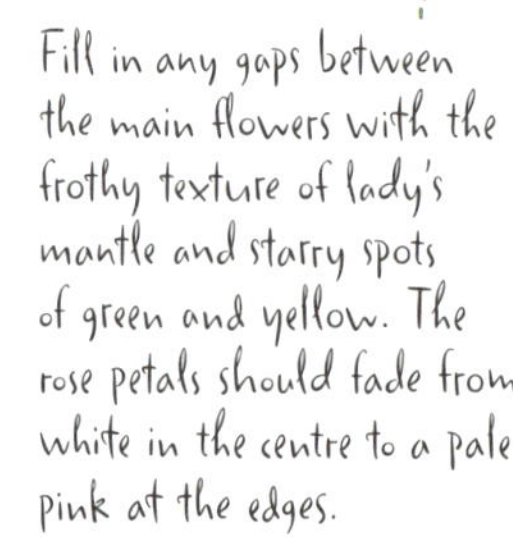

Fill in any gaps between the main flowers with the frothy texture of lady's mantle and starry spots of green and yellow. The rose petals should fade from white in the centre to a pale pink at the edges.

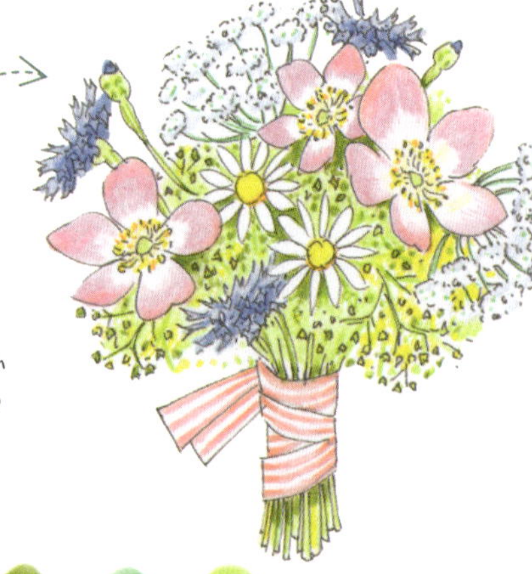

Lilac Bouquet

This is a beautiful bouquet of calming purples, pinks and light blues that looks luscious thanks to the full lilac blooms.

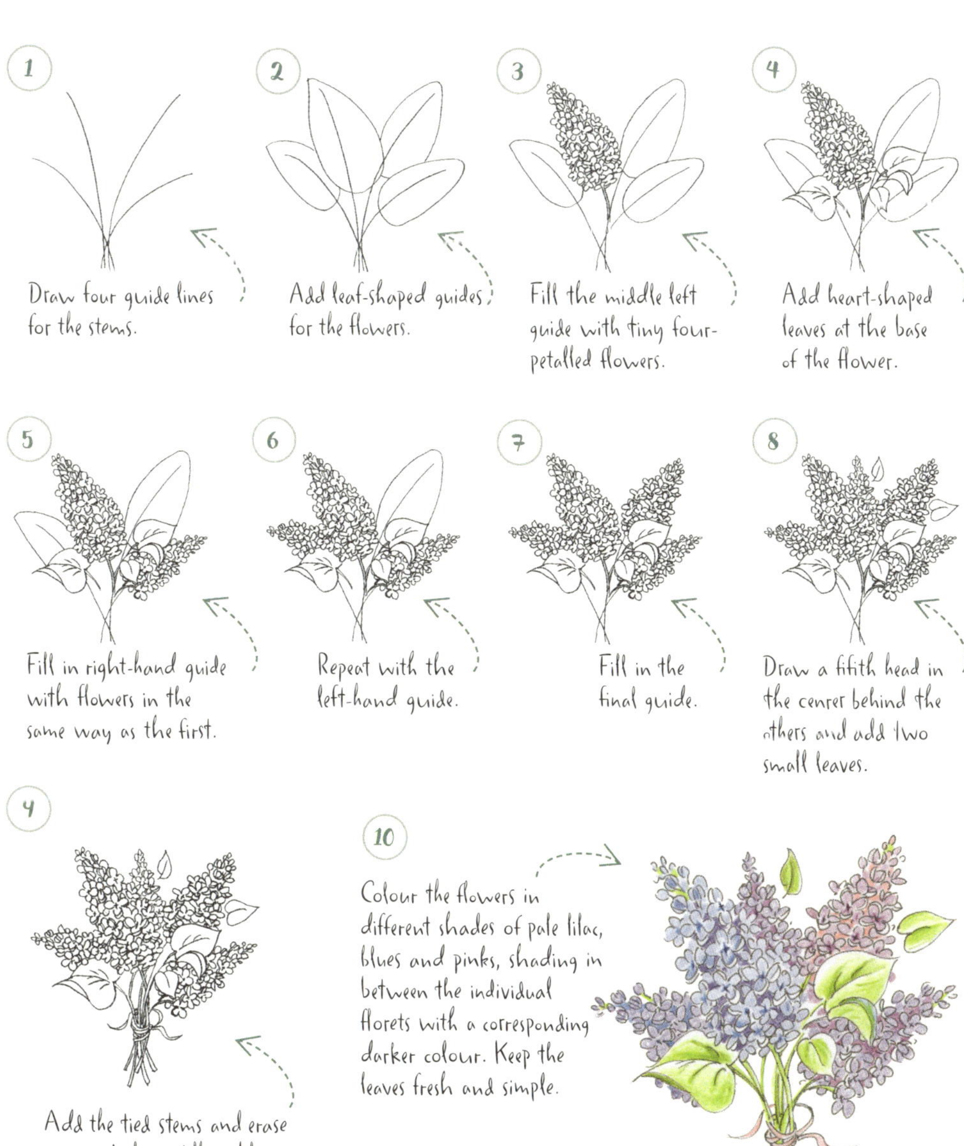

Winter Flowers

Gone are the bright colours of spring here, and instead we have the more muted blues and greens of winter with a bouquet made of white anemones, pine cones, fir sprigs, eucalyptus and berries.

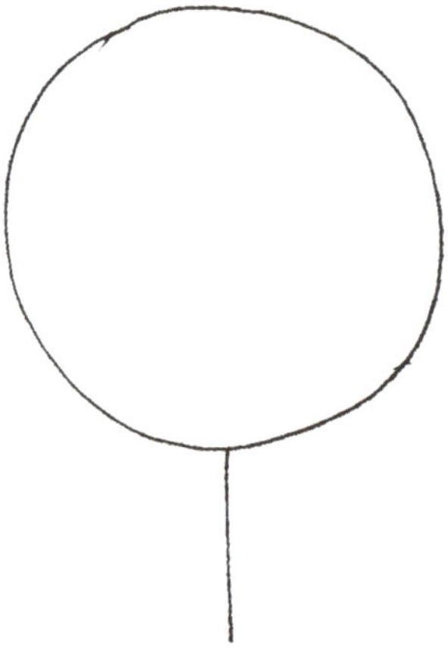

1

Sketch a guide circle on a vertical line.

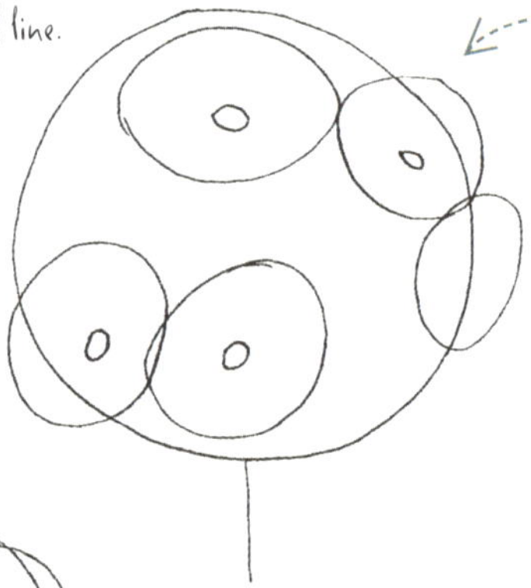

2

Add circle outlines (with a small circle in the middle) as guide positions for the five anemones.

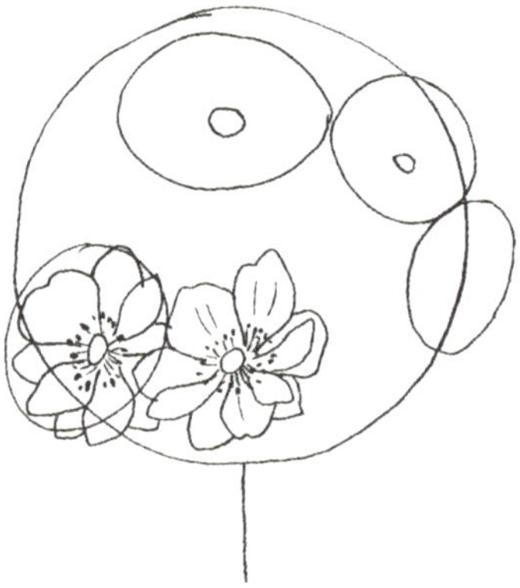

3

Draw the first two anemone flowers with curved, slightly overlapping petals.

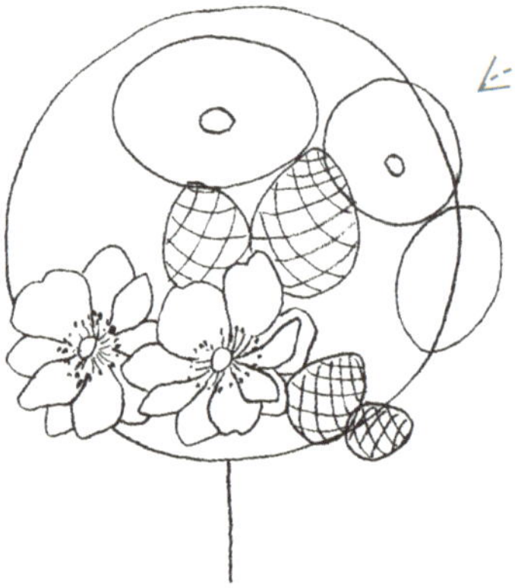

4

Draw guide shapes for the four pine cones and lightly sketch a spiralling crosshatch on them.

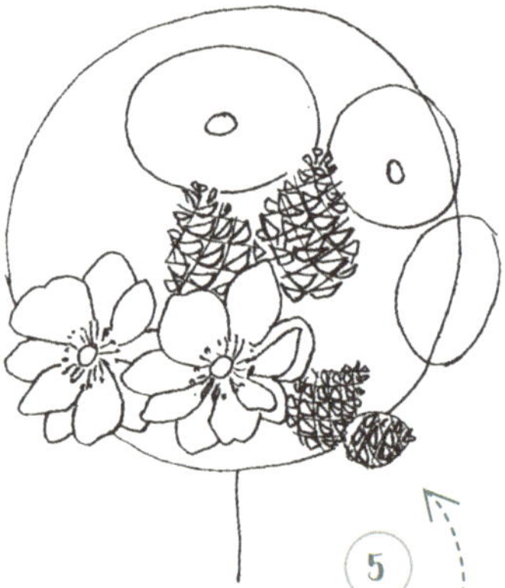

5

Using the sections created by crosshatching, draw in the pine cones.

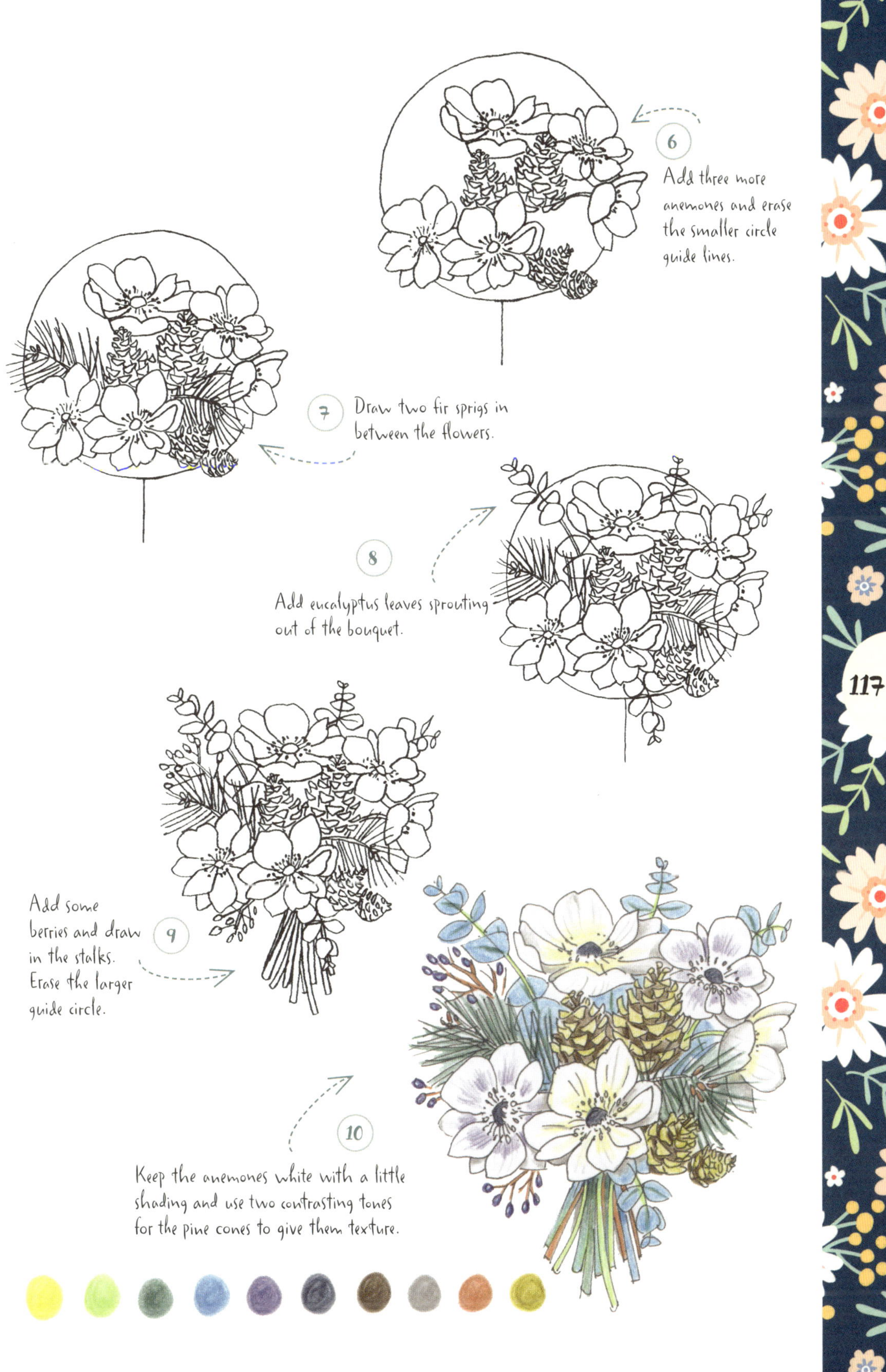
6
Add three more anemones and erase the smaller circle guide lines.
7
Draw two fir sprigs in between the flowers.
8
Add eucalyptus leaves sprouting out of the bouquet.
9
Add some berries and draw in the stalks. Erase the larger guide circle.
10
Keep the anemones white with a little shading and use two contrasting tones for the pine cones to give them texture.

Magnolia Wreath

Magnolia is a beautiful spring flower with a lovely full shape, making it perfect for this simple but elegant wreath.

1

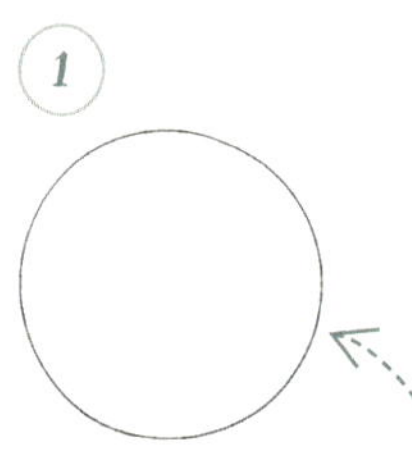

Draw a circle as a guide line for the wreath.

2

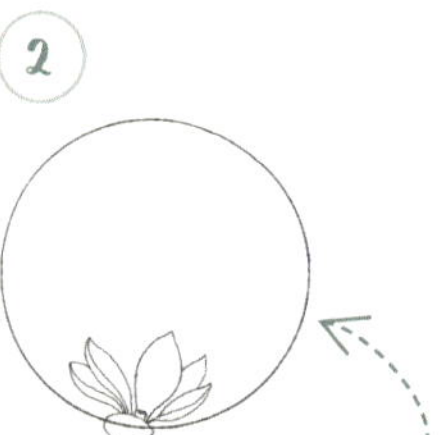

Draw an open magnolia flower (see pages 66–67 for guidance).

3

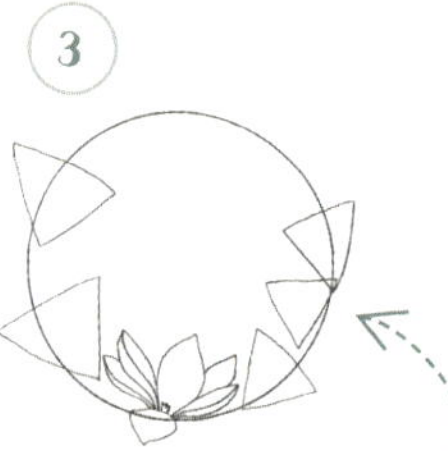

Position five triangles around the circle.

4

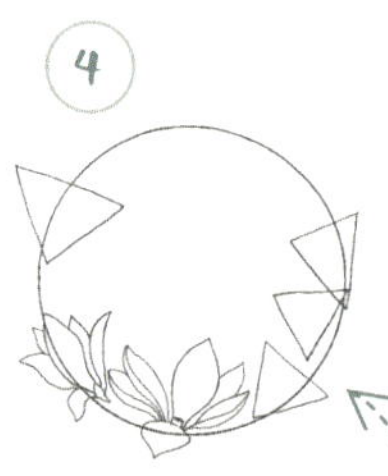

Draw in the second flower.

5

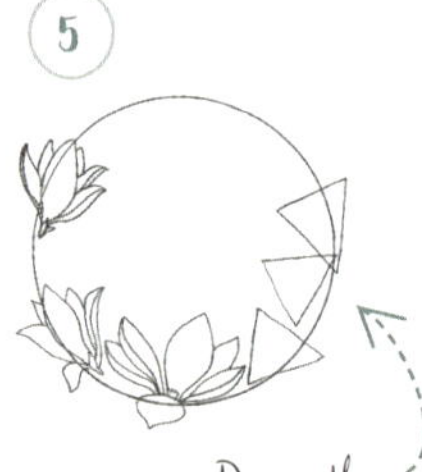

Draw the next flower.

6

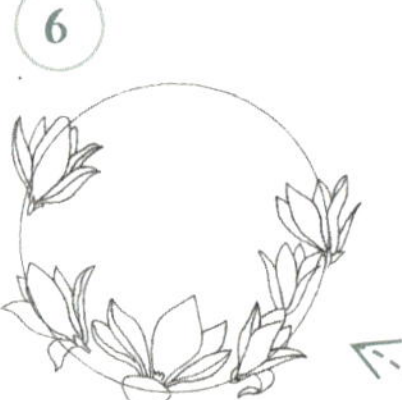

Add three more flowers, starting with the lowermost bloom.

7

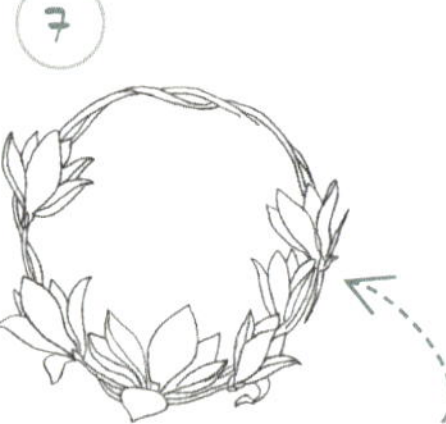

Complete the circle with two intertwining twigs and erase the guide lines.

8

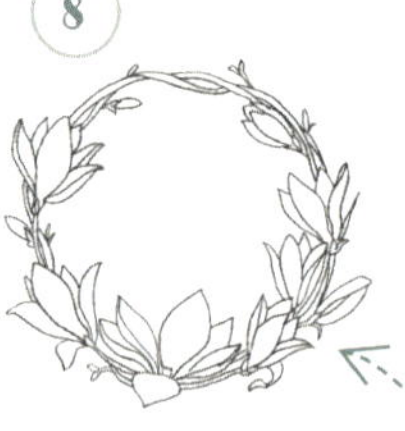

Add some magnolia buds around the wreath.

9

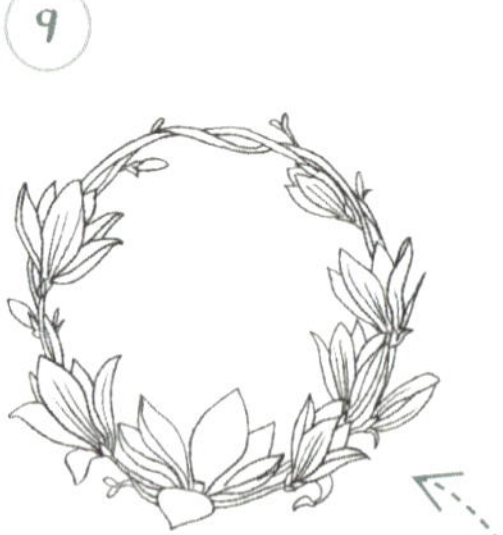

Add vein details to the outer face of the petals.

10

Shade the outside face of the petals from deep pink at the base, fading to white at the edges. Use very light yellow and gray on the inside face to create depth.

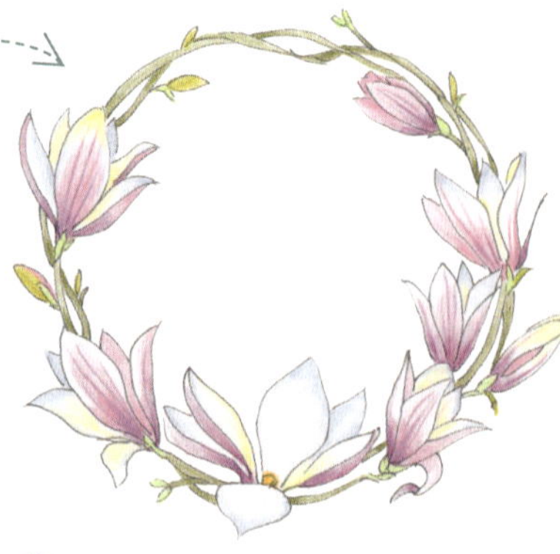

 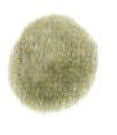 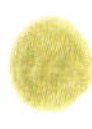  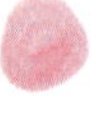 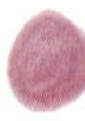 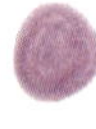 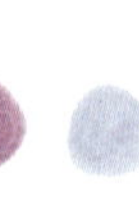

Spring Bouquet

This fresh and pretty bouquet is made up of stocks, anemone and grape hyacinth.

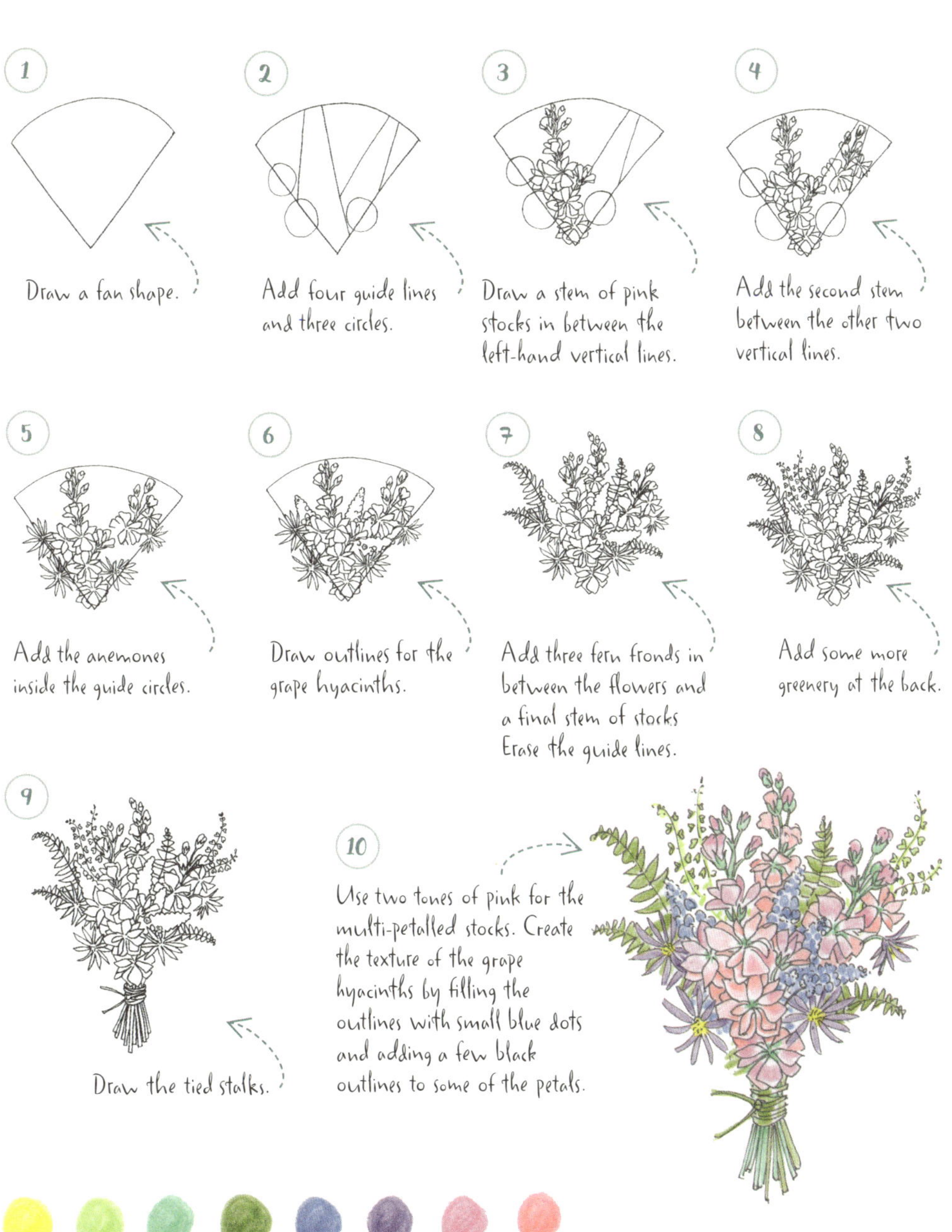

Hyacinth Bouquet

This pretty bouquet has a lovely contrasting selection of flower shapes, with the long, multi-petalled hyacinth and the cleaner lines of the tulips.

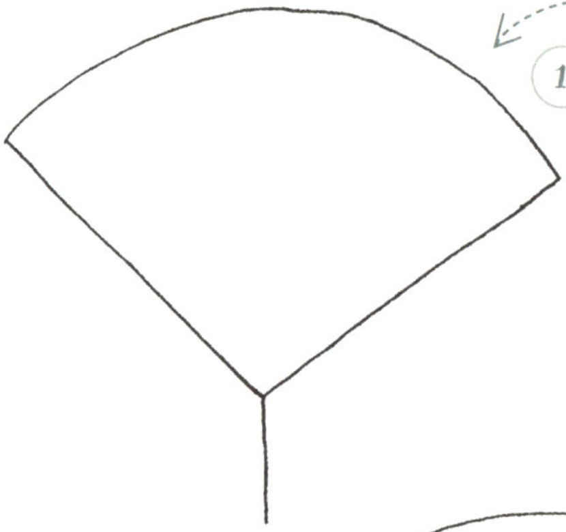

1 Draw a fan shape on a vertical line.

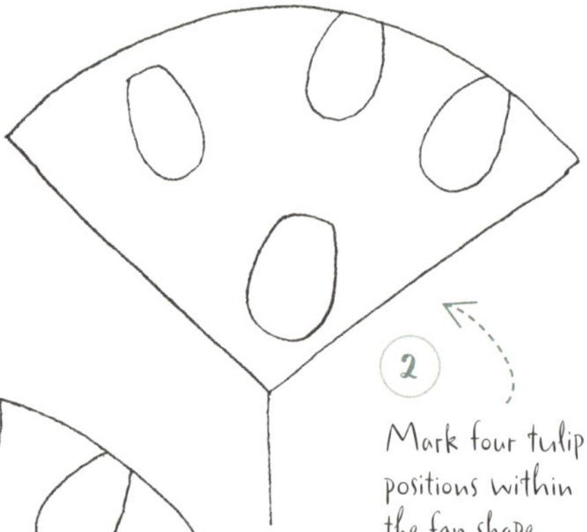

2 Mark four tulip positions within the fan shape.

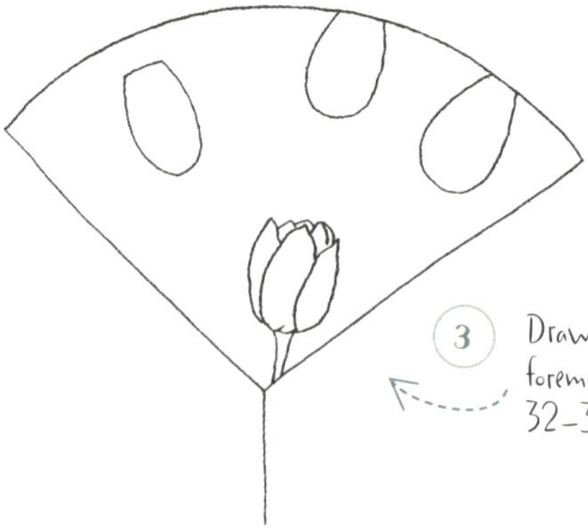

3 Draw the petals on the foremost tulip (see pages 32–33 for guidance).

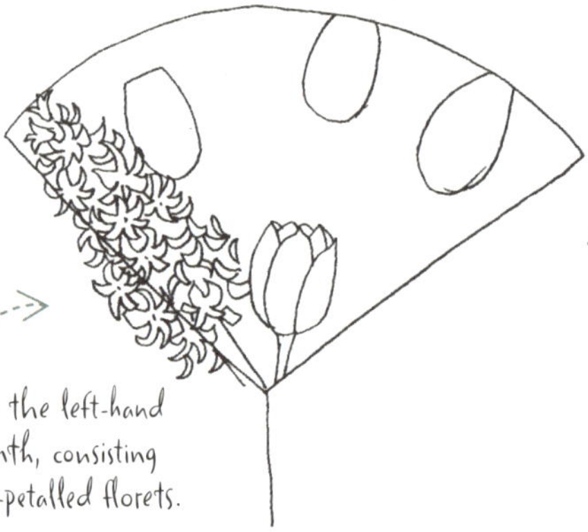

4 Draw the left-hand hyacinth, consisting of six-petalled florets.

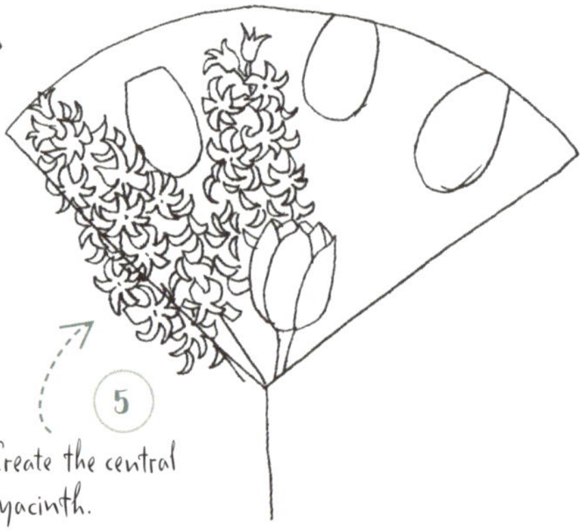

5 Create the central hyacinth.

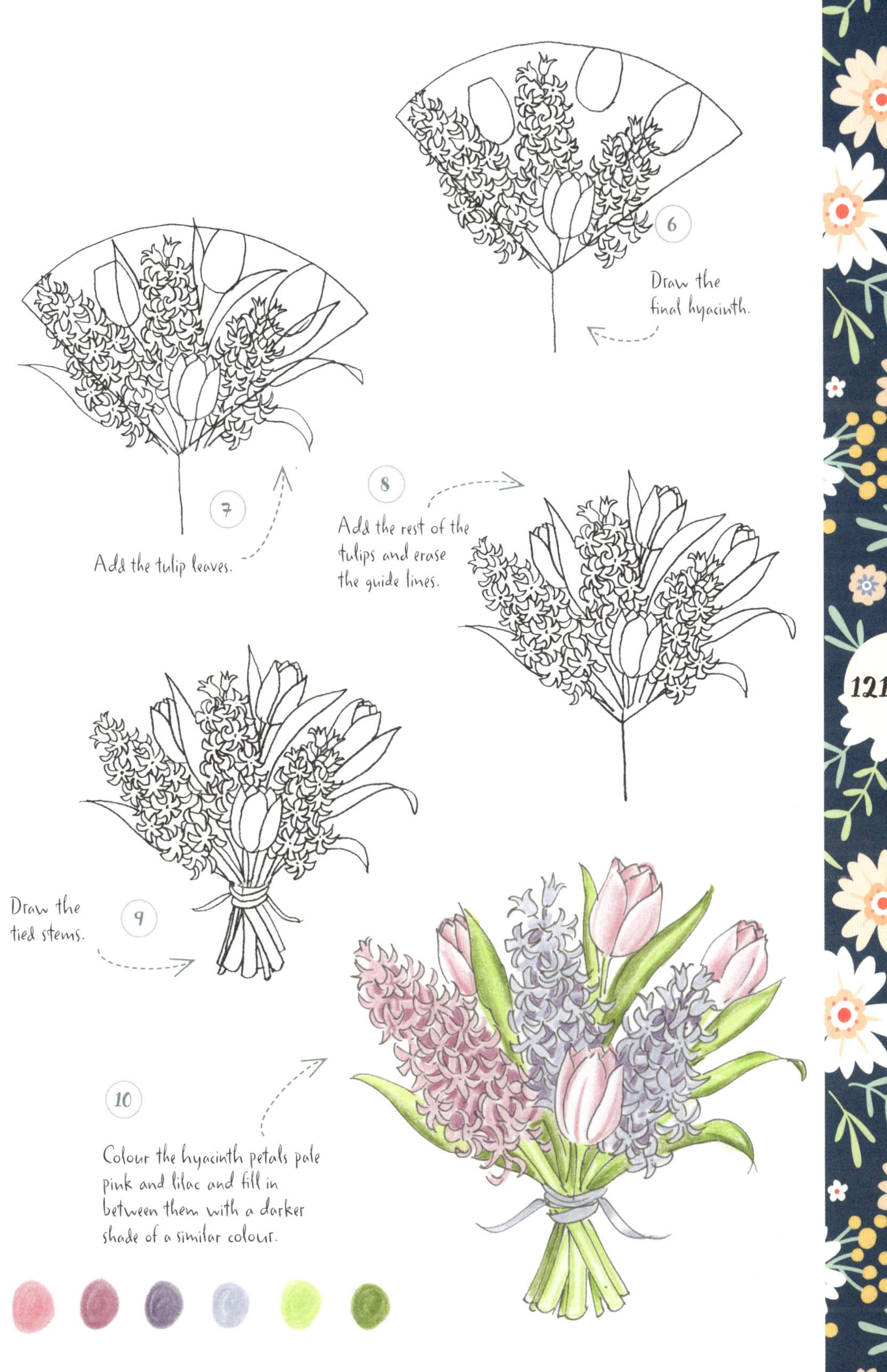
6
Draw the final hyacinth.
7
Add the tulip leaves.
8
Add the rest of the tulips and erase the guide lines.
9
Draw the tied stems.
10
Colour the hyacinth petals pale pink and lilac and fill in between them with a darker shade of a similar colour.

Tulip Bouquet

The simple shape of tulips (see pages 32–33) and the varying shades they come in make for a perfect spring bouquet. Choose a palette of colours to suit your personal taste.

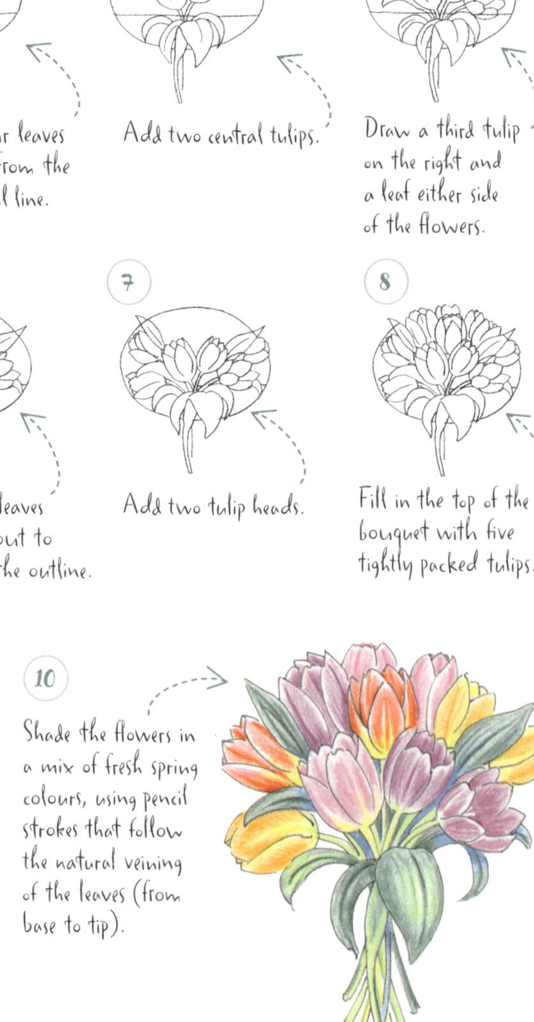

1. Draw an oval with a horizontal line two-thirds of the way down and a central stem.
2. Add four leaves hanging from the horizontal line.
3. Add two central tulips.
4. Draw a third tulip on the right and a leaf either side of the flowers.
5. Add a tulip on the left, tucked behind the leaves.
6. Add three leaves extending out to the top of the outline.
7. Add two tulip heads.
8. Fill in the top of the bouquet with five tightly packed tulips.
9. Draw in the stems and erase the guide lines.
10. Shade the flowers in a mix of fresh spring colours, using pencil strokes that follow the natural veining of the leaves (from base to tip).

Thistle Buttonhole

This striking bouquet filled with spiky thistles (see pages 84–85) makes a change from more gentle, prettier flowers. Use a blend of blues and purples to really add a punch of colour.

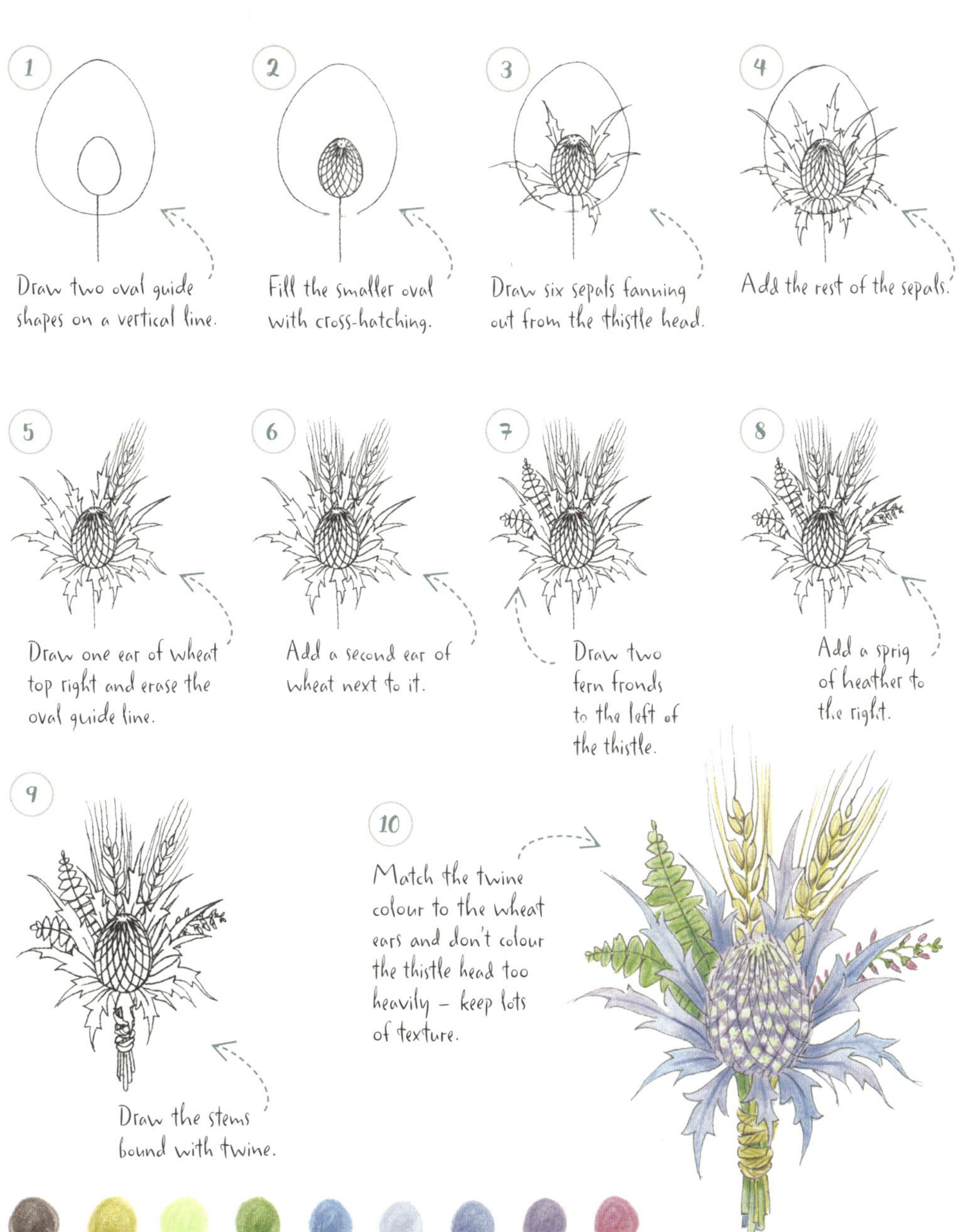

Bouquet of Grasses

This foliage-heavy bouquet is perfect for practising blending of different shades of green, with an added splash of colour.

1 Draw two guide lines in a cross.

2 Draw rough outlines for two achillea heads.

3 Add three nigella seed heads.

4 Sketch four grass heads.

5 Draw the guide lines for the barley ears.

6 Draw in the barley ears.

7 Draw the twine around the base of the bouquet.

8 Add the stalks.

9 Fill in the final grasses and erase the guide lines.

10 Keep the black outlines sketchy and colour to accentuate textures rather than shapes. Fill any gaps between elements with shading to create density.

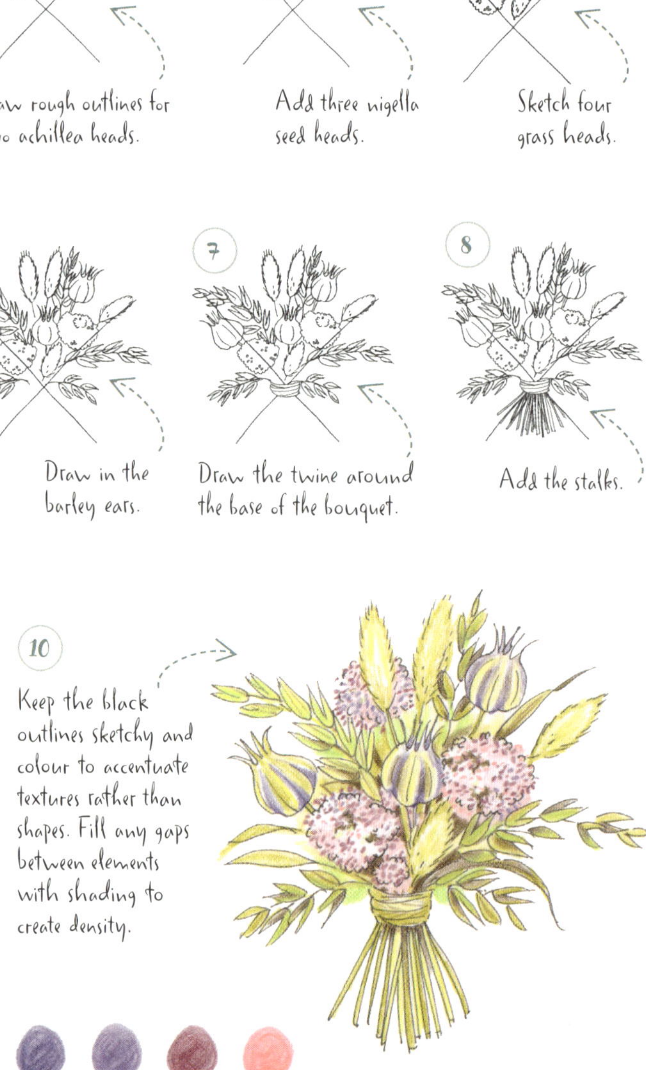

Rose Wreath

This horseshoe-shaped wreath is full of traditional roses. Change the colour scheme to suit your personal preference and refer to the rose instructions on pages 10–11 for help with the individual flower shapes.

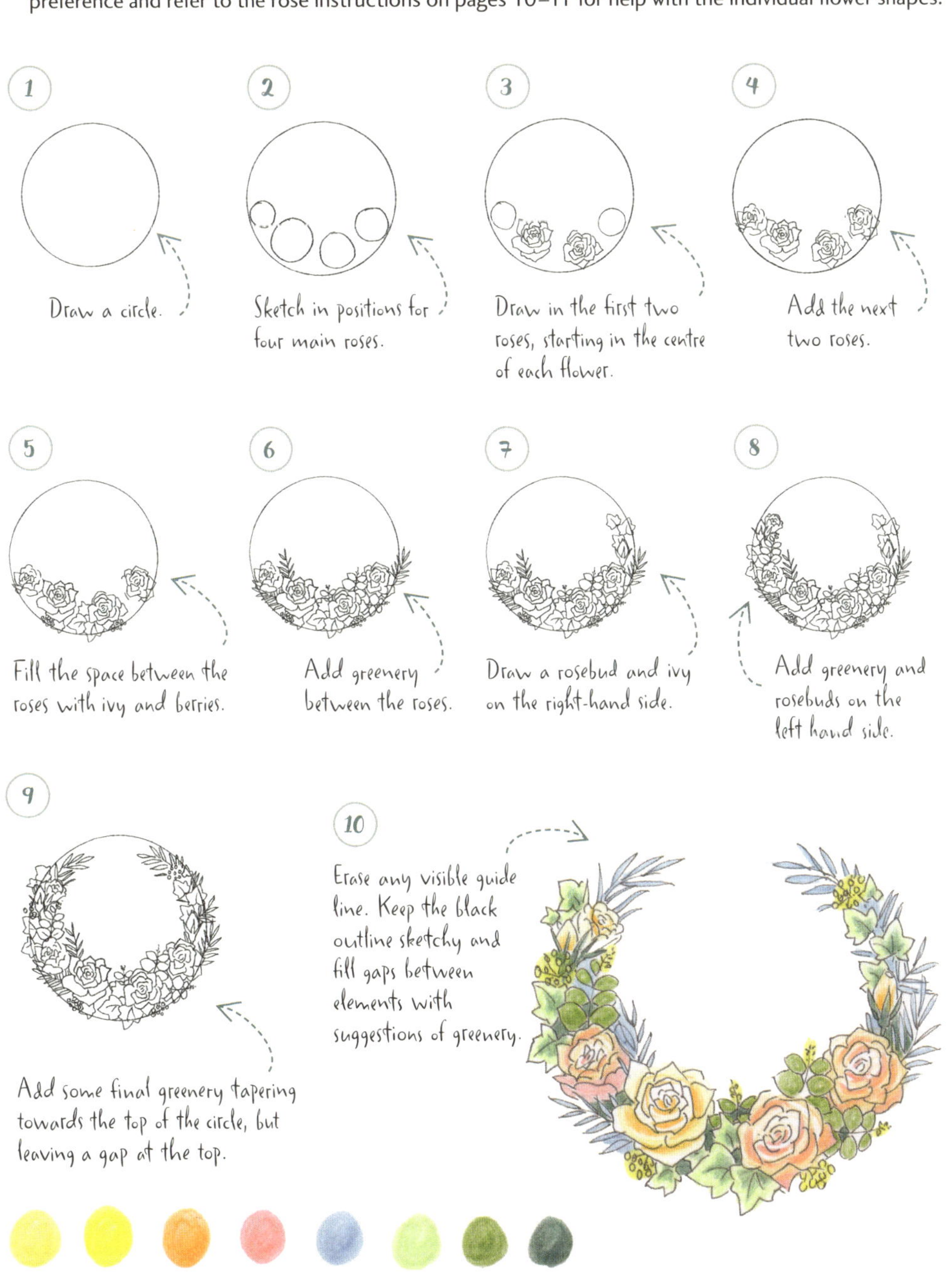

Orange Blossom Bouquet

The slightly angled, sloping shape of this bouquet makes a change from the normal hand-tied upright design.

1. Draw a semicircle guide at an angle.

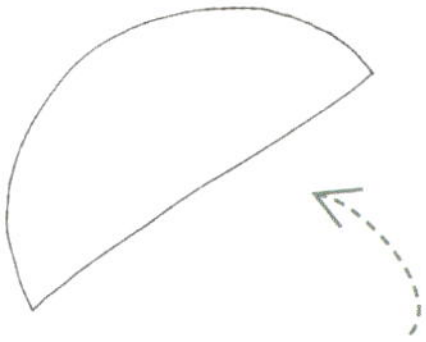

2. Position guides for the orange blossom.

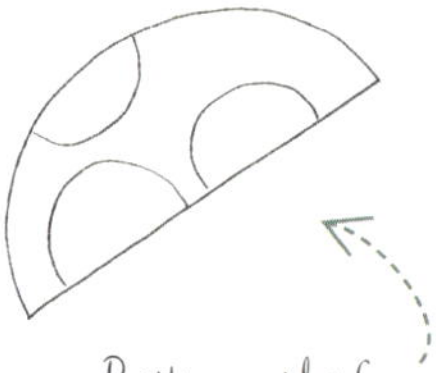

3. Draw the first group of blossoms, made up of smaller five-petalled flowers.

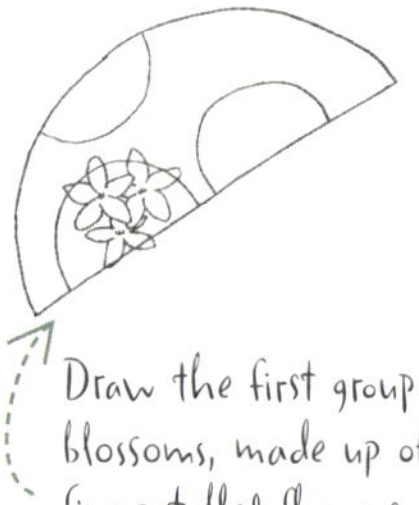

4. Add the second group of blossoms.

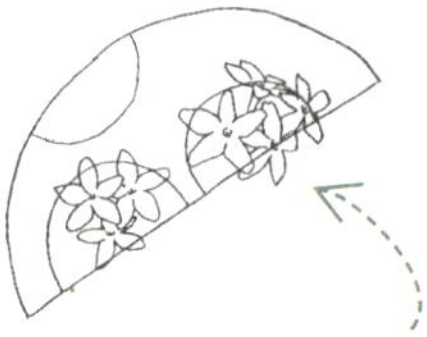

5. Add the third group of blossoms.

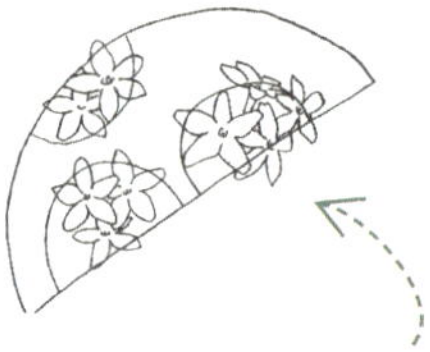

6. Draw lily of the valley stems fanning out from the lower blossoms.

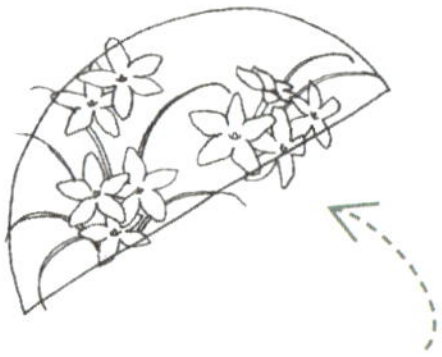

7. Add bell-shaped flowers along the stems.

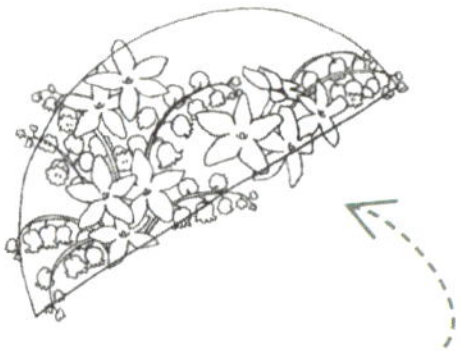

8. Tuck leaves between the flowers, fanning out from the bottom left.

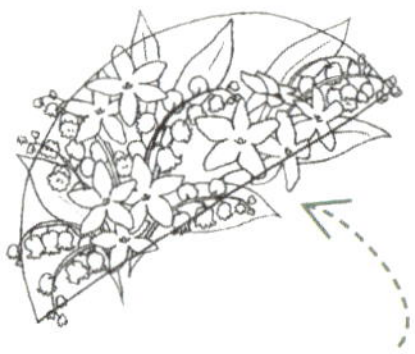

9. 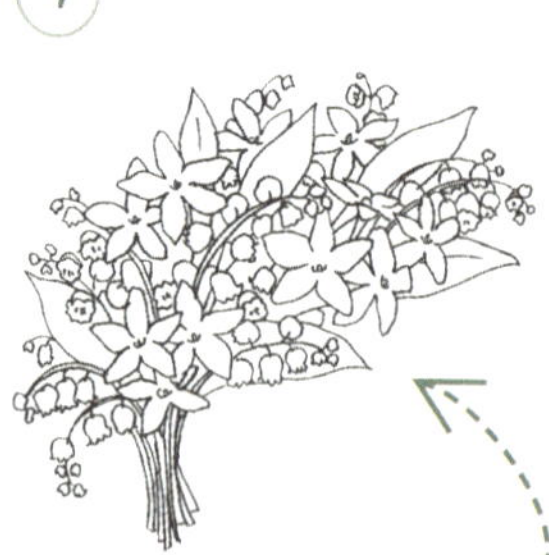

Fill in any gaps with more flower heads and draw in the stems. Erase the guide lines.

10. Keep colours to a minimum and shade delicately, keeping the greens pale. Add small dots of blue to fill any gaps – this will keep the drawing looking fresh and pretty.

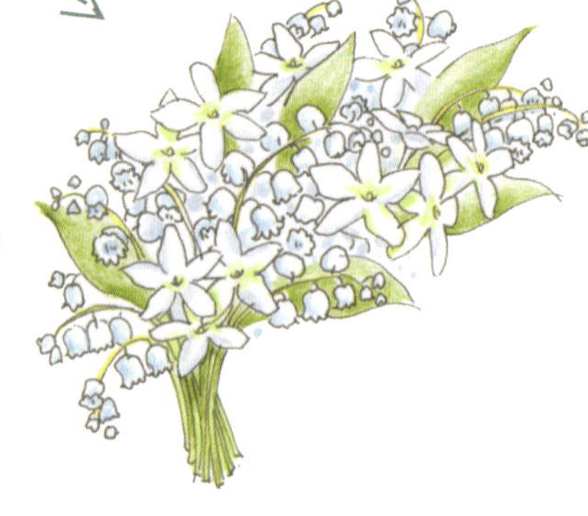

Gerbera Bouquet

This bright and colourful bouquet will brighten up any picture. Refer to the guidelines for drawing a gerbera on page 33 if needed.

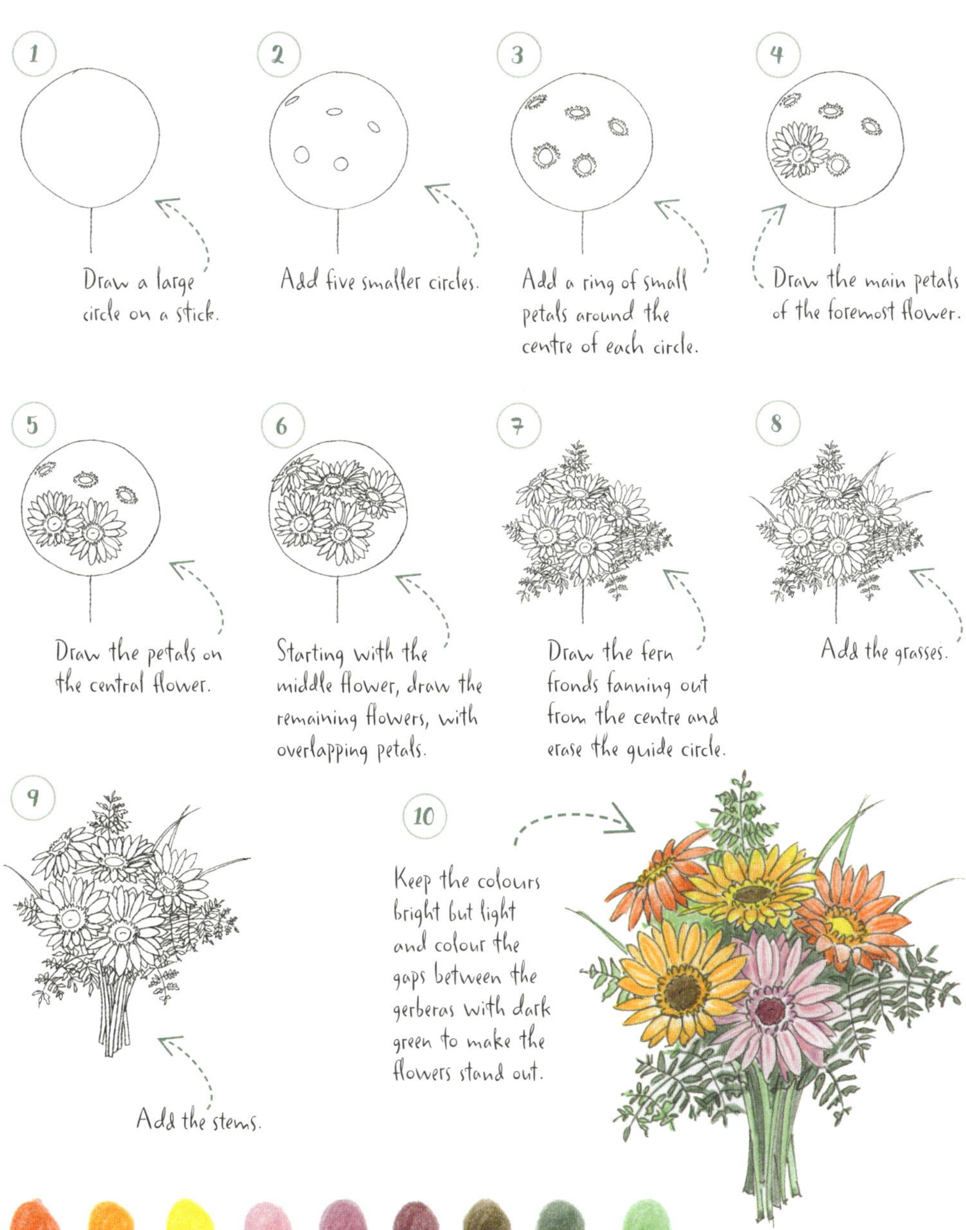

About the artist

Mary is an artist and illustrator based in Suffolk, UK. She specializes in painting natural subjects and produces artwork for everything from stationery to ceramic tiles. Mary's interest in the outdoors has inspired a number of publications, including *The Painted Garden Cookbook* (a collection of illustrated recipes that were produced in her own garden) and *Drawn to the Country*. Her most recent clients include Waitrose, Tesco, Grand Central Publishing and *Country Living Magazine*.

If you'd like to find out more information or to see further examples of her work you can visit her website: marywoodin.com.

Acknowledgements

A big thank you to my husband Andrew Martindale, for holding the fort while I was barricaded in my studio, eyes only for my deadline!

And as ever, I'm very grateful to Lucy, Steph and Alex at The Artworks Illustration Agency for masterminding this project.